Big Bend Country

Number Seventy-four:
The Centennial Series of the Association
of Former Students,
Texas A&M University

BIG BEND

Land of the Unexpected

Texas A&M University Press
College Station

COUNTRY

KENNETH B. RAGSDALE

The paper used in this book meets the minimum requirements
of the American National Standard for Permanence
of Paper for Printed Library Materials, Z39.48-1984.
Binding materials have been chosen for durability.

Library of Congress Cataloging-in-Publication Data
Ragsdale, Kenneth Baxter, 1917–

    Big Bend country : land of the unexpected / Kenneth B.
Ragsdale. — 1st. ed.

        p.   cm. — (Centennial series of the Association of Former
Students, Texas A&M University ; no. 74)

    Includes bibliographical references and index.

    ISBN 0-89096-811-X (alk. paper)

    1. Big Bend Region (Tex.)—History. 2. Big Bend Region
(Tex.)—Biography. I. Title. II. Series.

F392.B54R28   1998

976.4′932—dc21   97-49196

                                                CIP

Another one for Janet,

who makes writing possible

and living a pleasure.

A Special Place in Time

Any book on the Big Bend country should include the following beautifully poignant and often quoted description of that region of Texas that lies in the bend of the Great River. Most likely miscredited to "a Big Bend cowboy with the soul of a poet," it states:

> *You go south from Fort Davis until you come to the place where rainbows wait for rain, and the big river is kept in a box, and the water runs uphill. And the mountains float in the air, except at night when they go away to play with the other mountains.*

Contents

Illustrations

Preface

I have written two previous books on the Big Bend country of Texas. This will be my last; the reason is quite personal.

The region I first discovered as a child in 1928, and rediscovered some three decades later, exists today only as history, myth, and legend. What is missing are the people who made the history, created the myths, and lived the legends. Those who pioneered the Big Bend and represented that region to me no longer live there. Most have gone on to their reward carrying with them their memories, their experiences, and their eyewitness accounts of how one of America's last frontiers succumbed to a measure of something called modern civilization.

Those people represented a wide spectrum of lifestyles along the Mexican border. Some were ranchers, traders, soldiers, lawmen, smugglers, murderers, movie stars, miners, journalists, and humanitarians. Each in his or her own way contributed to the history and culture of the region. I was privileged to have known most of them personally; others I knew through their friends, enemies, victims, relatives, and associates. All shared their experiences and all created within me a personal indebtedness for their kindness and generosity. They *were* history; their living record fills the pages that follow.

Midcentury marks the dividing point in Big Bend history; socially, culturally, and economically, the region today bears scant resemblance to the place I first visited some sixty years ago. During the last four decades the lower Big Bend—the "river country"—witnessed an almost total population shift. Only the physical terrain, and the memories and the records of the past—those that still exist—lend a sense of continuity to Big Bend history.

The region possesses a rich and varied history. Anglo intrusion into the lower Big Bend began in the post–Civil War era. Ranchers and traders led the vanguard of settlement, followed closely by farmers, miners, and merchants. Population peaked in the post–World War I era; by the end of the next war the exodus was under way. The closing of the Terlingua quicksilver mines and the opening of the 788,682-acre Big Bend National Park in 1943, dispelled hundreds from their native haunts. They left in their wake a treasure land of natural beauty that continues to attract an ongoing migration of largely temporary citizens; permanent occupants are noticeably few.

Change is most evident in the once isolated villages and trading posts. Lajitas, the former cavalry post and legendary Rio Grande crossing, now suffers from urban face lift. Tom Skaggs's trading post, where farmers and ranchers, both Mexican and Anglo, once purchased coal oil, phonograph needles, bib overalls, and buggy whips, has been replaced by a tacky western movie set village that dispenses designer fashions, turquoise jewelry, Western art, and fragrances by Estée Lauder. Affluent tourists now park their Airstream trailers and play golf in a riverside meadow where Rex Ivey once grazed his livestock.

Driving east from Lajitas, one passes the new airstrip on the right, the vacant ruins of Terlingua on the left (the former Chisos Mining Company store and cantina have been reopened), and a little farther on another trailer park on the banks of Terlingua Creek comes into view. License plates on Mercedes, Jaguars, Lincoln TownCars, and Chevrolet Suburbans document a new transient population that bears no relationship to the past. Just across the Terlingua Creek bridge stands a real estate sign that seems to summarize the new regional philosophy: "Everything For Sale." Arriving at Study Butte, another former mining village, visitors stop at a modern service station to ask directions in strange accents that some locals find difficult to understand. Others occupy luxury motel suites, watch color television beamed in via satellite, and read same-day editions of the *New York Times* while munching bagels and cream cheese. My God! Whatever happened to barbecue, chicken fried steak, chili and tamales? And so the ever-changing panorama of history continues along State Highway 118.

To understand the spirit and character of a geographic region, one must first understand the people, places, and events that give a region its singular identity. Of all the regions of Texas, none is more readily identifiable as the Big Bend. Such terms as Panhandle, South Plains, Piney Woods, Rolling Plains, and Lower Valley are geographic generalizations lacking specific boundaries. The Big Bend, on the other hand, is a well defined region locked in by a meandering river that plunges deep into what might have been Mexico, leaving a residual peninsula containing some of the most magnificent, yet some of the harshest, most forbidding, and most unyielding land in the nation. (Local tradition identifies the Southern Pacific Railroad as the region's northern boundary.)

The Big Bend country is also a region of vast ethnic, cultural, economic, and geographic contrasts. There are flat plains and towering peaks, searing heat in the lowlands and frequent snowfall in the highlands. The Rio Grande, "that perverse and individualistic stream that gives character to the border of Texas," binds two nations of great diversity, a factor that frequently spawned misunderstanding, mistrust, and conflict. This is also a region of extreme wealth and abject poverty, where the illiterate far outnumber the literate, where political decisions have traditionally been made by the few, and where primitive men and methods once recovered some of the world's rarest and most precious metals. And this is where men in airplanes have invaded the once sacred domain of men on horseback.

Still comparatively remote and isolated even in the late twentieth century, the region unquestionably placed an indelible stamp on all who elected to live there. One longtime resident explained: "Man does not modify this country; it transforms him deeply." These are a rare breed. Ask them and they will tell you they would live nowhere else; their regional loyalty and patriotism is without parallel. Explaining his lifelong Big Bend tenancy, rancher Roy Stillwell claimed, "I'd rather be dead in Marathon than alive anywhere else in the world!" Yet fundamentally, the citizens of the Big Bend differ little from people in other regions of the state. The bad were sometimes very, very bad, while the good frequently performed deeds of exemplary kindness. And they all had to work to survive.

To comprehend more fully these elements of Big Bend society one has only to examine the region, a remote desert wilderness that yields grudgingly of life's necessities. In the ongoing struggle there would emerge inevitably persons representing the two extremes of human responses—compassion and conflict—those devoted to others' welfare and those who sought only self-gratification. Personal values aside, it was, however, the desert environment that added final parity to life in the Big Bend country; in order to survive, all were forced to conform to the region's bitter dictates. Therefore, in evaluating life along the Great River, most human experiences can be examined within the context of compassion, conflict, and compromise.

While the foregoing conditions may also exist to varying degrees in other regions of the state, the combined impact of remoteness, scarcity, and geographic location have helped give the Big Bend country and its people their individual identity. However, as I developed this study, I began to realize that, although these events did indeed occur in isolation, and in most cases, over a half-century previous, they nevertheless possess a marked relevance to contemporary urban culture. And while this is essentially regional history, the fundamental social, cultural, and economic factors examined within the specific confines of the Big Bend country, do indeed possess universal relevance.

Some years back during the televised Academy Awards presentation, the winner of the best foreign film acknowledged the award in his native French, apparently thanking everyone from his grandparents to the upstairs maid. At the end of the recipient's interminable speech, master of ceremonies Bob Hope quipped, "He said he did it all by himself." Since then I have secretly relished the idea of jolting academia, and the literati in particular, by beginning a preface with a similar claim: "I did this all by myself; I owe nothing to anyone." Of course, nothing could be further from the truth. Historical research is a grand experience, much like creating a great mosaic; hordes of thoughtful and generous people contribute their individual experiences, materials, and data to enable the author to assemble the final work. Specifically, I owe much to many.

The materials for this manuscript were collected over some three decades. As the following stories emerged while researching other Big Bend topics, I could not resist collecting the data for some future publication. Hence, the beginning of many lasting friendships. I first met Hattie Grace Elliott on the morning of December 29, 1964, while researching *Quicksilver*. During that interview she showed me her mother's diary. I recognized the historical merit of this rare document, which, thanks to Hattie Grace, is reproduced in this volume as the *Prelude*. My friendship with Hallie Stillwell dates from June 7, 1966, also while researching *Quicksilver*. Hallie contributed not only to that project but to *Wings Over The Mexican Border* as well. In fact, no reputable author writes about the Big Bend country without interviewing Hallie. And no one south of Marathon makes better burritos than Hallie and daughter Dadie. (Historical research requires physical as well as intellectual sustenance.)

I met Lee Bennett in 1968 while serving as education director for the Texas State Historical Association. At that time Lee was gaining national recognition for her work with the Marfa High School Junior Historians; items from their extensive collections greatly enriched the chapter on Mary Coe Daniels. (Information gained from the Junior Historian collection was available from no other source.) Also, Lee's recollection of her father's treasure-hunting venture, as well as her role as a *Giant* extra are found in chapters 9 and 11. Her contributions greatly strengthened the documentation of these two episodes. I deeply appreciate the help and guidance the foregoing ladies provided, as well as their enduring friendship. Southwestern Bell, AT&T, and Sprint also extend their appreciation; we all still talk frequently.

Fort Stockton attorney (and later district judge) Alex Gonzalez well remembers Sunday afternoon October 22, 1972. That was the day he left a Dallas Cowboys telecast to translate my interview with Valentin Baiza. Without Alex's presence, Valentin would have never divulged his personal involvement in the volatile Baiza-Acosta feud. The same appreciation is accorded Fort Stockton history teacher Joe Primera, who translated my interview with Francisca Acosta, who shared with me the Acosta family perspective of that conflict. Special thanks are due another history teacher, Jim Cullen, who conducted on-site Big Bend interviews for me when I was committed elsewhere. Roger Conger, another good friend, contributed greatly to this undertaking by sharing with me his dramatic narrative (as well as photographs) of the modern-day treasure hunt at El Muerto Springs, which was supplemented by extensive oral interviews with Herbert Hamilton and Robert F. Coffee. I am also indebted to actors Robert Nichols and Earl Holliman, who shared their personal recollections of the location filming of *Giant* in Marfa, Texas, as well as to George Stevens Jr., whose thoughtful correspondence explored his father's philosophy of filmmaking, especially as it related to the film adaptation of the Edna Ferber novel.

Of course, there are the librarians and archivists, bless them all. The staff at the Margaret Herrick Library in Beverly Hills, California, that houses the archives of the Academy of Motion Picture Arts and Sciences, made available to me the extensive George Stevens *Giant* collection. Patricia Dick at the Fort Stockton Public Library responded to my many calls for help, as did Ralph Elder, assistant director at the Center for American

History at the University of Texas at Austin, and his associate, Bill Richter, reference archivist. As I researched the chapter on W. D. Smithers, Roy Flukinger, senior curator of photography at the university's Harry Ransom Humanities Research Center, provided many rare items on this remarkable Big Bend photographer. To these many generous and talented individuals—and every other person cited in the notes—I owe a deep debt of gratitude. No author could have hoped for a richer body of data with which to work.

A special word of thanks is due two other good friends. Mike Cox, journalist, author, literary critic, and public relations executive, and my son, Jeffrey, read the manuscript and made well-informed suggestions from which I benefited greatly.

The person who helped launch me initially on my Big Bend research and remained my constant consultant for some three decades was Dr. Ross Maxwell. I first met Ross in 1964, when he was serving as resident geologist with the Bureau of Economic Geology at the University of Texas at Austin. Ross was the first superintendent of Big Bend National Park and knew the country and the people from firsthand knowledge. He became my friend, my mentor, as well as my most sought-after critic. Requests for help and guidance were never refused. Our first meeting remains graphic in my recollection.

Before embarking on my first Big Bend research trip, I met with Ross in his office. He was a no-nonsense kind of guy and came right to the point. "Mr. Ragsdale, you are going to meet some of the finest people in the world. And they are going to tell you some wonderful stories. But Mr. Ragsdale, you are an outsider, and you look like an outsider." (At that point I began wondering just what an outsider looked like.) "So you are going to have to be patient, be honest, and be straightforward with those folks and you will get a lot of information. *But most important of all, put on a pair of pants!*" (I was wearing walking shorts.) "You can't go out there looking like that," he explained. "They'll know you are an outsider and some probably won't talk to you."

And Ross had some additional advice. "Mr. Ragsdale, I understand you are a musician." I said I played saxophone and led a dance orchestra. "As a musician, I suppose you drink a lot." I explained that I was not that talented; I had to stay sober to perform. "Well," he continued, "Frank Dobie learned that a little liquor will loosen a lot of tongues. So it might be helpful if you will carry a bottle of bourbon with you. Don't take Scotch, that's what sissies drink. Stick to bourbon." Then he explained the methodology. After meeting my interview subject and after getting acquainted, I was to remove the bottle from my briefcase (backpacks were not in popular usage then) and ask the subject if he wouldn't like to join me for a drink. "Two things," Ross added. "It's okay to drink out of the bottle, but let him drink first."

And so I headed for the Big Bend country with high hopes, a new tape recorder, and a bottle of inexpensive bourbon. (I have never been able to get a research grant. If I had, I would have purchased a better brand of booze.) Anyway, in one of my first interviews, I followed Ross's advice to the letter. I wore pants, got acquainted with my subject, visited, and then went for my bottle of bourbon. Suggesting that we enjoy a drink together, I removed the screw top and offered him the open bottle. But somehow things didn't work out exactly as Ross predicted. After carefully studying the brand on the bottle, my interview subject returned my bottle to me and retrieved his own. He drank from his bottle; I drank from mine.

Ross, however, was indeed correct. I met a lot of fine people, established many lasting friendships, gathered a lot of information that I have used in writing three books on the Big Bend country. And I never offered anyone else a drink of cheap bourbon. While it may have worked for Frank Dobie, I never found it necessary. But I followed the rest of Ross Maxwell's sound advice: "Be patient, be honest, tell 'em what you are doing, and you will get a lot of information." I did, and in the process—just as he predicted—I met some of the finest people in the world. This book is about some of them. And to them, and to Ross Maxwell, I will end by saying, "Thanks for the memories."

Big Bend Country

They Came in Covered Wagons

THE DIARY OF IRENE ROGERS

They came in logical sequence, all seeking new homes and new opportunity in a new land. First, the Indians, then the Spanish who were followed by the Anglo explorers and the military surveys, and as the nineteenth century drew to a close the final occupants had begun taking possession of one of America's last frontiers—the Big Bend country of Texas. Cattlemen moved into that area in the early 1880s and quickly claimed the land containing the springs, creeks, and isolated water holes. James P. Wilson and Clyde and Louis Buttrill began ranching the Rosillos range in 1884, and the following year General Richard M. Gano established the Estado Land and Cattle Company on 55,000 acres in Block G-4 in southern Brewster County.[1]

I never met James Wilson, the Buttrills, or General Gano. They were gone long before I arrived. They were, however, the predecessors of those who helped make the history, create the myths, and live the legends, and who, in turn, had followed their mythical dreams to an unknown land. Those were some of the people I knew, who shared with me their history, their myths, and their legends, and who accepted me into the family of the region of which I came to feel so much a part.

As news of this virgin land spread across Texas, these watered oases became the nuclei for broader settlement patterns. Immigrants soon began filling up the land. Brewster County, organized in 1887, reported a population of only 710 in 1890. Ten years later that number had increased to 2,356, which by 1910 reached 5,200, more than doubling in population during the previous decade. In that same period Presidio County population increased from 1,698 to 5,218, representing an increase of almost 500 percent.[2]

Alpine, located in northeastern Brewster County, became the marshaling point for immigrants seeking new homes in the lower Big Bend country. By the turn of the century the *Alpine Times* was trumpeting the region's assets: "Alpine is a good town now and new buildings are going up all the time.... Alpine now has a population of about 1,200.... We feel safe in saying more people have visited Brewster County during the past year than during the previous ten years."[3] Wagons arriving from the East bringing in new settlers became an ongoing *Times* theme. Although the Southern Pacific Railroad began serving the region in 1882, the covered wagon in its varied forms became the transportation of choice for most Big Bend settlers.

The Thomas Henry Rogers party, which embarked from Pearsall, Frio County, Texas, appears typical of those who heeded the *Times*'s call. Although their initial destination was New Mexico, the route they followed, their mode of travel, their motivation, and their expectations all bore a striking similarity to thousands of other westward-bound settlers. The Rogers party's trek across Southwest Texas recorded in Irene Rogers's diary may be examined as a metaphor for all wagon travel bound for the Big Bend country in the early twentieth century. Nothing escaped the teenager's incisive scrutiny: flora and fauna in a pristine wilderness, horrendous road conditions, the loneliness of wagon travel, new towns springing up along the way, other people she met immigrating west, and the daily lifestyle of wagon travel are all described in this highly personal document.

Rogers's narrative also dramatizes the hardships of wagon travel in 1900. Poor road conditions—where there were roads—were an ongoing problem for the Rogers party. They opened gates, crossed pastures, removed rocks, forded rivers and creeks, double-teamed on hill climbs, locked wheels on steep descents, inquired for directions, took wrong turns, and frequently were unsure of their location. These were problems encountered by most wagon travelers in Texas at the turn of the century. And these problems were not new. During the late 1860s, one Texas traveler wrote, "Our roads are not worked, the waggoner makes his own way. ... Road laws in this magnificent State, like other laws, [are] seldom executed."[4] Three decades later, little had changed. According to the Texas Highway Department, "The turn of the century could almost be charac-

Irene Rogers, whose 1900 diary documents her six-week
wagon train trip from Pearsall, Texas, to Capitan, New Mexico Territory.
Courtesy Hattie Grace Elliott

terized as an era of 'no roads.' Travel was an adventure. The automobile was a curiosity."[5]

In 1900, road conditions in Frio County differed little from those in other areas of the state, and remained largely unchanged during the ensuing two decades. The first Texas road map issued in 1917, the year the Texas legislature created the State Highway Department, indicates no established road system over the initial segment of the Rogerses' journey, Pearsall to Sonora via Uvalde and Rock Springs. However, the conditions the emigrant family encountered once they began driving northwest toward Frio Town probably gave them a false sense of optimism. The gently rolling farmland of their home community would shortly give way to the rocky hills and valleys of Uvalde County, and as the Rogers party began negotiating the approaches to the Edwards Plateau, travel conditions would grow progressively worse.

Irene Rogers graduated from Pearsall High School on April 26, 1900. Two days later, following a round of graduation parties, she began making final preparations for her departure. That same day she began her journal "that is to cover our trip at least and possibly longer. . . . it is for my profit and pleasure and for future reference that this is penned." On the morning of May 3, 1900, the family departed Pearsall. Rogers's account follows:[6]

May 3rd. Nooning. *Left home at 8:30 this A.M. Mrs. DeVilbiss and family and Prof. Etta Bohon [her teacher] were over to bid adieu. We did very well this A.M. The mules, Pete and Katy decided to camp in a mud hole, but the drivers persuaded them to move to Elm switches this side of B. I. Gilmans ranch to noon (13 miles west of Pearsall). A place of lovely grass and numerous mosquitoes, red bugs, etc. Our dinner was sumptuous. Miss Priscilla's cookies, Mrs. Ferries light bread and pickles, and lots of good things. Turkey gob-gobbled nearby, and Papa and George tried in vain to put salt on his tail. More anon.*

May 4th, Friday. Nooning. *Last afternoon we traveled until we were about 24 miles from Pearsall on this side of Frio Town.[7] We camped on a slope about 2 miles from the C. B. Woodward ranch. Just down to the right was a level hole of fresh water and on the opposite side of the road were some pretty mesquite and blackberry bushes. The night, our first out, was a lovely moonlight night, and with our faithful dog "Tiger" to guard us, we lay down to rest, undisturbed by dreams of uneasiness. The biddies [baby chickens] went through the night O.K.*

There was a heavy "fall" of dew that caused our bed quilts to be sunned this morning while we "rest." We travelled very well till this noon. Crossed numerous mudholes, black flats, etc. I've met Jesse Davis this A.M. Passed Mr. Hardin and wife who were stalled on acct. of one horse being snake bitten. After freely bestowing turpentine, we bade them farewell and journeyed on till we reached the 12th gate from home (out on the Uvalde road) and stopped for dinner. This place lacked the shade of yesterday, till a wagon sheet was stretched. Hal and I tried "Herbine" [a patent medicine?] which was bitter sweet. May and Hal made a swing of a mesquite limb—to a hobby horse. Time to catch horses, dog, and chickens. So will quit.

May 5th. Nooning. *Nooning just east of Uvalde, on a lovely body of water; under large Elm trees giving a dense shade; another dinner of quail, rabbit, Miss M. P. DeVilbiss's cookies, light bread and pickles.*

Last night we camped by a lovely mudhole and drank "blue" soup [dirty water] night and morning. The mosquitoes were so large and strong there that, this morning on the road travelling . . . they helped prize us out of bog holes. The gnats were not so large but just as loud. We have only double teams twice, though the road this morning has been very rough.[8] We camped this morning right on the road. Saw many passer's [sic] by. Many of these mosquitoes are as large as my fist. I must write to Allie and Hixie, so will stop.

Sunday, May 6. *Camped on the Nueces, will write up later. (Next Day)—We drove 13 or 14 miles to get this side the Nueces for stopping. . . . The river was easily crossed, rock bottom—the water about 18 or 20 inches deep. It is truly called the "swiftly flowing Nueces." A wide bottom with gently sloping banks, then rising abruptly as if chopped off. Little fish, big fish—all kinds. Yet too smart to bite at bait. The boys fished— but we didn't have fish for supper. Hal, May, Ida, and I went down stream two or three hundred yards and had a fine bath in the swift, clear, deep (8) [feet?] water. The boys, after failing in the fish business, went in swimming, but 'twas most too cold for them.*

Mama baked light bread, washed towels, had early supper. All retired early under a perfect sky lighted by a brilliant moon and twinkling stars. But alas how deceptive a clear sky may be. About one o'clock Mama waked us with the startling statement that "'twas going to rain." All dressed and the boys soon had the tent stretched, which, by the way, had not been used before. We girls folded quilts and rolled mattresses and moved into our 12 x 14 [tent]. Ray ditched it on the North side—the highest. We all (save Geo., who retired to his downy (?) couch in the top of the loaded wagon) went to sleep in our tent—in the face of the thunder storm. It came on directly and presently our bed was most floating in water.

We withstood the storm, however, and woke (with the exception of Mama) about as well as usual. This morning we dried wet bedclothes and allowed the tent's moisture to evaporate and left the grand camping ground rather late. The shower had muddied the ground considerably but never-the-less we have pushed about 26 miles from Uvalde and camped in the Nueces Canyon for noon. The boys found a stream a little muddy and decided to fish again. Hope they will be more successful than previously. Hal and May have gone to explore a nearby mountain that they never reached. Its about time to travel, I must finish a letter.

5/9/00. Monday Night. *Crossed the river again and camped just this side on the left bank. Fished. Had fish for supper and breakfast. Stretched tent again. Lightning in the North. No rain and very little dew. Next day for dinner camped on an elevation in the Canyon. More fishing, but with little success. More reports of the bad road ahead of us. In the afternoon crossed the River and its tributaries several times. Rocks getting numerous. Traveled lots in the low bottoms. The road across the river is walled up by . . . rock. Pass one large hill after another. Round a bend in the road and drive along a bluff nearly perpendicular. The area is covered with shrubs, here and there a large cedar or oak to break the scene—vines—grapes—wild flowers—red, white and blue. Just at the base of the cliff flows a stream of water clear as crystal, dotted with dark spots, still pools full of fish. Rocks. Later the road grows rougher and rougher. May is sick and doesn't very much enjoy the road.*

Last night camped near a dwelling house. Found water in a spring. Saw fish a foot long swimming in the stream flowing there from. Could catch none. Stretched tent again—heavy dew. George killed a big tarantula on his bed. Turned out to be Mama's tucking comb. Greased the wagons so got rather a late start. The road grows worse and worse. Round one bend and travel a mile or so in the low bottoms, with a stream to our right, walled on its other side by bluffs of solid rock. Then cross, and presently we reach another high bluff on the other side; rocks! rocks!! rocks!!! Hills grow more numerous, banks more steep. Have to double teams. . . . Pete and Katy [their mules] weren't equal to it. Now another hard pull—up single teams. Stopped for dinner in rather a "ticky" place. More people to tell us how bad the road is ahead. We are still 12 or 15 miles from Rock Springs at noon.

Wednesday, May 9th.[9] *George and all the rest save Papa and I went to a spring. Geo. wanted a snap shot. He got two. Hope I may live to see some of them. . . . Tis a blessed thing I wrote even the little I did last Wednesday the 9th. I have not had any time to write since and so much has transpired that I will have to scratch a bit. . . . Well, nobody exaggerated about the roads. We left our dinner camp that noon rather early. The road is rather rough. Presently we enter a "flat"—crossed it and*

*slightly ascendly [sic], then turned due south. What a funny way to
go when we have been travelling north all the time. Now the road
forks. Which shall we take? One is a gradual ascent. The other very steep.
We take the gradual—wind about among rocks and up inclines. Now
we reach a down hill. All walk except . . . May who is sick. We must be
on the wrong road. Tis the roughest thing, in the way of a road, I ever
saw. . .*

    *Down this hill us girls trot behind the "Chuck-box" for one hinge is
broken and we are afraid things will fall out. Now the other breaks—we
stop and tie the box shut with ropes. . . . Trot down hill some more.
"Stop! This hill is too steep, we must double teams." Every body works
the road—throwing out rocks, grading up the most abrupt pulls. Then
all get behind and push. Then some take hold of hind wheels and turn.
One big jolt follows another. Now a mule falls on his knees. Now stop
and scotch—somebody carries a big rock all the time. Now Alf. is ready
to give up—"Only one New Mexico trip for me," he says. Every-one
looks* tired, cross, *and* full *of the trip—nearly an overdose. Three times
they double teams.*

    *Here comes a horse backer. "Yes," in reply to our questions, "you are
on the wrong road." "It's three miles nearer but ten miles rougher." We
travel on—jolt! jolt!! Jolt!!! Somebody says—"If a worse road than this
leads to purgatory, I think I will change my route at once." No wonder
E. U. Cooke wrote—"Hell in Texas."[10] It is a good thing he didn't come
from Barksdale to Rock Springs through Hackberry Draw. For then the
poem would have been too forcible.*

    *At last we spy a wind mill. Oh, blissful thoughts. "Yes." They will let
us camp in pasture and get water from the tank. The lady is very kind,
gives us good words and brings down a bucket of milk—appreciated.
Next morning another. She tells us we have about a mile more of rough
road. . . .*

    *Then we drive on and now we are in Rock Springs. We must stop,
get oat meal, cornmeal, salmon, get the wagon fixed (we broke it
doubling teams up a steep bank.) We admire the Court House. Wonder
how people can live so far from any railroad and yet do so much. Meet
up with people going our way, we gladly welcome them (they wore their
welcome out) for it's no fun getting off the road. We have tried it twice.
. . . This man has lately returned from Mex. [New Mexico Territory]
and says he knows all about the road, so we feel better.*

    We leave Rock Springs, travel two or three miles, and stop for dinner near freighters, who have one wagon broken down. Mr. Hill and his outfit passes us. Later we pass them, all camp together, about a mile from a windmill. Carry water in jugs and kegs. Drive horses to water. Start early next morning, travel 8 or ten miles and stop for dinner in a flat. No water! Just after dinner decide to move on three miles to water and wash. We don't much like the idea, not the washing, but the slow moving. But we halt with the rest about a quarter mile off the road. Meet a very pleasant lady, she too contemplates moving to New Mexico. How many more? She lets us have her tub and wash board, etc. and we wash up all dirty clothes. Fear we can't wash any more before we reach our destination.

We have six wagons, a hack, and a buggy in our crew tonight—and about twenty or twenty five head of horses and mules. We are all tired so I had better stop and help get supper for tis growing late. The roads are growing better at this point, about 35 miles from Sonora.

5/11/00. *Wrote above. I was too tired last night to sleep well, but managed to get through the night. Next morning we all rushed thro. the work and pulled out, without thanking Mrs. Neil and Mr. Allen for their special kindness to us. Such is life.*

We had quail stew for supper and dove and quail fry for breakfast. Passed through some pretty country, and halted for dinner in a draw of the best grass we had seen since we left Pearsall. . . . No shade save a few mesquite bushes, but we enjoy a good short rest. Papa tries to trade his horses for mules, to a passerby but doesn't. One of the crowd killed a prairie dog. Oh! Yes Tiger, with the aid of two other dogs killed a rabbit. All cheered him. (It makes me think of an English Chase.)

We left camp at 3, and passed on through more lovely country. Stopped at a tank and windmill; watered the horses; filled kegs and jugs; and moved on, stopping for the night in a draw, the main prong of Devil's River (it ought to start in East Hackberry).

Threatened rain; all stretched tents and wagon sheets, but it didn't rain. Planned to move within a few miles of Sonora Sunday morning, but have camped near a rancho. . . . Mr. Hill just came up and said we must move on through Sonora. All of us are put out. Geo. is the only one that got to bathe. Now all must hustle around just like it wasn't Sunday. Oh, hasten blessed day, that shall usher in cow men, merchants, farmers, etc. who appreciate and hold sacred the Sabbath day. I must quit and do what I can to help.

Sunday, May 13, 1900. *Changed plans again, Mr. Hill decided that as Mama didn't want to go on we would stay right here till Monday morn. Had quite a little stew over it. I was politely told to keep my mouth shut, and I'm polite by doing so. We think it is going to rain. . . . Will write about it later. Will stop and write letters, read and sleep, while we are resting.*

May 15th 1900. Last Sun. we stayed where we were when I stopped writing. It kept threatening rain till we moved the tent after much discussion, a few yards to the higher portion of the flat. The wind continued to rise; the boys ditched the tent; and we retired only to be buried alive in black dirt.

Twas rather late next day before we leave for Sonora, 3 miles distant, but 6 miles the way we must go. The road is fine, tis early yet when we reach the city. Tis the prettiest since we left Pearsall. A Court House resembling that of Rock Springs but more beautiful and better situated for prominence. Part of the lawn is built on a hill, 3 windmills gracing it. The court house is near the base at the end of Main St. This is an enterprising town, everything clean, fresh and bright, as should be in the only town in the county.

The Rogers party reached Sonora thirteen days after departing Pearsall. By estimating the distance actually traveled at 195 miles—about 150 miles via a straight line—they averaged approximately fifteen miles a day. This was the most difficult segment of their trip across Texas, and road conditions in that region changed little during the next two decades. The first road map issued by the State Highway Department in 1917, showing the "proposed system of state highways," indicates no organized road system between Pearsall and Sonora.[11] A 1918–1923 Rand-McNally map, locating "principal highways" in Texas, identifies a road between Uvalde and Rock Springs but nothing between Pearsall and Uvalde.[12]

Within this time frame, intermittent postal service over this segment of the journey also reflects the sparse population, as well as the difficult travel conditions. In 1906, the Post Office Department provided delivery service between Pearsall and Frio Town three times a week, none between Frio Town and Uvalde, six times weekly between Uvalde and Rock Springs, and once-a-week service between Rock Springs and Sonora.[13]

In the next segment of their journey, the Rogers party traversed a far less difficult terrain, possessing a longer and better documented travel history, especially that portion between the Pecos River crossing near Sheffield and Fort Stockton. This was part of what was known as the

"Southern Route" across West Texas, the course pioneered by the San Antonio-San Diego mail service in 1857. This also was the route followed by various frontier military operations and wagon roads that connected San Antonio and Indianola on the east and the military posts and trading centers in West Texas and Chihuahua.[14]

Postal service in this area differed little from that in the region the Rogerses had just left. For example, six years after the Rogers party traveled from Sonora to Fort Stockton, the Post Office Department still had not initiated mail delivery between Sonora and Ozona. Those living between Ozona and Sheffield had mail service three times weekly, while the Sheffield-Fort Stockton segment had once-a-week service.[15]

As the wagon train headed west from Sonora toward Fort Stockton, it would follow generally a route that would become known as Interstate Highway 10-290. And it would traverse a region vastly different geographically from that over which they had just traveled. Irene Rogers noted this change in scenery, which she describes as "our prettiest country yet." Her narrative continues:

> We leave Sonora and for the first mile the country is open and green, then we enter a lane four miles long and rather rough, then into a rolling prairie of Soto [sic] plants on an eminence, in this we stop for noon. Find a little stock water at rather a distance. Have Sonora bread, cake, and potatoes for dinner. Also a shower (slight). In the afternoon strike out northwest, pass a gate, and travel through our prettiest country yet—Prairie bounded by gently sloping hills. Also some rather rocky road, but we call it fine—after our East Hackberry experience.
>
> Later it grows more cloudy and is raining ahead of us. We have some rather rocky abrupt jump-downs for the wagons and after watering at a windmill decide to camp . . . on the base of a hill. It is getting late and very threatening. We hurry supper. Find things broken in chuckbox —Before supper is ready it begins to pour. Mama is sick in the wagon— the rest in the tent. I take refuge on the wagon seat until it slacked up. Then fly to the tent amid blinding flashes of lightning and deafening peals of thunder. . . . We make out a fair supper. This morning we have waited for drying off, climbed hills and now I must make bread, eat dinner and travel on. . . .
>
> 5/17/1900. Thursday—We left our camp and travelled to the long prairie and got another rain. . . . Coming up, Ray drives over one of the few bushes of our ground. Directly, he has unharnessed and discovers a

pretty rattler in the bush. . . . All try *to kill it, but I believe George cut it in two with the ax. Alf. wanted to pull it's [sic]tail out to find its head.*

We were slow getting up next morning, fooled away time, and then had to travel six miles over a muddy road and only reached Ozona about noon. No mail as usual. I appreciate the kindness of my dear friends; so nice to get such long interesting letters. Bought bacon, corn, mollasses [sic], pickles, crackers, cheese, etc.

Ate dinner just west of Ozona. This is the prettiest town we've struck yet. Built on an elevated part of the country—partly on a hill—it is a clean, fresh, bustling town. Some of the residences are sure pretty. The Court House reminds one of Frio's, only it's a more exaggerated state of affairs. . . . an ugly old frame building, looking shame faced, standing so near a handsome, new, rock jail. But I hear the people have started a petition—are carrying it over town today.

5/16/00. . . . We left about three o'clock and camped nine miles this side of Ozona. Mama, who has not been well at all, is worse—has high fever—must take medicine—pills. This morning she is better and we rise early and travel for New Mexico. The roads are fine, only two bad hills, and they are passable. Today for noon we are in a draw—the hills on both sides, in front, and behind. Arthur and Alf. have been tumbling rocks down the side of the most abrupt hill. . . . Mama is lying down, so is George. The rest are talking or washing dishes as I ought to be—but there'll come a time someday———.

5/18/1900, Friday. Did we ever come over a high divide? . . . . Oh yes, one Thursday afternoon, about the 17th of May we went up a hill, winding around considerably to avoid steep pulls. Ray goes to level ground and brings his mules back to help George up. The divide is long and in some parts quite rocky. Here one sees lots of the "wire" grass, which has been quite plentiful along our route for the past week or ten days. The cowmen have begun using it for food. Just chop out a large pile of a bush and two or three cows "go after it," and "they" say, do well on it———.

The divide is high, rough, and wide, but at last we reach the down part, and it is sure down, too. We walk, except Papa, Mama, and drivers. About two-thirds of the way down hill they stop and tie wheels and after some severe jolting, finally land safely in the valley. Travel till we reach water. Water teams, fill kegs, and watering all done we move on across hill, plain, valley and glen till we are within 18 miles of Sheffield.

Spend a very pleasant night except for the thought of bugs, for its rather brushy and buggy here. The night is fair and we try to rise early and pull for the next stop, but are a little late. We travel faster than usual this morning, don't meet such bad roads. Strike a new creek—Live Oak—a pretty clear stream, but carries in stock small fish, only. We drive off the road, hem and haw and finally decide to come on, but Mr. Hills' crowd stay. Wonder whether or not we'll ever see them again? (Yes we most certainly saw them again, they are not anxious to part from us.)

We came within sight of Sheffield and cooked dinner. The sun was most hot enough to cook without any fire. Immediately after dinner the horses are harnessed and we soon reach the Pecos River. Quite ugly though, muddy, with a high mountain on the left bank and flat as can be on this side. We stopped here, stretched our tent and intended staying all night, but are about to change our minds and go on to some springs— mile or two from here. Hope we will, as I would like a cold drink of spring water.

It remains unclear at what point the Rogers party reached the Pecos River, a traditional barrier to east-west travel in Southwest Texas at that time. Apparently they encountered little difficulty in negotiating the crossing, as Irene Rogers makes no special mention of the event. For others traveling west in horsedrawn vehicles before the mid-1920s, a Pecos crossing was an experience fraught with danger. Historian J. Evetts Haley describes that treacherous stream as being "generally so deep as to be impassable— a pocket edition of the lower Rio Grande."[16] Wayne R. Austerman is even more dramatic in his appraisal. He saw the Pecos as "a considerable obstacle to emigrant wagons and stage coaches . . . between the Concho [River] and the Rio Grande. Men often prayed to find it, and then cursed when they attempted to traverse its steep, mired banks. They sometimes died violently in the tangled grease-wood and mesquite thickets that marked its course."[17]

After crossing the Pecos, the party elected to continue on toward Sheffield before making camp with the hope of finding fresh spring water. They were successful, as Miss Rogers explains:

5/20, Sunday. *Yes, we went to the spring at least in that direction. We took the first right hand road and then decided it was wrong. Waited for Ray to gallop ahead and prospected. He returns and we go on, stop, and repeat the act. Finally camp within a short distance of the spring. We walk and bring water in buckets. The boys water the horses. After* stretching the tent and eating supper, Ray and Papa go set hooks. Early next morning, while Arthur and Alf. go in search of horses, they go to bring in their fish, but only one cat can they capture. We salt it down and bring it on for dinner. It is a mile or so to Sheffield where we enquire [sic] about the road, buy soda, corn, bacon, and medicine and pull for Fort Stockton.

It is a rough (?) cloudy day and we travel briskly, camping at 12 in a pretty grassy spot. Eat fish fry and stew. Hal, May, Ray, Bud, and Alf. go mountain climbing while Ida Neal and I wash dishes. Directly George pulls out and goes to the top of the highest mountain in sight. Hal and I follow and all get back just in time. We trot off down the valley and when we reach a fork in the road, take the left hand. Meet a man. . . . We are on the wrong road, will follow him and get back in our road. . . .

Meanwhile, Mama is quite sick, in fact, isn't enjoying this brushy road. At last we are in our road and after a little bit, camp for the night, on a dry (?) creek. Kill two tarantulas for scene I. George gets up next morning with a vicious headache. Mama doses him with P.P.P. [a patent medicine]. . . . By twelve we are ready to stop for Sunday dinner—our third on the road. We have dinner, a la ashe, and I crawl into the tent while the others wash dishes. The weather the last two days, Sat. and Sun., May 19th and 20th, have been cold as Feb. or March (usually) at home, but we must get used to it, for to Mex. we go.

Mr. Hill passed us this noon, we left them Friday. They expect us to overtake them tomorrow, if not will wait for us in Fort Stockton. We are booked for a short supper tonight. The boys are returned from watering the horses at a nearby windmill. (1½ miles). Tig captured a rabbit for breakfast. The girls have returned from their walk and its [sic] time I should quit.

Mama is still wondering and worrying because of no word from Allie. George has written for his pass. We are about half way on our journey and hope in two weeks, by the third of June, to be in New Mexico, if not in Capitan [New Mexico Territory], 17 more days on the road. & Oh! those nice letters my friends were to write me, how I have enjoyed them!

May 23rd, 1900. Wednesday—Last Sunday, how long ago it seems. . . . We had a slight supper and retired early. It was very dark, dreary— doleful. About 11:30 I was awakened by a slough of water under my pillow and shoulders. . . . Directly Ray got up and ditched back of the tent, but 'twas too late! Presently we are all either standing or wading in water. Oh, 'twas nice, fine! Don't you wish you had been there? Hal and May absconded to the wagon. Now George follows (poor sick boy). We hold tent poles for fear of its falling. How delight-fully(?) cool this water is to my bare feet! Let's all emigrate. Where to? Why the wagon, of course.

On go our shoes then splish! splash, splish! splash! Draw our feet out of the sucking mud, stand on the wagon tongue, jump, pause on the seat, remove heavy-laden shoes, fall behind seat and enter pleasant dream land, if you call it pleasant when one's neck is bent two ways and one's legs doubled into the least possible space. But thus we slept, Mama, Ida and I . . . May, too closely quartered in her place of refuge—seeks admittance and is not denied.

At last the day dawned. What blissful cooking, but it's accomplished at last and we breakfast at 11:30 and are off for dryer regions. Soon overtake the Hills and decide to tarry for the evening. We wash towels and try to dry things. We get ready to sleep, and sleep—full till morning. Now off again and travel past more hills and better hills; through mud, past sunny springs, windmills, ranch houses; through more mud, water and so on, to a dryer looking hill for New Mexico Territory.

How nice. Now the brilliant sun comes out. We don't know how to appreciate its beauty and warmth till we've been deprived of it three or four days—especially in camp. God's blessings are manifold, but of all, the sun, glorious sun is greatest, greatest of all.

We dry the bed clothes, clean . . . out the wagons, but Grandma Hill walks in and overtakes us. They stopped behind us. We talk, listen, and now Mr. Hill is coming and we harness up and "Fall in line boys, fall in line." On through more nasty mud-holes and to a pretty grassy camp ground, the first for several days. A pretty clear night like our first out in C. B. Woodward's pasture [in Frio County]. I'm tired, wholesomely hungry, truthfully dirty, while Mama enjoys no such bliss, but is sick all the time. "On to [Fort] Stockton." "Two o'clock now."

5/24/1900. And its [sic] little while till we come in sight of our town. It looks pretty in the distance. To the northwest of us is a lovely line of trees—cotton woods, I suppose. We are in sight of town a good bit before we are in it. . . . A prettier House of Justice that we've seen before. . . . I like this place better than any other since leaving home, and haven't yet seen the place. I would exchange old Frio [Town]. But I think it would be nice to live here 3 or 4 months. It reminds me pleasantly of last summer—idle happy yet busy, prosperous moments—gone all too soon, *leaving the sweetest of memories. How often in these long seemingly useless days, I long to live that short vacation over. I would have but few changes, but one grave one.*

This courthouse is also of rock and built on a slight eminence. On the top are eight, yes nine towers—one large one in the center, freely supplied with windows. . . . The people here are, to my taste, more than [those] of Sonora, or Ozona, or Sheffield either. Well, we disposed of our loose change. . . . Oh, yes, George got 5 (five) letters, just think of it— pause and consider, you who have beguiled the hours away for me by your sweet long loving letters. . . . I heard I had 3 mailed to me down in Pecos City. In this instance I hope "There's more pleasure in pursuit than [in] possessing," will prove false, for it is rather tedious, if comforting, to think of letters ahead if none read. 10 miles north of Fort Stockton. . . . Saturday 1:30. And we went wiggling for Pecos.

Irene Rogers's enthusiastic approval of Fort Stockton overlooked one important aspect of this frontier village. Fort Stockton and adjacent Comanche Springs had been an important urban oasis on travel routes across West Texas for more than a half century. The Old San Antonio Road, the Comanche Trail, and the San Antonio-San Diego Mail Route all intersected at this site. This was also an important stop for military traffic serving the West Texas forts, as well as a junction for wagon traders bound for Chihuahua.

That portion of the Chihuahua Trail extending southwest from Fort Stockton—both segments—became a major entrée for emigrants heading for the Big Bend country. Those bound for the eastern sections of Brewster County and the Boquillas area followed the "cut-off road" by way of Camp Pena Colorado, near present Marathon, and then south to the Chisos Mountains and the Rio Grande. Others bound for Alpine, Marfa, and points in Presidio County followed the right fork of the trail via Antelope Springs and then down Alamito Creek to the Presidio Area. Federal Highways 385 and 67 now follow generally these original wagon routes.[18]

Some twelve years after the Rogers party reached Fort Stockton, the nine-member James William Green family, bound for the Big Bend country, passed through this well-traveled intersection and followed the Chihuahua Trail cut-off to Marathon. Arriving there three days later, they camped, pastured their livestock, and purchased supplies before continuing on to what became their Maravillas Creek homestead. Cheap land

and a healthy climate had lured the family to this picturesque setting. They liked what they found there; eight decades later two members of that family, Aaron and Willie Green, still resided in the region they helped settle in 1912.[19]

The Rogers party, however, chose neither of these routes; Irene Rogers's Big Bend residency would be delayed for almost a decade. And thus she continued northward with her family for a brief interlude in New Mexico Territory. Unaware of what fate held in store for her, Irene Rogers was, unknowingly, enjoying what probably would be the happiest times of her life. Her teenage friends, memories of graduation, and last summer's vacation were visions of the past that would ultimately be dimmed by the events that lay somewhere in the future. But this was today and thoughts of yesterdays seemed to ease the discomforts of wagon travel. And as the Rogers party "went wiggling for Pecos," the only thing that seemed important to Irene was receiving letters from home.

Following a northwesterly course along what is now Highway 285, the Rogers party reached Pecos City, on Wednesday, May 30. It had not been a pleasant journey; instead of rocks, steep hills, and river crossings, they encountered seemingly endless seas of sand. "In the last three days since we left Fort Stockton," Rogers writes, "we have pulled through enough sand, and salt grass, past sufficient alkalai [sic] land to do an ordinary appetite for years, but ours is 'insatiable,' so here we are in sand, sand, and rough grass." And rattlesnakes—George Rogers made his fourteenth kill of the trip.

Irene Rogers's arrival in Pecos City, however, proved to be a mixed blessing. It was at this point that her favorite half-brother, George Rogers, decided to leave the wagon train and return to Pearsall. "We must bid George good bye," she writes. "Just now it seems all is going wrong. (But the human heart in time grows accustomed to all things, and while we sorrow when we must say farewell and long for the companionship of absent ones . . . time and reason tells us 'tis for the best and we seek new objects of adoration. Nature's hands are ever full of gifts for her poor children.)"

Pecos City, however, meant letters from home, "yes five or six of them. One from dear old Hixie, a blessed good girl. Her letters did me *more* good and furnished me more down right pleasure and food for thought." Then her thoughts turn to the absent George; "we all know it's going to be lonesome now." But not for long; a young man named Kimball asked to join the wagon train as he also was going to New Mexico. Irene was delighted as "its something new and he partially fills the vacuum made by Geo's removal. . . [and] developed into a fine fellow, why he'd wipe the dishes, make fires, get wood, drive for you, talk for your amusement—tease you mercilessly about an old friend (??), or in short, keep you from having the blues." However, Kimball's tenure with the Rogers family was brief; sometime later, without explanation, he also left the wagon train.

After leaving Pecos, the Rogers party followed the Pecos River Valley northward, and on May 30, "crossed the fence [into New Mexico Territory] and bade farewell to Texas." Two weeks later, on June 15, 1900, after six weeks in transit, the Rogers party reached Capitan, New Mexico Territory. For the next decade this would be Irene Rogers's home; her Big Bend tenure remained somewhere in an indefinite future. But for the interim, her primary objective was securing a teaching position. On July 11, 1900, she traveled to Alamogordo, New Mexico Territory, where she stayed with "dear Lillian" while studying for the qualifying exams to become a public school teacher. The success she hoped for, however, was not forthcoming. Although her diary entries for the remainder of the year document a period of disappointment and frustration, she nevertheless remained optimistic. The final entries are as follows:

> Have been trying to find out about schools but it seems I can't. . . . How I wish I had a school. I know its [sic] naughty to complain, but really old journal, it bothers you less than my friends, so there. My dreams I will yet realize so help my heaven. . . . No school . . . yet. Hope on. Trust ever. . . . No school . . . but I am not ready to starve. Not Much! Long live the hopes of youth. . . . I have joined the Peacock's Teachers' Agency. No school yet.

On December 9, 1900, she notes that "the year is nearly gone. Papa was crippled on his Roswell trip. Got a letter today [and] was disappointed, have the blues and here it is nearly Xmas." It remains uncertain whether it was the lack of time, interest, or information to report, but on January 1, 1901, Irene Rogers abruptly ends her journal with a terse two-line entry. Other than noting that the day was cold and dreary, the content is without significance.

The bleak New Year's Day appears to have foreshadowed the months of frustration that lay ahead; the teaching position that Irene Rogers so desperately sought continued to elude her. The following year, still unemployed, she accepted a position as governess on a ranch in a remote area of the Capitan Mountains. For sixteen dollars a month, she had to walk five miles each Sunday afternoon to the ranch, and remain there all week. The following Friday afternoon she would walk back to the Rogers homestead. The inconvenience and hardships of negotiating the rocky mountain trails on foot, however, led to an unexpected discovery.

Late one cold Friday afternoon as she made her way home, she heard what sounded like a cry for help. Although frightened, she investigated the matter and found a baby Angora goat tangled in the branches of a thorny bush. She sat down beside the little animal, removed it from the branches, and carefully picked the thorns from its matted hair. Seeing no other goats in the area, she wrapped the little animal in one of her petticoats and carried it home.

A few days later a handsome young man came to the Rogers home, introduced himself as George Peters, and asked if they had seen a baby goat that was missing from his herd. Irene produced the rescued animal, which Peters identified as his. They talked briefly and he left with his goat but returned in a few days to "call on" Irene. Romance blossomed and sometime in 1903 they were married at the courthouse in Lincoln, New Mexico Territory.

A member of a wealthy Ohio family, George Peters had interrupted his medical studies to join the United States Army during the Spanish-American War, and while stationed in Florida developed tuberculosis. On the advice of his physician, he subsequently moved to New Mexico Territory seeking relief in that arid climate. He found the change beneficial and by the time he married Irene Rogers the disease appeared to be in remission.

Theirs was indeed a happy and productive union. During the ensuing four years Irene Peters gave birth to four children, and George, apparently recovered from his malady and enjoying a secure home life, decided to continue his medical studies at Fort Worth University. The strain of medical school, however, ultimately took its toll. Immediately following graduation, "while preparing to go to his home, he was stricken with pneumonia."[20] Irene accompanied her ailing husband back to Capitan, but there appeared little hope of recovery. Ten days later, on March 1, 1909, George Peters died. He was twenty-nine years old.

At this point Irene Peters faced the major turning point in her life; she could not support four children on sixteen dollars a month, and securing a permanent teaching position in the Capitan area appeared unlikely. On the advice of an aunt, Ida Newton, the family decided to return

Peters family portrait. Irene and George Peters pose with their four children,
left to right: Hattie Grace, Oscar Sherman, Mary Josephine, and George Thomas.
Photograph taken shortly prior to George Peters's death
on March 1, 1909. Courtesy Hattie Grace Elliott

to Texas, and during the summer of 1909, they established residence in
Alpine. Irene found the vast stretches of the Big Bend country highly appealing, and after pooling her resources with those of her parents, purchased an entire city block along what is now East Holland Avenue. Here
she planned to remain; Alpine, Texas, would be her permanent home. In
retrospect, it appears ironic that, in the wake of this great personal tragedy, Irene Peters's lifelong dream was about to be fulfilled. In September,
1909, she began teaching the fourth grade in the Alpine school system.

According to her daughter, Hattie Grace Elliott, "this was the happiest time of Mama's life. We kids were growing up, Mama was receiving a
good salary, and she was doing what she had always wanted to do—teach
school." But misfortune still seemed to lurk in Irene's shadow. After some
twenty years of dedicated service, her teaching career was about to be
abruptly terminated. Her spanking an undisciplined child led to complaints
to the president of the school board who, under the guise of a promotion,
had her reassigned as the principal of the Madera School, a segregated
Mexican elementary school. After one year there, she resigned and accepted another teaching assignment at Marathon, a small ranching com-

George Andrews Peters served in the U.S. Army during the
Spanish-American War prior to settling in New Mexico Territory.
Courtesy Hattie Grace Elliott

munity located some thirty miles east of Alpine. She objected to the weekly commuting, and when Sheriff Everett Townsend offered her a position as an office deputy, she decided to give up teaching in order to be home with her family.[21] But even this assignment was temporary. When W. O. Hale replaced Townsend as sheriff he owed a political debt that he planned to repay with Mrs. Peters's position. "He didn't have the nerve to tell her to her face that he didn't need her any longer," Mrs. Elliott recalls. "So he wrote her a note and mailed it to her [saying] that he no longer needed her services."[22]

Irene Peters, however, emerged as a survivor. Like many other members of the Big Bend community, she had learned that the capacity to compromise was a prerequisite for tenancy. So following her release from the sheriff's office, she found employment in the Brewster County Tax Assessor-Collectors Office, from which she later transferred to the city tax department. Adversity sometimes brings blessings in disguise. The skills and information Mrs. Peters gathered in the tax departments enabled her to achieve a level of personal independence she had so long been seeking. Discovering that absentee property owners frequently need local tax counseling, she began compiling a list of potential clients to whom she offered her services. There were many takers, and her new business prospered; Irene Peters could again look to the future with confidence and optimism.

But just as she began enjoying her newly found success, she was suddenly taken ill. The diagnosis: cancer. There was a brief exploratory operation, and the following day, September 6, 1943, she died in her sleep. She was sixty-three years old.

It has been almost a century since Irene Rogers began her westering adventure that morning in May, and nearly a half century since she was laid to rest in the tree-lined cemetery on the outskirts of Alpine. Time takes its inevitable toll; few people living in that region today remember Irene Peters. However, the young teenager from Pearsall, Texas, unknowingly seemed predestined to preserve her story for posterity. Latter-day scholars examining the westward movement of civilization across Texas and the ultimate settlement of the Big Bend country, can see in Irene Peters an enduring symbol of that process. She not only lived history but recorded it with a skill, perception, and insight that belie her age, education, and cultural background.

Irene Peters's tenacity, her determination, and above all her unbridled optimism were typical of the others who accepted the challenge of the Big Bend country and remained there to make a life in that harsh and forbidding land. She, therefore, emerges as a symbol of my verbal lament for the region's past. And while Irene Peters may have faded from the realm of human recollection, she, nevertheless, has etched for herself an enduring niche in the annals of Big Bend history. She will not be forgotten.

"I've Been Seeing Other Women"

Over a period of some thirty years I made many trips to the Big Bend country conducting interviews and gathering information for various research projects. Each time, on my return home, my wife asked the same question and received the same answer: "Yes, I had a very successful trip, but I must confess, I've been seeing other women."

A survey of my Big Bend bibliographies yields a disproportionate number of female contributors, many the widows of men who helped make the region's history. But there were others who made history themselves and, other than my wife, were some of the most fascinating women I ever met.

The region, especially its remoteness and scarcity, imposes a great responsibility on all its occupants; survival becomes a way of life. In the ongoing struggle there evolve two distinct classes of people, those who succeed and those who do not. In most disparate societies the plight of these less fortunate has awakened within a few individuals the latent spirit of compassion, the desire to help those unable to help themselves. The history of the river country, and especially the lives of some of the region's less prosperous, have been greatly enriched by the personal commitment of four outstanding women. I was fortunate to have known three of them.

When I made my first Big Bend research trip in December, 1964, Maggie Smith was in the twilight of her career. She died two years later. Although we never met, the stories I heard of her deep compassion for other border residents prompted me to learn more about this remarkable woman. Two facts became readily apparent: one, Maggie Smith was a local legend; and two, she represented what I admired most about the Big

Bend country—people helping people. I further recognized that she must be included in any social history of that region. However, it fell to friends and fellow scholars to provide the details of the rich and abundant life of Maggie Smith.

"Her name lives on with the reputation she earned as a fearless, generous, honest, independent woman and general godmother," writes folklorist-historian Elton Miles. "In her long Big Bend career she was a border storekeeper and trader in *candelilla* wax, respected by Anglos, and almost revered by her Mexican neighbors."[1] She also instilled in her children her personal philosophy of humanity, generosity, and compassion. Daughter Madge Smith Gravel explained, "she was a very generous person. She believed there was good in everyone. She always told us when we were growing up that it wasn't the color of a person's skin and it wasn't their religion or creed, it was what was inside that was important. She was never prejudiced in her life. She always said there was some good in everybody and nobody was all bad. . . . She always had a helping hand for everybody, and she did good in more ways than just helping people—like raising children that didn't belong to her."[2]

Maggie Smith was born on June 5, 1895, at Carrizo Springs, Texas. While still a teenager she moved with her family to her grandfather's ranch south of Sierra Blanca; the borderlands culture placed an indelible mark on Maggie. She worked cattle with her father, acquired the language and folk remedies of the Mexican people, learned to handle firearms, and married twice.[3] Maggie's Big Bend tenure began in 1940 as the proprietor of the store at Boquillas, Texas. Three years later the State Parks Board asked her to take over the store and bath house at Hot Springs, originally established by J. O. Langford.[4] She remained there until December 31, 1952, when she moved to San Vicente, where she maintained a store until the National Park Service acquired the property in 1960.[5] Within this two-decade time frame, Maggie became a Big Bend legend. She served the less fortunate on both sides of the Rio Grande as "doctor, midwife, justice of the peace, ambassador, and friend to those in need. She raised her own five children and more beside."[6] Maggie's friend and neighbor, Mrs. Frank Wedin, remembered her as "a mighty good person" but "a little bit rough. . . . She didn't have time to stop and pretty herself up such as that. She was doing things for other people." Mrs. Wedin adds that the community held Maggie in high esteem "because lots of lots of people down there on the river would have almost starved if it hadn't been for Maggie. . . . There was never a day too long or a night too dark that she couldn't go help people."[7]

Maggie had two primary sources of income, the store and the *candelilla* wax trade. According to historian Clifford B. Casey, "Maggie Smith aided the Mexicans smuggling *candelilla* wax across the river in the darkness of night. She was often seen far from Hot Springs . . . making contacts with Mexican producers along the Rio Grande."[8] Some of Maggie's contacts came from the interior of Mexico with whom she negotiated with both cash and merchandise. D. D. Thomas, a Marathon, Texas, appliance dealer, explained that on several occasions he sold her gas refrigerators, not available in Mexico, which she traded for smuggled *candelilla* wax. He recalled delivering a refrigerator one night to San Vicente, a remote riverside village where the exchange was scheduled to be made. Arriving at the site, Maggie told Thomas, "'Well, let's just park here by the river and we'll just get out and wait a while.' . . . And so we sat there for almost an hour." She explained to Thomas that the wax business was a high-dollar operation, adding, "'there's many a time when I sat right here with $80,000 in cash to pay for the wax.'" Around one o'clock the next morning a wagon forded the river from Mexico on which they loaded the refrigerator. When Thomas inquired about the appliance's destination, Maggie explained, "'It goes to a Mexican army captain about two hundred miles in the interior of Mexico. . . . She just bought the refrigerator and gave it to him. . . . That's what she bought the wax with. . . . Never was another person in this world like Maggie Smith."[9]

Between the wax business and the store, Maggie maintained a steady income, little of which she kept for herself. She made her living off the Mexican people, explained Ross Maxwell, former director of Big Bend National Park, "but she was godmother to many of them and gave back most of what she made in the way of food, clothing, medicine, and services. A Mexican never left Maggie's store hungry or cold."[10] She never deviated from this policy. Shortly before her death on April 8, 1965, she instructed daughter Madge to purge her books of all Mexican accounts and destroy the records.[11]

And so the legend of Maggie Smith endures, an inspiration to all who share her compassion for those who have been denied life's amenities in a harsh and forbidding land. The other three women whom I was privileged to know fall within Maggie Smith's category of social benevolence. Each person—Kathryn Casner, Mary Daniels, and Lucia Madrid—chose by circumstance a role to play in the ongoing drama of survival in the Big Bend country of Texas. Their stories follow.

1

Kathryn Casner

SHE PRACTICED MEDICINE
WITHOUT A LICENSE

In appearance, personality, and cultural background, no three women could have been more dissimilar; their common bond was their intractable concern for the less privileged. I am not sure if any of them were acquainted, and certainly none worked in concert with the others. Kathryn Casner undoubtedly knew of Mary Daniels, but they moved in different social circles. Probably neither Casner nor Daniels knew Lucia Madrid, and while Madrid also knew of Mary Daniels, there is no record of them meeting socially.

Taken as a group, they were what is usually termed ordinary middle-class women who had little in common except their social concerns. None were wealthy, none were poor, and two were, or had been, schoolteachers. All three were storekeepers who successfully bridged the ethnic gap between the Anglo and Mexican cultures. All were married and all had children.

The Big Bend country provided the setting for these women to fulfill their desire to serve others. Two of them regarded the border environment as their natural habitat; they would have lived nowhere else. Kathryn Casner, on the other hand, moved to the river only because of her husband's health. And unlike the stereotypical women of the American West who were dominated by the "patriarchy of masculine power and prerogatives," these women encountered no domestic encumbrance.[1] All were married to men who were either supportive, tolerant, or disinterested in their wives' social concerns, and all were free to pursue their special interests. And because of their strong commitments, they are still remembered along the Great River for bringing hope to many where there was no hope.

Of the three, Kathryn Casner arrived on the scene possessing the fewest prerequisites. As the wife of Stanley W. Casner, businessman and mayor of Marfa, Texas, her daily routine included women's club activities, church functions, community fund drives, and the responsibility of raising two small children. This was destined to change. Stanley Casner, a World War I United States Air Service veteran, was the last of the four brothers to enter the family business, Casner Motor Company.[2] In the early 1920s, the business prospered as did the Casners; they became local symbols of civic pride and leadership. It was during this period that Stanley met Kathryn, who was then attending Sul Ross State Normal College in Alpine. Following a brief courtship they were married in Mertzon, Texas, Kathryn's hometown. In December 1924, after a monthlong honeymoon, they moved to Marfa where Stanley's responsibilities with the family business multiplied manyfold.

This proved to be an unwise move. "Stanley had taken on too many jobs," Kathryn explained. "He was working under too much stress and was on the verge of a nervous breakdown."[3] Army doctors at the Fort Bliss hospital recommended rest, a change of pace, and a move to a warmer climate. After considering the coastal area, they chose instead Chinati Ranch, the family-owned property on the Rio Grande, located some thirty-five miles upriver from Presidio. "It was a quick decision," Kathryn explained. "In a week we were moved."[4]

Although a mere sixty-five miles separate Marfa and Chinati Ranch, they were socially, culturally, and economically worlds apart. Remoteness and ethnic diversity were the conditioning factors. So when the Casners arrived at the riverside farm and ranch in April, 1932, they were totally unprepared for the new lifestyle that awaited them in that vague twilight zone that existed between the two bordering nations. The change was startling; their only neighbors were Mexicans who migrated at will across the shallow waters of the Rio Grande. Neither spoke the other's language, and each viewed the other with equal measures of suspicion and distrust. Thus the natives and the newcomers found themselves at a marked disadvantage. If the cultural impasse was to be resolved, the responsibility would fall mainly to the intruding Anglo minority.

With the specter of banditry still shrouding the borderlands, Kathryn saw danger where danger no longer existed. "The Mexicans all looked like

Stanley and Kathryn Casner enjoying a rare moment of relaxation at Chinati Ranch. Farmers, ranchers, merchants, and humanitarians, the Casners helped to enrich lives of the Mexican people living along both sides of the Rio Grande. Courtesy Stanley W. Casner, Jr.

bandits," she explained. Time and experience, however, changed this. She soon learned their different personalities and "the one that first looked like a bandit . . . was one of the most kindly of all. And he was good to my children."[5] Stanley also gained the confidence and respect of the Mexican staff who worked the twenty-four-section farm and ranch, as well as the confidence and respect of his neighbors along both sides of the Rio Grande. As the local symbol of Anglo prestige and authority, he projected a new and welcomed image; he went unarmed and treated the Mexicans with consideration and respect.

Of the two, Kathryn was forced to make the greater adjustment. She helped Stanley in the company store, served as postmistress, and accepted the teaching position at Chinati School. The Casners owned the school building, but with no teacher, there had been no school at Chinati for several years. So with a measure of civic responsibility and concern for her children's education, Kathryn accepted the position; she received seventy-five dollars a month.[6] This new position required considerable preparation. Her daughter, Ann, who attended Chinati School, remembered that the room "had the old-fashioned desks of assorted sizes, which mother repainted. She made curtains and put up bird prints and decorated the walls with posters made by the children. . . . Mother made a very nice coat closet out of two large packing crates."[7]

Chinati School opened with some thirty-five students in grades one through three. Thirty-three of the students were Mexican; two were Anglo. Ann Casner was five and Stanley, Jr., was three. According to Ann, "Mother really seemed to like to teach the Mexican children more than Stan and me. . . . I'm sure the Mexicans, most of whom had never owned a pencil, crayon, paper or book was, for her, more interesting to teach because everything was new, and simple things were often so difficult for them. But they were always thrilled when something turned out well."[8]

Education at Chinati School evolved as a two-way process. As the Mexican children gained English reading and writing skills, the Casners also developed rudimentary use of borderland Spanish. The children, however, progressed faster than their parents. "They knew . . . [Spanish] before I knew they knew it," Kathryn recalled. "I heard Stanley, Jr., just a

Ann and Stanley Casner, Jr., enjoying a ride on their favorite burros, "Cleopatra" and "Socrates," at Chinati Ranch. Growing up as minorities in a Mexican community, gave these two youngsters deep insight into race relations. Courtesy Stanley W. Casner, Jr.

little tot, telling Salome Garcia in Spanish to 'Shut your mouth, you old goat,' because he did something Stanley didn't like. He sounded just like a little Mexican child."[9]

In order to help the Mexican children develop bilingual skills, Kathryn encouraged her children to use only English at school, but to no avail. They preferred Spanish, claiming English "slowed up their games too much."[10] Ann remembered that her father "did fine [with the language] if he was doing the talking, because he had probably rehearsed what he planned to say. He often turned to Stan and me for translations of what was being said to him. . . . Mother invented her own Spanish."[11]

With school, the post office, the store, and the house, Kathryn led a busy life at Chinati. The store, stocked with groceries, work clothing, piece goods, and sundries, evolved as the major trade center between Presidio and Ruidosa. All customers were Mexican; the ranch employees charged their purchases, while those from Mexico paid with both United States and Mexican currency. In the beginning Kathryn found this confusing, but "I learned my lesson the hard way. I took a Mexican twenty dollar bill [for some purchase] and thought how wonderful." Her enthusiasm was premature. When she checked up at the end of the day she discovered her error. The bill was worthless rebel currency bearing the image of Pancho Villa.[12]

As the Mexican people gained confidence in and respect for the Casners, they came to expect more and more of the newcomers to the Rio Bravo. It was this confidence that created a new responsibility for Kathryn, and one for which she possessed no prerequisite. She long remembered her first patient at the Kathryn Casner minor emergency medical clinic. Having no alternative, a farm worker came to her with a badly mangled hand. She was startled at the sight: broken bones penetrated the skin while infected proud flesh covered the back of the hand. Kathryn made no attempt to reset the bones; "it was too far gone for that." As a last resort, she turned to the only remedy she knew, and the only one available at Chinati Ranch—Epsom salts. After days of soaking the hand in this solution, the infection disappeared and the wound began to heal. "I never thought I could save that hand," she recalled, "but it got well and wasn't too badly scarred."[13]

With Kathryn's reputation as the "Miracle Worker of the Rio Bravo," her front porch clinic became the destination of all the sick and injured from both sides of the river. There were doctors in Presidio and Ojinaga, but she was the only hope for many Mexicans. "Roads were terrible on either side [of the Rio Grande]," she explained, "and almost impassable on the Mexican side." Lack of funds, however, was another factor that attracted the Mexican people to Kathryn. "They had to have the money before a doctor would look at them in Ojinaga," she added, "and my services were free. So I developed quite a large medical practice. It was literally forced on me."[14]

Although her first venture into medical practice proved successful, Kathryn realized she needed professional assistance. "That's when I got the doctors in Presidio and Marfa interested in helping me," she remembered. "No one had been doing anything for the Mexican people before, and when I asked for their help they were really generous. They gave me advice, as well as lending me their medical books."[15] And while this material proved helpful, she credited two other factors for her success at Chinati: on-the-job training and luck.

Minor surgery became Kathryn's greatest challenge. With most Mexicans working without shoes or gloves, thorn-induced infection sent many patients to see "La Doctora." This required opening the infected area to establish drainage. For this procedure, Kathryn used a makeshift scalpel, a double-edge razor blade, and a bottle of CO_2, which the doctors provided to ease the pain.[16] It was while assisting Kathryn during a surgical procedure that Stanley first learned of his wife's venture into medicine. She recalled his being visibly shaken seeing her open a patient's infected heel. Up to that day "I don't think he even realized how dangerous it was and what a strain it was [on me] to cut into somebody when you know that if you slipped or erred, you could kill 'em.... That was not long after we went there."[17]

In the absence of traditional clinical supplies, Kathryn, through necessity, turned to whatever was available. Before performing surgery on an old Mexican woman with an infected hand, she explained to her that "I can't keep it from hurting, because I have to go deeper than I can freeze it [with CO_2].... So I gave her a small glass of sotol [a fiery native liquor made from the sotol plant]. I thought it was enough to put anybody out, but it wasn't near enough for her," Kathryn recalled. "When I finished, she got out her own bottle of sotol and took an even larger drink.... My patients used sotol as an anesthetic [and an intoxicant] and I used it as a disinfectant when I didn't have alcohol."[18]

Most patients came to Chinati Ranch for their medical needs; for those unable to travel, Kathryn made house calls. Since poor roads made automobile travel difficult, she usually walked or rode horseback, carrying her meager medical supplies in saddlebags. These were usually emergency cases, and thereby, the most traumatic. A runner from Mexico arrived at the ranch one Sunday morning, reporting that a teenage Mexican boy had been stabbed at a dance the night before. His parents wanted Kathryn to come immediately and try to save the boy's life. Arriving at the home, she quickly examined the wound but, not knowing the depth of the incision, confessed later that "I was scared half to death."[19] She, nevertheless, proceeded to bathe the patient with wet towels to lower his temperature and calm his excitement. Next, she disinfected the wound with sotol. Realizing that the bleeding wound had to be closed, Kathryn again was forced to improvise. With small strips of adhesive tape, she carefully drew the wound together and dressed it with strips of cloth torn from a pillow case. She would not, however, leave her patient until the bleeding had subsided. Fearing internal hemorrhaging and a possible secondary infection, she persuaded her husband to take the boy to a doctor in Presidio as soon as he was able to travel. According to her daughter, Ann, the doctor praised her mother's emergency procedures, explaining that "since the knife just missed the heart, he would have bled to death except for what Mother did for him."[20]

Delivering babies was one procedure that Kathryn always tried to avoid, and with one exception, she had a perfect record. Before leaving on this particular delivery call, she sent Stanley for a local midwife, "five miles down the river over bad roads. Of course, the baby came before he could get back with the midwife." Kathryn, however, proved herself a competent obstetrician. When the midwife finally arrived "she complimented me on the way I handled the delivery. Said I had left the length of two fingers of the cord and had tied it properly. . . . I don't know how I did it. Just instinct, I guess."[21]

Kathryn's success record at Chinati was not without blemish. Cruz Mavarette, a local bootlegger and friend of the Casners, was also a frequent customer at the store, and during Prohibition provided their friends with quality liquor from across the border. Even under the close scrutiny of the Border Patrol, Cruz's ingenious smuggling technique enabled her to prosper while others fell victim to the law. Stanley recalled one occasion when she arrived at the store to make a delivery and unexpectedly encountered a border patrolman. There was no indication she was carrying the illegal contraband, which she had carefully sequestered between her two ample breasts. While her customer sat awaiting the exchange, Cruz eyed her adversary carefully while supposedly scanning the shelves for merchandise. Finally, when something diverted the patrolman's attention, she moved quickly in front of her waiting customer, made a deep bow exposing her femininity, as well as the cache of liquor. Permission was not requested, nor was it granted. The waiting customer quickly reached inside her loosely fitting blouse, withdrawing his prepaid bottle of liquor. Cruz continued to peruse the merchandise for a few minutes, then quietly departed toward the river.[22]

Later, the Casners became concerned when they had not seen Cruz for several weeks. When Cruz finally sent for her, Kathryn knew there must be a problem. One look at the old bootlegger confirmed her worst fears. "Her whole body was just a mass of blood boils," she recalled. "When I lanced them, they would get well, but soon more would appear." Kathryn finally explained to Cruz that there was nothing else she could do; she would have to go to the hospital. Cruz refused, explaining that if Kathryn could not cure her, then she would live out her final days at home.[23]

Even if the old bootlegger was ready to give up, Kathryn was not. "I rode over there—in Old Mexico—every day and took ice—none of them had ice—and milk and soup or some kind of broth," she recalled. But it was all for naught. After several days she drifted into a coma and died shortly thereafter. "I was there when she died," Kathryn added. "I checked her pulse, found nothing, and told the family she was gone." They immediately began lighting candles around her bed, with a cluster near her head. Kathryn remembered it was a long, lonely horseback ride back to the ranch that night. "It upset me, of course," she explained. "It was a personal loss because I had taken care of her for so long and had gotten attached to her. And she had such great confidence in me."[24]

After years of treating the Mexican people in their native setting, Kathryn concluded that poverty, nature, and ethnic tradition greatly limited her potential for success. Malnutrition, she believed, was the greatest obstacle to good health among the Mexican people. "One reason I saved so many lives was probably the food I took with me rather than my medical skills," she explained. Her two nutritional standbys, hot soup and milk, were seldom found in the Mexican homes along the Rio Grande. She believed their restricted diet—frijoles (beans), green chilis, tortillas, and sometimes chicken and eggs—constituted their greatest health hazard. Fruits and vegetables were virtually excluded from their diet, and when considering that so many of her patients suffered from blood poisoning, she reasoned that better nutrition would have better enabled them to resist infection. And so Kathryn Casner discovered along the Rio Grande in the

1930s and 1940s what the United Nations confirmed a half century later. On May 1, 1995, that organization issued the following statement: "Poverty is the greatest underlying cause of death, disease and suffering worldwide, the United Nations said today in its *first survey on the state of World's health*" [italics mine].[25]

In 1946, the Casners sold the ranch and moved to Presidio. Their fourteen-year tenure at Chinati left an indelible mark on the family, and they, in turn, helped instill in the Mexican people a different and more positive view of Anglo society. Kathryn and her front-porch clinic touched the lives of many Mexican people living along the Rio Grande. "I guess this was one of my biggest contributions to humanity. I didn't think I was doing anything unusual," she explained. "There was no heroism involved. No one paid for anything. I never expected to be paid. I was just doing what I could for the people."[26]

Kathryn agreed that the Mexicans' attitude toward them differed from that displayed toward other Anglos along the border. She believed it was mainly a matter of kindness, consideration, and understanding. Daughter Ann agreed. She remembered that "my parents did not try to change the way people lived. They did try to help them with what they had. I remember my Dad [trading] ... one of his young Hereford bull calves [to a Mexican] for a scrawny river calf. It was an even trade. Dad knew that bull would immensely improve the quality of the Mexican's herd with the birth of the first calf." Ann was equally surprised when her mother traded "all her wedding finery for a long legged heifer. ... I could not understand how she could sell all of those things at any price, much less [for] an ugly cow. [But] she felt it was the right thing to do. ... Mother did not want to insult them by giving them things they fully intended to buy."[27]

The Chinati experience had an enduring impact on the Casner children, Ann and Stanley, Jr., especially through their association with the Mexican children. "[They] often seemed superior to us, even though they could neither read nor write, but because they really belonged to the country," Ann wrote. "Their destiny was tied up with [the country]. They seemed to know that they would be doing just what people had been doing there forever. I had a feeling of not belonging, of some uncertainty about a life I felt I should be a part of, but was not. I hated to think of leaving the security of what seemed to me to have the safeness of eternity."[28]

Economics conditioned by drought, the Depression, and hard times, ultimately dispersed the Rio Grande society that once found hope and security at Chinati. Many of the Mexican people preceded the Casners in their exodus from the valley. Some found farm work at Pecos and Balmorhea, while others were attracted by the good salaries in the Permian Basin oil field. "But there were still some to tell us good-bye when we left," Kathryn recalled. "And whenever one of them came back from . . . wherever they had gone, they would always come by to see us. They never forgot us."[29]

2

Mary Coe Daniels

SHE LIVED *MUY A GUSTO,*
A GUSTO

It was late afternoon when Stanley Casner and I returned to Presidio. We had spent most of the day traveling upriver, visiting sites at Candelaria and Ruidosa. I told Stanley that before I left the area I wanted to meet Mary Daniels. "Should be no problem," he explained. "She lives in her store and stays open as long as there is anyone to talk to." He then laid down the ground rules for my visit. "It's getting late so she will probably invite you to dinner across the river in Ojinaga." Should that occur, he emphasized, I *was not* to offer to pay the check; that would be a breach of protocol. "Her money, and yours if you are with her, is no good over there," Stanley added. "She's done so much for those people, that's their way of saying thank you. When she crosses that river, they open up the town for her."[1]

As Stanley and I parted that afternoon he said his wife had made plans for the evening; otherwise, he would enjoy going with me to Mary's. I soon realized the import of his statement. I spent the evening with a delightfully charming lady and a well-known Big Bend personality. From Porvenir to Boquillas, from Marfa to Ojinaga, most people either knew or knew of Mary Daniels. Mary, Maria, Dona Maria, and later just plain "Ma" Daniels was, and so remains, a Big Bend legend and an institution. During her nearly six decades along the Rio Grande, she brought hope, happiness, some security, and much good cheer to those who passed her way. Possessing that rare quality of human sensitivity that endeared her to all people, she unquestionably left the river community a better place than when she found it.

Mary Franklin Coe was born on September 28, 1892, in Colorado City, Texas, the daughter of Judge A. J. and Mary Martha Bender Coe. "It was under the guidance of these two dignified parents that the unpredictable Mrs. Daniels grew up," wrote Susan Godbold. "Her father fondly called her 'Jim' and allowed her to take on such un-lady-like chores as taking care of his horse and buggy."[2] With the exception of art and music, Mary found school boring. Upon graduation, however, she enrolled in Carlton College in Bonham, Texas, later returning to Colorado City for a brief stint as an art teacher.

Meeting John Ringo Daniels in a Colorado City drug store marked the turning point in Mary's life. When she first saw the handsome young stranger supporting himself on crutches, she knew immediately he was her man. "Mrs. Daniels was a belle and enjoyed the attentions of the male

At age sixteen, Mary Franklin Coe, the belle of Colorado City, Texas, strikes a formal pose. Courtesy Junior Historian Files, Marfa Public Library

population of Colorado City," Godbold wrote, "but none turned her head like Daniels."[3] Recovering from a recent railroad accident, John walked with great difficulty. Mary felt deep compassion for this lonely young man and immediately wanted to be his friend and companion. Concern for those who could not help themselves became a dominant force in her life. She confessed years later, "I have always been interested in the downtrodden and the handicapped."[4]

Although her family disapproved of Daniels—"'they wouldn't let him come on the place'"—she and John, nevertheless, began dating and were married in March, 1913. According to Mary, her parents "'just had a wall-eyed fit.'"[5] Judge Coe's objections were well taken. "'What'll happen,'" he predicted, "'is that he loves the river [Rio Grande] and she will tramp right in after him the rest of her days. She'll be right on that river.'" Time proved the judge correct.[6]

The newlyweds began life together on a ranch near Sweetwater, Texas. When that venture failed, Daniels, as his father-in-law predicted, turned his attention to the lower river country. In late 1914, John and Mary, accompanied by John's parents, embarked in a dilapidated Mitchell automobile for Dugout, a small Big Bend ranching community located east of the Chisos Mountains in southern Brewster County. Finding no accommodations there, they continued on to Boquillas, where Jesse Deemer allowed them to spend the night in his store. Although young Daniels foresaw opportunity along the Rio Grande, his father's illness interrupted his immediate plans. The following day John and Mary drove the elder Daniels back to Alpine, where they boarded a train for Merkle, Texas, their hometown.

Left alone in Alpine, the newlyweds faced a very fundamental problem: Big Bend distances required a better automobile. And there was another very practical problem; they had no money for a down payment. Mary offered a solution; John was hesitant. Jim Casner, the Alpine Ford dealer, recalled the event with some amusement. Following a brief conversation with this very strong-willed young woman, he "suggested that she go to the local bank, which she did and hocked her diamond ring . . . for enough to buy the car which sold for about $500."[7] This event marked the beginning of another Daniels life pattern; Mary made the business decisions. "John was very different from her," explained Presidio merchant Carlos Spencer. "John would never tell her anything to do or not to do. She was the boss. John was a very quiet man."[8]

In their new car, the Daniels embarked for Marfa, where Mary found

*Mary and John Ringo Daniels at their Chisos Mountain cabin. As young
pioneers they cut the logs for the cabin, hauled water in barrels strapped
to a burro, cut their firewood, raised a few crops, and hunted for their food.
Courtesy Junior Historian Files, Marfa Public Library*

opportunity waiting. Marfa was the hub of a booming Mexican cattle
trade, and "they were crossing lots of cattle out of Mexico [at Lajitas],"
she recalled. "So we used this automobile . . . for a service car running
[cattle buyers] from Lajitas to Marfa." Although the money was good, the
roads were not; "took twenty-horsepower and one mule to get you out of
there [Lajitas]." The Daniels prospered, and profits from the cattle trade
gave them time to assess other opportunities in the Big Bend area.[9]

Mary soon tired of the taxi service, and she and John decided to do a
little pioneering on their own. Their objective: the mile-high Chisos Mountains. They had fallen in love with the lofty Chisos on their 1914 trip to
Dugout and vowed to return. It was a precipitous journey. After selling
the car, they hauled their possessions in a wagon from Marfa to Terlingua,
thence down Terlingua Creek to Terlingua Abajo, where everything was
transferred to pack burros for the final ascent up Blue Creek to Laguna
Meadow.[10] "We had to carefully pack everything to keep it from getting
broke," Mary explained. "I had some nice things, beautiful Haviland China
and silver. The sewing machine was the hardest thing to pack. Well, we
packed those burros, and the only thing that was broken was a coal oil
lamp."[11]

This was indeed a pioneering experience; life at Laguna Meadow afforded few amenities. The Daniels camped out for two months, cut logs to build a house, hauled water from a spring in barrels strapped on a burro, cut their firewood, raised a few crops, and hunted for most of their food. "I didn't like to hunt, [but] Mr. Daniels took care of that part," Mary explained. "We raised goats and sheep, [and] there were lots of bear." But despite the hardships, those were happy times for the Danielses. Mrs. George Crosson visited them in their mountain retreat and observed "their very marked devotion to each other. She, high spirited and intelligent and he, slow, sure, and calm at all times. They enjoyed life very much in those days."[12]

When Mary became pregnant with their first child, they realized their mountain sojourn was nearing an end. And there were other problems. This was the high tide of border depredations, and all along the Rio Grande people lived under the constant fear of attack. "We didn't get raided but there were warnings of raids," Mary explained. "I went to Marfa to get help. They wanted to give me the [Texas] rangers. I said, 'Just give me the bandits, I don't want the rangers, that's a cinch.' They couldn't do anything until it happened. I said, 'We won't need help after it happens.' I called the government up and the next day here came a whole slew of them [cavalry soldiers] riding on horseback."[13] The protection the cavalry provided fell far short of Mary's expectations. She recalled with some amusement that Mexicans from across the river later stole the cavalry mules. Apparently the Mexicans were not the only violators of the international boundary. The Daniels received another warning when several "officers came up there and arrested Pappy [John Daniels] and took him away for something. . . . But they turned him loose." Mary chose not to elaborate.[14]

In July, 1917, following the birth of their first child, Mary Sue, the Daniels left the Chisos, and John found employment on the Brite Ranch, located some thirty miles southeast of Valentine, Texas, near the Mexican border. Tragedy, however, seemed to follow the Daniels. Soon after arriving, Mexican bandits raided the ranch on Christmas Day, 1917, stole a number of horses, sacked the commissary, and killed the stage driver and two of his passengers.[15] Although the Danielses were not injured in the raid, they were, nevertheless, destined to experience another tragedy. On April 27, 1918, their year-old daughter died of ileocolitis.

Distraught over the loss of their first child, the Danielses decided to relocate. Again they felt the lure of the river. Using her recent inheritance,

Mary purchased a cotton farm at Porvenir, a cattle ranch across the river in Mexico, and established her first store near Harry "Hawkeye" Townsend's cotton gin at Porvenir.[16] Mary explained these were good times for them: "I never lived anywhere in my life that I enjoyed living any more. The [Mexican] people were the poorest people I ever [saw] in my life, but I am interested in the downtrodden, the handicapped, and retarded people. And we just lived *muy a gusto, a gusto* [very happily, very happily]."[17]

The primary source of Mary's happiness was the love and friendship she shared with the Mexican people who lived in Pilares, a small village across the Rio Grande in Mexico. In a region seething with racial conflict and distrust, "Dona Maria" offered their only ray of hope. She fed them when they were hungry, doctored them when they were sick, mediated their domestic quarrels, and delivered their babies. The Danielses also prospered in their new riverside setting. They enjoyed abundant yields from their irrigated cotton farm, and the Mexican cattle ranch emerged as "a nest egg for us." In addition, Mary was appointed Porvenir post-mistress, and her new store drew steady trade from both sides of the river. "I've had a store ever since we lived in this country," she explained. "Some kind of a little old trade-out store. And you take everything in trade but children. It doesn't make a bit of difference what it is, you take it. Not much money changed hands." She added that she had traded for thousands of furs: coyote, bobcat, ring tails, "and thousands of arrow-heads."[18] And Mary even once violated her no-children rule. "I once took a five year old Mexican boy and reared him," she explained. "He's a fine, fine boy. . . . He's married [now] and lives up here at Morton, Texas."[19]

Although Mary enjoyed good relations with the Mexican people, such was not the case with her Anglo neighbors. Their distrust and suspicion probably stemmed from her close ties with the Mexicans, especially with those living across the river in Pilares. The law enforcement agencies had targeted this village as the region's primary bandit stronghold. During that period of border depredations, members of the United States Cavalry, Texas Rangers, and local ranchers staged at least two punitive attacks on Pilares, killing an undetermined number of suspected raiders, as well as some innocent civilians.[20] Mary assumed an unpopular stance; she openly denounced the invaders as bloodthirsty murderers. Others agreed. Texas governor William P. Hobby dismissed Texas Ranger captain James M. Fox and his entire company for their role in the raid, and the Carranza government filed a protest with the United States Department of State. Mary further alienated herself by the company she kept. Chico Cano, the notorious bandit leader reportedly visited in her home, and she claimed she knew "the old lady who held the horses for the bandits when they killed [in ambush] Mrs. Howard's husband [United States mounted inspector John S. H. Howard]."[21]

The local Anglos' dislike and distrust for Mary ultimately prompted overt response. According to her, they conspired to enforce an economic blockade of her activities. "They didn't want me to buy anything [there]," Mary recalled. "Old man Coronet [unidentified] had the [cotton] gin and didn't want us to buy cotton or seed. Old man Carr [unidentified] didn't want us to buy feed, and the Snyders [Thomas W. Snyder] didn't want us to buy cattle. . . . They finally put the clamps on me . . . but they never found a striped dress [meaning a prison garment] to fit me."[22] Mary, nevertheless, came perilously close to wearing that proverbial striped dress.

Transporting smuggled cotton, however, afforded her enemies an opportunity to silence this annoying newcomer to Porvenir. Retribution was soon forthcoming. Since Mary also boycotted the local gin, she was forced to haul her cotton some 250 miles to gins in McNary, Fort Hancock, or Esperanza. This long haul made her vulnerable to customs inspection. Late one afternoon she drove her truck to Casa Blanca, an adjacent community, to pick up a load of cotton for ginning. This was all American cotton except for four sacks of smuggled Mexican cotton "that was put on my truck and was all covered over." Mary returned to Porvenir, spent the night, and departed for Fort Hancock at four o'clock the next morning. As she approached "Hawkeye" Townsend's residence, two armed customs agents stepped in front of her truck and ordered her to stop. There was no question in her mind what the charges would be—transporting smuggled cotton. They explained that they were taking her to El Paso where she was to appear before a federal magistrate.[23]

Although under arrest, Mary was still among friends. "I knew every customs officer from El Paso to Presidio," she explained. "And you'd thought I was Pancho Villa because they had the whole outfit after me." One customs official, a Mr. Morgan, joined Mary in her truck, and as they drove west toward El Paso he began his interrogation. "He would ask me about the Carrs, and he'd ask me about the Snyders, and he'd ask me about 'Hawkeye' [Townsend]," she added. "And I'd say, 'I don't know,' and he'd say, 'Of course you know. You couldn't live down there all this time and not know anything about those people.'" Although Mary divulged nothing, she also raised some pointed questions and received some potent answers. The truth finally came out. This was not a coincidental arrest; Mary had been set up. Morgan admitted "they [her Anglo neighbors] had literally deviled the life out of them [the customs officers] about me . . . until they had to do something." The source of this protest, she believed, was "old man Carr the *chi chi* [tattletale]."[24]

Knowing the four sacks of smuggled cotton was sufficient evidence for indictment, Mary was careful to present an uncharacteristic helpless and appealing image. "'I hate to put you in jail,' Morgan said. 'I'm just not in the habit of putting people like you in jail.'" When Mary offered no protest—"I'm at your mercy. I'm your prisoner."—he agreed to release her upon her own recognizance with the understanding that she would be in his office the following morning at eight o'clock.[25]

Morgan obviously did not know with whom he was dealing. As the daughter of a judge, Mary had long since learned the mechanizations of the legal system. "When you have trouble . . . honey, don't ever start at the bottom rung of the ladder," she rationalized. "The top rung of the ladder is the place to start." After checking into an El Paso hotel, she called an old friend, a Judge Ivey. "He was a very prominent man and a very, very good friend of mine," she explained. "It never occurred to them that I knew anybody that could lend a helping hand." The judge met Mary the following day at the federal courthouse, where a United States commissioner presided at what Mary described as "kangaroo court . . . [where] they thrashed it all out and put me under $2,000 bond. And it was all over four sacks of smuggled Mexican cotton."[26]

Although Mary was free to return to Porvenir, the authorities impounded her truck and the load of cotton at Fort Hancock. The matter "rocked along for a while," she explained, and again her friends proved to be her greatest asset. While visiting relatives in New Mexico, Mary received a call from Judge Ivey, instructing her to be at the federal building in El Paso on the morning of January 27. (Mary could not remember the year.) He told her not to "'come down here looking like you usually do. You wash behind your ears; clean yourself up real good." Mary arrived looking her "Sunday best." Although the presiding judge, whom she also knew, had been reassigned, his replacement, nevertheless, ruled in her favor. "'Mrs. Daniels,'" he explained, "'there's nothing in the world we are going to do to you, because it wouldn't be fair to [punish] you because there [are] too many other people involved. But be awfully careful what you do from here out, because this must never come up again.'"[27]

The judge's admonition fell upon deaf ears. For Mary, the border remained a challenge and an opportunity; the land beyond the river represented abundance—cattle, cotton, furs, *candelilla* wax, and liquor—that for the mere crossing, would yield a handsome profit. And the borderland Mexican, strapped with poverty and social immobility, continued as the object of her humanitarian concern. This was her primary mission in life, and no matter the difficulties or the obstacles placed in her path, the Rio Grande would remain her home and the Mexican people her friends.

Other than her hostile neighbors, unforeseen factors were conspiring to force another change in Mary's life. Who could explain it better than she?—"the river ran dry!" Completion of the Elephant Butte dam in New Mexico ultimately impounded the water that formerly fed the lower stretches of the Rio Grande. By the late 1920s, the downriver cotton fields, once irrigated by river water, became arid, and many farmers and ranchers left the area. After almost a decade at Porvenir, the Daniels sold their farm, closed their store, and joined the exodus.

For her next location, Mary chose a site she and John first visited in 1914, the Boquillas area in the lower Big Bend country in Brewster County. The land was cheap and the Rio Grande ran full, fed by the waters of the Conchos River out of northern Mexico.[28] Following negotiations with John O. Wedin, the Danielses purchased Section 4, Block G-19 in 1930, and established residence just east of what is now Rio Grande Village in Big Bend National Park.[29] Except for location, little had changed in the life of the Danielses. John ran the ranch (sometimes stocked with cattle of questionable origin); Mary opened a store, became the postmistress, raised cotton and sometimes other people's children.[30] "I've delivered lots of babies in this country," she recalled. "Six hundred of 'em. . . . And every time we'd move, which wasn't very often, Pappy would say, 'Now, honeybee, I want you to promise me one thing, that you'll stop delivering these babies. . . .' Well, I didn't hardly get in my house down there until here they came. Lucille Hannold [a neighbor] came after me. Well, I went up there and delivered the baby and everything turned out beautifully."[31]

Geographically, the Danielses still lived in a bad location. The nearest cotton gin was located at Balmorhea, a distance of some 150 miles over poor roads, as was Fort Stockton, where they purchased most of their supplies. Visits to the outside, however, became more frequent when Mary received the Boquillas-Marathon mail contract. But even in that new location, her travels sparked the imagination of the gossip mongers. "Everybody thought she was peddling dope," Mrs. Frank Wedin reported. Mary was unmoved: "'doesn't make any difference to me what they think.'" Regardless of what she transported, Mary felt insulated by the nature of

The Daniels home and store at Boquillas, Texas. While John Daniels ranched, Mary ran the store, served as postmistress, raised cotton, and sometimes other people's children. Courtesy Junior Historian Files, Marfa Public Library

her cargo: "'Don't you think they'll stop the United States Mail!' She warned, 'They won't get by with that.' And she carried a gun . . . with her."[32]

Although the dope smuggling accusation probably lacked validity, Mary, nevertheless, continued to engage in illicit international trade with a special skill and finesse. "I well remember one time we were going to cross a big bunch of furs," she explained. "There wasn't too much of a problem of crossing furs. Now, what you want to do if you're going to cross anything [and not get caught], be sure to tell somebody, just kinda in a real easy way. And they'll tell 'em [the customs agents] that Mary is going to cross so many furs tonight . . . at a certain place. But be sure you want to be crossin' 'em at some other place and be out of the country with 'em before they know it."[33]

Unquestionably, the borderlands leaves its imprint on those who survive its inhospitable environment. Mary was no exception. Journalist Leon Hale viewed her as "a student of the sometimes strange ways of border life. She knows what gets a man in trouble there, and more important what gets him out." To Mary, life along the border was never a black-and-white matter; there were always gray zones to be considered. "Nobody down here has a completely clean skirt," she explained. "We don't do anything criminal you understand, but people on one side of this river can't live without those on the other, and we do what we do. . . . we ranched a little, we farmed, and we smuggled."[34]

Mary's father's early premonition that her marriage to John Daniels would lead to a lifestyle vastly different from his, and would, in turn, estrange her from her family, was indeed valid. In the following letter written to her father on January 31, 1938, Mary cites the pluses and minuses of her life with John, her enduring concern for the Mexican people, while obviously lamenting the loss of family relationships. She wrote:

> *Dearest Daddy—I'm a poor letter writer—But here goes—When a fellow is as busy as I am most of the time, he doesn't do very much writing. . . . We have had to scramble this year to make ends meet with such low prices for what we had to sell. But we are still eating three times a day and well, and going on for another year, clearing more land and getting ready for more cotton. Its the only money crop. Have just finished two nice little adobe houses up at the pump for the Mexicans to live in, and am moving out of the old house I was in when you were here. Going over to the road—better location for my store.*
>
> *Have had good business all thru the fur season—But furs are a very low price—So it makes it hard buying on [a] declining market—Just like playing cards.*
>
> *Lots of sickness among the Mexicans—as well as the Americans. Everywhere you go you contact sickness—I was in Ft. Stockton last Thursday and will go to town this week about the latter part.*
>
> *Would love to run down to see you one day, but its [sic] so far. I get a monthly letter from Sis, telling me of my short comings [sic], and if you [were here] . . . you could see just about how much effect they have on me.*
>
> *I have neither time nor the money to galivant [sic] around—and if*

there's any visiting done, she has an automobile, the roads are good and
plainly marked, and most any one west of the Pecos river can tell you
where I live. We love this country and are happy here. You would enjoy it
if you were not afraid. By By—
    Maybe I can run down a day or so this spring—love to all—Mary.[35]

When Mary wrote this letter she was fifty-four years old. Time, work, and weather had all conspired to erase the beauty of the former belle of Colorado City. And there were other visible changes. Men's work clothes had long since replaced feminine attire, and while her engaging personality endured, she developed a manner and a vocabulary commensurate with the region and the responsibilities she bore. Bill Ivey, then operator of the Trading Post in Lajitas, recalled only one encounter with Mary during this period. "She came in [the Trading Post] with some dogs with her," he recalled. "And I remember one dog in particular that she carried around with her. That was the ugliest dog I ever saw in my life," which Mary addressed affectionately as *precioso* [little precious]. Bill added that "she talked real rough . . . and kinda slammed things around." Later she opened her purse to get a handkerchief and "a .38 revolver fell out there on the counter. . . . It was no big deal; just like her compact had fallen out."[36]

As the Daniels approached the decade mark of their lower Big Bend tenure, the unexpected once again conspired to uproot them from their homeland. After clearing additional cotton acreage, building houses for the employees, and moving the store to a better location, they received notice that the State of Texas was exercising eminent domain in purchasing the entire region for a national park. The survey included Section 4, Block G-19. By the end of August, 1942, some 691,338 acres had been acquired, and the Danielses were gone.[37] They did, however, remain faithful to the river; they acquired more cotton acreage one mile east of Presidio on the Redford road. This would be Mary's last, and probably most successful stopover during her some six-decade trek through the Big Bend country. Here the fertile valley soil produced bumper cotton crops. One journalist reported that cotton on the Daniels farm "stands head high and heavy with bolls" with yields as high as "four and five bales to the acre."[38] Another writer noted that, in addition to the economic benefits, the Danielses also "lived a happy, pleasant life farming along the banks of the Rio Grande." Their home became the showplace of Presidio, where they "entertained people from all over the country. Their Christmas dinners were a specialty, and you didn't have to be invited to attend."[39]

Mary was enjoying the best of times. Her second daughter, Jane, had graduated from Presidio High School and married a young pharmacist, Frank Smith. Mary persuaded them to return to Presidio, where she opened a drug store and gift shop, which they operated jointly. "People came from miles around to trade there," explained Carlos Spencer, president of Spencer Brothers, Presidio's only department store. She carried "nice China, nice table cloths, nice crystal, silverware, very beautiful things —lamps, mirrors—and a complete fountain service."[40] And with this new endeavor came a new personal image; Mary began wearing makeup, designer dresses, fashionable jewelry, and high heels. Edmundo Nieto, another Presidio businessman, remembered that during this period cowboy types from the outlying ranches would come in and ask her for a date. She would respond, "'Sounds good to me, but let me ask Pappy!'"[41] Mary traveled annually to the Dallas market to purchase stock for the store and, according to Carlos Spencer, made a lasting impression on the vendors. When he began going to market and vendors saw his name tag, they would respond, "'Presidio. Say, I'll bet you know Mary Daniels!' Everybody knew Mary Daniels."[42]

That venture, however, was short-lived. When her daughter and son-in-law moved to New Mexico, Mary closed the drug store and moved back to the river where John was managing the farm. But she missed the people and the challenge of bargaining with customers. Some two years later she opened another store on Presidio's main thoroughfare, a combination liquor and dry goods store. During what was probably the most economically productive period of her life, tragedies struck in quick succession. In 1957 and 1958, her home and store burned in successive years, and on July 26, 1960, John Daniels died. He was seventy-five years old; they had been married fifty-seven years. Mary was devastated. Although John was Protestant, she requested a Catholic priest conduct the ceremony. Crowds of her friends from Mexico came to console her. "'*No commodre. No, no, shed no tears for John, he has gone to rest,*'" she responded. "'The tears should be for us who are left behind to miss him.'"[43]

Following John's death, Mary opened her third and last store in Presidio. Located in an L-shaped adobe house about a block off O'Reilly Street, it was the same type of store she operated before but with greater emphasis on piece goods. "She loved to deal in piece goods," Carlos Spencer explained. "She would fill that station wagon up with all of those piece goods and go around the country selling those door-to-door, or rather ranch-to-ranch."[44] Mary made a lasting impression driving down the highway in her old station wagon with her five dogs seated beside her. Distance was no concern; she would "drive 260 miles to 'dicker' with merchants for stock for her store and drive home, 260 miles, the same day. Bright and early the next day she is greeting customers in her store."[45] Veteran Big Bend rancher Travis Roberts remembers seeing her in the late 1960s in Marathon, where she spent the night in the Gage Hotel and was "on her way to Presidio with her car loaded to the top with merchandise."[46]

Concern for the Mexican people, however, remained paramount in Mary's mind. She frequently visited the cantaloupe farms along the river in her trailer, and the farmers would give her their rejected melons. She would then park the trailer in front of her store and "here comes her friends from Mexico and they would help themselves. They loved her." But to Mary, love and trust were synonymous. Carlos Spencer would warn her, "Mary, you need to watch that store more, people are stealing from you. And she would say, 'Well, they can't steal it all!' "[47]

The last time I saw Mary Daniels was in her Presidio store; we talked late into the night. Mary was seventy-six. Although the years had taken their toll, she remained mentally alert and still bore faint traces of the beauty of her youth. Yet hers was the image of old age: stretch slacks, jeans, over blouses, and sandals had long since replaced designer dresses, fashionable jewelry, and high heels.

During the evening Mary entertained me with sacred hymns played on an electric organ and introduced me to Rex, "a marvelous dog," who slept on her bed, undisturbed by the music and conversation. But mostly Mary talked, mainly about herself: her successes and failures, her love for John, her estranged family, concerns for other people, and their views of her. "I don't suppose there is an old lady that lives in this country that has any more friends than I do," she explained. "I love people and if people don't like me, [then] I've done something to 'em to make them dislike me."[48]

If anyone disliked Mary Daniels, it would not have been politic to express those feelings in either Presidio or Ojinaga. Mary loved everyone, and most everyone returned that love manifold. Companionship, however, remained her primary concern. Later that night, seemingly eager to reveal her deepest feelings, she asked me to read a letter she had just received from Robert L. Cartledge, former general manager of the Chisos Mining Company in Terlingua. He wrote:

> *My Dear Love: It has taken me a long time to answer your sweet letter. However, I have been writing you daily . . . but just have not been able to find words to express my feelings. It touches me deeply down in my heart, and made me just want to get up and pull out for Presidio. However, as much as I would like to hold you in my arms and kiss you and show my love for you, I can't help but feel that it would be an imposition on you.*
>
> *You have always had lots of push . . . and anybody but you, would have given up after those two losses you had by fires. . . . However, you have held up, head up, shown you cannot be defeated. . . . You have always made a success of any venture you started. . . . Lots of love and love and kisses from Bob.*[49]

When I finished reading the letter she asked quietly, "Now, how would you like to be an old lady of seventy-six and get a letter like that? I'm sort of a romantic old sister. I love the boys." Then, after pausing for a few moments as if in deep thought, she added, "When people grow old, you need companionship."[50] Mary had indeed grown old, but the companionship she sought was never forthcoming. Bob Cartledge never came to Presidio, nor was he ever able to demonstrate his love for the aging Mary. He died a few months later of emphysema.

Although plagued by failing eyesight, Mary continued to maintain a busy schedule. No longer able to drive, she remained a familiar sight along O'Reilly Street in Presidio, frequently visiting Spencer's department store. Unable to recognize people, she would hear an unfamiliar voice and say, "'I'm Mary Daniels, now who are you?'" And she still trusted everyone. Since Presidio had no bank, merchants either drove to Marfa to make deposits or sent them by registered mail. Not Mary. Carlos Spencer remembered "she would be in the store here and hear someone say they were going to Marfa, and she would ask: 'You're going to Marfa? Would you mind taking my deposit to the bank?' *And this was cash!* She would trust anybody."[51]

Mary's acquaintances were not limited to the river country. She transacted out-of-town business from a pay telephone at Spencer's department store. After dialing the long distance operator, Carlos Spencer would overhear the conversation: "'Ladybird, I want so-and-so in Del Rio.' The operator would ask her for the number and she would say, 'Honeybee, no I don't. But you are there . . . so you just connect me with John Doe and that will be just fine.' And her calls always went through. After a while all the operators got to know her. She never called anyone by name, always ladybird or honeybee."[52]

To Mary Daniels, those people—her friends—were her extended family, but the family she missed the most was her own. Reconciliation, however, was never forthcoming. And while her sister once called Carlos Spencer to ask about her, Mary never returned the call. "I know they don't want to have anything to do with me because of the way I am. They wouldn't dare introduce me to their friends, but that's all right. . . . I'm going to live my life the way I like to live it."[53] In later years Mary even became estranged from her daughter. "I have a lovely, exquisite daughter," she explained. "She looks like me but is not anything like me." After Jane and her husband moved to New Mexico they never returned to Presidio.[54]

Blindness eventually forced Mary to close the store. In the late 1970s she moved to Shafter, where she owned a home, and lived there briefly, but was not happy. She complained the people were not very friendly. Later she returned to Presidio and soon became ill. No longer able to care for herself, her daughter took Mary back to Tatum, New Mexico, to live with her. Reconciliation was brief; Mary died shortly thereafter.

Some three weeks later news of her death reached Presidio. No one remembers the date; there was no obituary. And while none of her friends attended the funeral, her passing was, nonetheless, mourned. Kindness is not easily forgotten by those whose lives were enriched by this strangely independent and compassionate woman. No one knows if a headstone marks her grave, but if one does, the inscription she would have preferred, would read: "Mary Coe Daniels. She dedicated her life to the down-trodden, the handicapped, and the retarded, and lived *muy a gusto, a gusto.*"

Today, the mainstream of Big Bend society remembers little of Mary Daniels. Those who do think of her casually as "Ma" Daniels, cotton farmer, junk dealer, who loved dogs and drove an old station wagon. Cecilia Thompson, in her *History of Marfa and Presidio County,* dismisses Mary Daniels with a single line: "a Presidio character known for her colorful dress and generous nature."[55] But along the Rio Grande, where poverty and social immobility remain the status quo, her memory endures. And when old-timers return to Presidio, sooner or later they make their way to Spencer's department store, where they always ask, "'Whatever happened to Ma Daniels?'" As one of her closest friends on O'Reilly Street, Carlos Spencer concludes, "She was a real landmark. I don't think there will ever be another person like her. She was genuine. She was one-of-a-kind."[56]

3

Lucia Madrid

PLANTING THE SEEDS
OF KNOWLEDGE

Even with the three gasoline pumps and two faded Coca-Cola signs, the looks are deceiving. It is what a motorist traveling the river road between Big Bend National Park and Presidio might expect: a welcome oasis in a land of dust and cactus.

And an oasis it is, a literary oasis. A prominent sign reads Madrid Store; first-time visitors never forget the initial shock on entering those welcome portals. Beyond the Coke machine, junk food, and ranch-style beans, loom ceiling-high shelves of books, thousands of them all neatly arranged by subject and reading level. And the surprises continue. Further on, around two large tables sit an ever-changing assemblage—toddlers, teenagers, college students, and elders—all quietly reading, oblivious to the world around them. The inquiries vary little, as do the answers: it's a library. Its creator? Lucia Rede Madrid. How it all started? Well, that's another story.

Lucia Madrid's personal objectives parallel those of the other "women I had been seeing." She shared their concern for the less fortunate. And while she never smuggled cotton, raised other people's children, or practiced medicine without a license, she did help enrich the lives of many living along the Rio Grande. But here the similarities end. Where Kathryn Casner and Mary Coe Daniels were preoccupied with others' physical welfare, Lucia Madrid advocated social and economic mobility through intellectual awareness. The tools of her trade: books. And there are two other dissimilarities. First, Lucia Madrid achieved national and international recognition for her work; and second, she was Mexican American.

Lucia had a proud heritage. Her grandparents were one of five families who settled on the north bank of the Rio Grande near what is now Redford, Texas. In 1871, her grandfather, Secundino Lujan, received a 160-acre land grant from the State of Texas, and during the ensuing years fought Indians, cleared the land, dug a sixteen-mile irrigation canal, and built a school, all the while expanding his holdings.[1] He and his siblings prospered in their new homeland; in the process of acculturation they came to enjoy the best of two worlds, Hispanic and Anglo.

Lucia's mother, Maria Antonia Lujan, recognized as a child the importance of learning to speak the language of her acquired homeland. An avid reader in Spanish, she was, nevertheless, intrigued by the sounds of English being spoken by the people for whom she worked. El Polvo in the late 1800s offered scant opportunity for a young Mexican girl to learn English. Maria, however, found a solution. She offered her labor in exchange for English lessons. Washing, cooking, and selling goat's milk door-to-door, her determination yielded unexpected benefits. Some thirty years later she became the first teacher of bilingual classes in the Big Bend area, and subsequently the first woman postmistress of Redford.

Eusebio Rede, Lucia's father, who farmed and worked in the Shafter silver mines, also was an avid and articulate reader. Lucia "grew up listening to . . . [him] discuss works by Cervantes, Dante, and Victor Hugo, in the process of stimulating Lucia's enduring love for literature that continues today." Lucia's home life, therefore, was unlike that of most children living in the Redford area; books and literature were part of the family's daily fare. "The older ones inspired the younger ones," Lucia explained. "I was in the middle."[2]

Otherwise, Lucia's early childhood differed little from that of other Mexican children living in that area. When she was eight years old she entered the overcrowded Redford elementary school—one teacher for about eighty students in all grades. Lucia shared a bench with two other little girls; the one in the middle held a single book. "I was on the side and couldn't see the complete sentence," she recalled. "I could speak English, but I couldn't read until I was in the tenth grade and had my own book."[3]

Believing his children's educational needs would be better served elsewhere, Lucia's father decided to move to Marfa, a ranching and trading village located some eighty miles north of Redford. His social naïveté, however, proved to be another asset. Marfa then was a segregated village; Anglos lived primarily north of the railroad tracks, while the Mexicans lived on the south side. However, in January, 1925, Eusebio Rede purchased a temporary residence on Marfa's north side near the elementary school. "My brother and I went to school there not knowing that Mexican Americans didn't go to that school," Lucia explained. "We invaded their sanctuary [unaware] we were on the wrong side of the tracks." School officials, however, ignored the matter; the following year about twelve other Mexican American students joined Edmundo and Lucia. "We had integrated Marfa Elementary," she explained later.[4] And that was before either knew the meaning of the word.

Eusebio Rede's decision to move his children to Marfa was indeed propitious. Lucia remembered she experienced no discrimination; the teachers were good to her, and she developed potent learning skills. After graduating from Marfa High School in May, 1932, she entered Sul Ross State College the following September to study education. Her progress was immediate. She received her teacher's certificate the following May and accepted a temporary position, teaching five children on a ranch near Van Horn, Texas. Her salary: sixty dollars a month plus room and board. Lucia returned to Sul Ross the following year, and between 1933 and 1937, when she received her bachelor's degree, she fulfilled other temporary teaching assignments (Porvenir and the Ochoa Ranch near Presidio), plus a four-year stint at Ballinger, Texas. There she taught in a Mexican-American school and had to "cross the tracks to go to school."[5]

In the meantime the Rede family had moved to Shafter, where Lucia's father worked in the silver mines. Between school terms she always returned home to be with her parents; the summer of 1940, however, had a special significance. Since childhood she had hated Enrique Madrid; he teased all the little girls and threw dead snakes on them. However, after completing Redford Elementary School, he began exhibiting more substantive qualities. While studying mechanical engineering by correspondence, he took high school courses at night from Lucia's oldest sister. And later, while attending diesel engineering school in California, he began corresponding with Lucia; after he accepted a position at the Shafter silver mines, their friendship matured into deep affection. Enrique wanted to get married; Lucia was hesitant. But after reconsidering his proposal, Lucia assumed a more positive attitude; she now recognized Enrique as an intelligent person, a hard worker who possessed "all the qualities I admired." Later she acknowledged "he was the best man I had ever met."[6] Lucia returned to Ballinger in September, completed the final year of her contract, and returned to Shafter where she and Enrique were married in the Catholic Church on May 3, 1941.

The Madrids' Shafter residence was brief. There were two contributing factors: first, the independent-minded Enrique objected to the industrial regimentation he encountered in the silver mines; and second, when his two younger brothers entered military service at the beginning of World War II, Enrique received a deferment to supervise the Madrid family farms, ranch, and store at Redford.[7] With the return to Redford and the birth of their first child, Jaime, on October 16, 1942, Lucia interrupted her teaching career, but not her love for books and learning. Both remained part-and-parcel of the Madrid household. And while Lucia aided Enrique in his wartime responsibilities, she nevertheless maintained a wholesome learning environment for Jaime, as well as those children that followed: Enrique, Jr., on September 26, 1947, and Lydia on August 24, 1949. Her devotion to her children's personal welfare yielded rich rewards; Lucia and Enrique produced a family of high achievers. From modest beginnings in one of the nation's most remote corners, the Madrid children have indeed scaled the academic heights. Their inspiration came from home; Lucia recalled modestly, "I wanted the best for them."[8]

For almost two decades, Lucia's life was devoted to raising her children. In the meantime, however, she was already looking forward to the time when she could return to teaching. Even while the children were small she attended summer classes at Sul Ross State College, working toward a master's degree. Ultimately time and opportunity converged. When her youngest child, Lydia, reached school age, Lucia accepted a position in the Redford schools teaching fifth grade. The pleasure she anticipated in the classroom, however, only led to disappointment. The source of her childhood frustration remained; there were still no books at Redford Elementary. But as an adult and a teacher she then had an option, which she exercised. Since the Redford school was part of the Marfa Independent School District, policy was determined at Marfa, some eighty miles away. And the policy that infuriated Lucia was that, while the Marfa library had books in abundance, they could not be removed. Lucia thought otherwise. Rejecting the status quo, she recalled, "every two weeks, on Friday afternoons after 4 P.M., and after I'd gotten the children off, I'd leave to drive the 75 miles to Marfa to get 25 books for 80 children."[9] They could use the books for one week before Lucia had to return them to Marfa. "And people wonder why our children don't have the advantages of Anglo children."[10]

Lucia, however, was determined that the Mexican students living along the Rio Grande be provided the same learning opportunities as those living elsewhere. This meant change, and change at Redford, Texas, was hard to come by, especially when there existed subversive forces over which she had no control. But change is for the change makers; age and experience had given Lucia both perspective and determination. Now in her mid-forties, she stood on the threshold of the most productive, most rewarding, and most revolutionary period in her life. Books and learning remained at the heart of the matter.

Lucia's opportunity for change came when the federal government launched the Project Head Start program in 1965.[11] (This was the same year she received her master's degree from Sul Ross State University.) She requested reassignment, and in September began teaching remedial reading during the long term and the Head Start program in the summer. It was the revolutionary approach to education that Lucia found the most challenging. She understood that "you can't nourish the mind of an undernourished body." When the four-year-olds entered the classroom "the first thing we did was give them a big glass of milk and cookies, and at lunch we gave them good food. . . . And you know, these children gained about four or five pounds in just a few weeks."[12]

Lucia also had a $400 budget for instructional materials—bilingual picture books, visuals, educational toys, and so forth—which she requisitioned through the Marfa Independent School District. When the materials failed to arrive in Redford, her inquiry led to more frustration. The Head Start materials had indeed been received, but the "trustees felt that, since there were so few children in Redford, the materials should be kept in Marfa." Following a moment of pensive thought, Lucia added, "I did get some, but not much."[13] She could not understand why the school trustees involved themselves in essentially instructional matters, especially since Superintendent H. G. Adams, supported her effort.

Although Lucia could still "borrow" some of the Head Start materials, provided she drove to Marfa, she nevertheless sought alternatives. "I'm going to the hills," she explained. "I'm going to the river with the children to find things that will help them learn." The countryside did indeed yield both the familiar and the accessible. Along the riverbanks they found reed stems, which the students cut into uniform lengths and arranged in imaginative designs on their desks. They gathered smooth rocks from the river on which Lucia wrote the days of the week, the months of the year, and the letters of the alphabet. "They learned the words in Spanish and counted in Spanish; then they learned the words in English," she explained. When a local rancher butchered a hog, he reserved the feet for Lucia's Head

Start class. The bones, when reassembled in their original order, will stand alone, and with these the students made toy soldiers. "They were resourceful," she added. "Everything that I took [to the class] had a purpose. They learned to love everything and they [even] brought [other native materials] to me to use in school. Instead of using cardboard and charts, I used these things, and the children loved them and learned from them."[14]

Although far removed from the mainstream of pedagogical change, Lucia unknowingly was working in accord with the profession's elitists. When Jaime, her oldest son, first observed her class, he asked how she learned to teach by the Montessori Method. Montessori Method? What is that? Later when Lucia traveled to Rome to attend Jaime's ordination, she visited the site where Maria Montessori once taught and developed her innovative methodology. This sparked her interest. When Lucia later studied the Montessori literature, she discovered that "sure enough [their methods] were the same."[15]

Lucia's innovative teaching methods did not go unrecognized. The small white stucco building on El Camino Del Rio became a mecca for many teachers seeking creative approaches to elementary education. They came to observe and learn. Later, Dr. Robert W. Miller, director of the West Texas Innovative Education Center at Sul Ross State College, invited Lucia to conduct a summer workshop to display her materials and explain her methods. This proved so successful that he suggested they send examples of her work to the Head Start regional headquarters in Albuquerque, New Mexico. Unexpectedly, the Marfa board of trustees blocked Dr. Miller's suggestion with the pretext that Lucia "did not go through the proper channels." Eventually, the truth came out.[16]

Some years earlier a Marfa citizen seeking election to the school board solicited Enrique Madrid's support among the Mexican people living along the Rio Grande. Although the gentleman was elected, he did not receive a single vote in Redford. Enrique had supported his opponent, a matter that the new trustee did not take lightly. Lucia eventually learned that "in essence, he told Enrique: 'You did not support me [in the election] and the children in your district will be the losers.'"[17] That incident left an indelible imprint on Lucia's memory. Decades later, when discussing the Head Start experience, one journalist noted "a hint of anger crosses her kind countenance before she gets her emotion under control."[18] Yet Lucia bears no grudge. "I have forgiven the person who was cruel to me," she wrote. "How mistaken some people are by having the delusion that personal gain is made by crushing others. . . . My dreams kept me going."[19]

And indeed they did. In spite of the administrative obstacles, Lucia prevailed. And contrary to the trustee's threat, the children in her district were not the losers but unquestionably the winners.

Far removed from local political vindictiveness, more enlightened minds began recognizing the achievements of people like Lucia Madrid. Acknowledgment could not have come at a better time. It was during this period of administrative rejection that Marfa school superintendent H. G. Adams received that memorable telegram. It became one of Lucia's prized possessions. The message on the faded yellow paper states that *Grade Teacher Magazine* had selected Lucia Madrid as "one of the nation's outstanding teachers of the disadvantaged." She was one of 135 men and women in the nation described by the magazine as "an inspiration to educators at all levels."[20]

When Lucia retired from teaching in 1978, she left the Marfa Independent School District with mixed emotions. Amidst the ongoing struggle with administrative reticence, she had, nevertheless, gained national recognition while partially fulfilling her personal mission: preparing disadvantaged Mexican children for a productive life in an Anglo society. That was the past; sixty-five years old and her children grown, Lucia passively awaited an uncertain future in that remote corner of the Big Bend country. But her most productive years still lay ahead; she was about to embark on the most exciting phase of her career. Again books and the desire to help others lay at the crux of the matter.

Attending school was a full day's work for Lucia's neighbor, Rosario Evaro. As one of about twenty-five Redford students who were bused to Marfa High School, she left Redford each morning at six o'clock and returned home around six in the evening. With no time for lesson preparation at school, Rosario began visiting the Madrids at night to use the family's personal library. It was during these nighttime sessions with her former Head Start student that Lucia realized that Redford needed a lending library. There were, however, two immediate problems: no books and no space. Lucia quickly solved the second problem; Enrique assigned her a corner of the grocery store to begin her library. To solve the second problem, Lucia again had to improvise. Because there were no bookshelves in the store, the local dairy products distributor gave her milk cartons to hold the original inventory: old magazines, newspapers, *McLean's Almanac,* and a Sears catalog. The latter became well circulated; with both words and pictures it served as a dictionary for Mexican children learning to speak English. Such was the modest beginning, but totally unforeseen to Lucia, great changes were about to occur.

The gasoline pumps and Coca-Cola sign evolved as the library's most unlikely assets. Travelers on the Camino Del Rio stopping at the Madrid store were intrigued with the incipient project and offered to help. And thus emerged an ever-growing support group, "the unorganized friends of Mrs. Madrid's library." None apparently knew the other—and most likely didn't even know Lucia Madrid—but all joined together with a singleness of purpose: to help build a library in one of the most unlikely spots in the nation. Books, money, equipment, and letters of encouragement began arriving with unexpected regularity. And as the library grew, so did the public awareness of what was happening along El Camino Del Rio. According to the *Fort Worth Star-Telegram,* "The news [of the library] brought donations by the hundred from strangers nationwide—a set of encyclopedias from Memphis, hundreds of paperbacks from Illinois, children's tables and chairs from a community center in Dallas."[21]

Publicity—both media and word-of-mouth—helped multiply the library's holdings. "People find out about the library and they donate

Lucia Madrid, in background, shares her grocery store-library with a group of local pre-schoolers. The library is the fulfillment of her educational philosophy: "When a child picks up a book, you are planting the seeds of knowledge." Courtesy Lucia Madrid

books, they send tables, they send shelves, other libraries send us their [used] books, so it's everyman's project," explained Enrique Madrid, Jr., one of the library's most ardent patrons. "Whoever likes the idea has co-operated. We receive books in the mail and from UPS once or twice a week from all over the United States, from people who have only heard, or read about the library."[22]

Within ten years, the library holdings grew from almost nothing to some twelve thousand volumes (which exceeds many small town municipal libraries), all acquired through donation.[23] The titles are as varied as the donors; the readers as varied as those traveling the El Camino Del Rio. On my first visit to the Madrid Library I met Victor Lujan, age fourteen, and his two sisters, Maria and Silvia, age ten and twenty respectively. They lived on a ranch some three miles from the Madrid Store and drove to Redford every third day to get their drinking water. Victor, who attends school in Presidio, explained he read a varied menu: horror-mystery books, entertainment, and modern science. He had recently written a research paper on computer design based on notes taken in the Madrid Library. Maria and Silvia, however, were less scientific in their choices—romance, travel, and entertainment. But like the collection itself, Mrs. Madrid's library offered something for everybody.

Age, obviously, is no barrier for using the facility. "We have all ages that come to the library," explained Enrique Madrid. "We have retired people and little ones, two-years-olds, who come with their mother and look at books."[24] Young people, however, comprise a majority of the library traffic. According to one journalist, the facility has evolved as the community's "central magnet," viewed by many youngsters as their home-away-from-home. "One young brother and sister spend hours there every day rather than return to their one-room dwelling they share with their parents and six other siblings."[25] Since the library is located only a half mile from the Rio Grande, it also enjoys a brisk international traffic. And with Redford an official port-of-entry, people living in the adjacent Mexican villages are accorded free access to the United States. "There is a rowboat down there," Enrique explained. "You give them a few pesos and they row you across [the Rio Grande]. They come over here to get their mail, do their shopping, and check out their books."[26]

The library has also emerged as a regional cultural center. On one occasion a visiting journalist noted the diverse array of individuals gathered in the reading room: an artist in search of inspiration, "a neighbor on a grant from the University of Texas at El Paso, collecting oral folklore, and a New York sculptor . . . studying Spanish." Also present were two local children immersed in Dr. Seuss and munching on an afternoon snack. "I think we're the only library in the state that allows ice cream and Popsicles in the stacks," explained Lucia.[27] On a more intellectual level, the library also evolved as a meeting place for scientists and scholars working in the Big Bend area. "They stop by for information," Enrique explained, "and I share my books and information with them. One day we had several scholars seated around the table and one suggested that we should have a Big Bend Scholars Society. It just became an informal group; the only by-law is that one of the members of the society buy another member a drink sometime during the year." Enrique concluded, "That keeps the society alive for another year."[28]

One of the library's greatest assets is its simplified checkout system; the Dewey decimal system never made it to Redford. Lucia's only record of circulation is a loose leaf notebook she keeps on her desk. Each patron writes the title of the books, along with his or her name and address. "See, I let them [the children] write because many are just learning to write [in English]. And that helps them," she explained. Surprisingly, the books are not cataloged; "I would never have time for that." She sets no limits; sometimes the children check out as many as fifteen or twenty books. Lucia added that she seldom experiences losses; "they learn to take care of the books."[29]

With growth came abundance; Lucia's initial concern of maintaining a minimum circulating inventory soon disappeared. Later when a shipment of books arrived in Redford, they were carefully inventoried and assigned where they could best be used. Duplicate copies of popular titles were shelved with the permanent collection to insure their continued availability. College-level mathematics and economics textbooks, considered inappropriate for local patrons, were dispatched to other libraries in Mexico where they were desperately needed. With shelf space at a premium, many incoming paperbacks were placed in a basket and given free to children. However, after reading them many return the books to the library to be given to others.

Unlike some librarians, Lucia never developed the traditional "jailer's complex." To her, books are to be read and enjoyed, not shelved, hidden away, and hoarded. She once suggested to one of her volunteer donors that when she collected books in the future she should take them to some store in a less privileged part of a city and place them in a box with a sign, "Free Books." "'Do this and you will be planting the seed of knowledge,'"

Lucia Madrid's smile is the smile of success. In 1990, Texas governor Bill Clements inducted the former Redford, Texas, school teacher into the Texas Women's Hall of Fame for establishing her library to combat illiteracy. Courtesy Lucia Madrid

she added. "'It does not have to be Redford, Texas, to benefit children. *When a child picks up a book, you are planting the seeds of knowledge.*'"[30]

From its humble beginnings in 1979, Lucia Madrid's library became one of the region's biggest success stories. Journalists came from all over to see "what must be the largest private lending library in the United States," and the lady who created it.[31] It was not an easy trip. Located some 250 miles east of El Paso and 350 miles west of Del Rio, Redford is further from a commercial airport than any other town in the lower forty-eight states. Distance, however, was no barrier. When a reporter from the *Fort Worth Star-Telegram* arrived in Redford to write a full-page article on Lucia, he was surprised to find Jane Pauley and an NBC crew in the library taping a two-day segment for the *Today* show. This national media attention prompted the *International* (Presidio) to report, "News of this incredible library in the tiny community of Redford was spreading far and wide."[32] In addition to NBC and the *Fort Worth Star-Telegram*, other coverage appeared in *National Geographic*; *Spirit,* Southwest Airlines' in-flight magazine; and most Texas metropolitan dailies; as well as news features on National Public Radio, various local radio stations, local television stations, plus both local and syndicated television shows. "It's a very simple idea," noted Enrique, "but it has captured the hearts and people throughout the nation and parts of the world."[33]

Modesty is Lucia's most distinguishing feature. Yet for all she achieved, it was inevitable that unsolicited honors would ultimately be accorded one so richly deserving. And they came in rapid succession. On March 27, 1990, Texas governor Bill Clements inducted Lucia Rede Madrid into the Texas Women's Hall of Fame. One of seven distinguished honorees, Lucia's category was education, specifically the "10,000 books in her private lending library which she started to combat illiteracy."[34] Momentarily ignoring the pomp and circumstance, Lucia seized the moment and solicited the governor's wife "for some extra books for her part of the world."[35]

One month later Lucia appeared in the White House, where President George Bush awarded her the silver medallion of the President's Voluntary Action Award. Established to "recognize, inspire, and encourage volunteer achievement in communities throughout the United States," Lucia was one of nineteen recipients (chosen from some four thousand volunteers) honored at the White House presentation. Following the formal ceremony, President Bush turned to Lucia and made an unexpected announcement. At that point she learned that she was also the recipient of the special Ronald Reagan Award for Voluntary Excellence, an honor conferred only on the occasion of outstanding achievement. Further recognition came from south of the Rio Grande. The *Internado Indigena*, an Indian boarding school in Chihuahua, Mexico, presented Lucia with a bronze medallion in appreciation for the tons of clothing, food, school supplies, and books she has sent to that institution. Also a high school in Delicias, Chihuahua, named the library in her honor.

Such recognition prompted the expected flood of congratulations. Senators, congressmen, university professors, business, and education leaders cited her for serving as a "role model for other Texans by your actions and your commitment to excellence," as well as being an "inspiration to many individuals. This prestigious award brings honor not only to you, but your family, your community, Sul Ross State University, and the State of Texas."[36] But probably the letter that touched her most deeply came from a fourth grader in Odessa, Texas. On June 15, 1990, following Lucia's return from Washington, Mayra Garcia wrote: "Thank you for letting us

*Recognized nationally for her crusade to combat illiteracy, Lucia Madrid
is presented with the silver medallion of the President's Voluntary
Action Award by President George Bush. Courtesy Lucia Madrid*

come and visit. Thank you for also letting us see your library. I had a nice
visit. When I grow up, I want to build a library of my own and do volunteer work and get metals [*sic*] like you did."[37] And thus Lucia had indeed
planted the seeds of knowledge; now she could watch them grow.

Although the faded Coca-Cola signs remain atop the Madrid grocery
store, the racks of junk food and ranch-style beans have long since given
way to Dr. Seuss, *Encyclopedia Britannica,* and *The Handbook of Texas.*
Enrique Madrid closed the store in 1991; by then Lucia had redirected the
family priorities. And while the traffic through those once-inviting portals remains brisk, the motivation has changed. Reflecting on her years of
caring for her neighbors, Lucia said, "I've long looked out for the poor
here, cared for them, tried to find food and clothing for them. But too
often overlooked are people's minds. The mind must be nourished, too.
And books are the best food."[38]

Lucia's books are there mainly for one specific purpose, to teach bi-
lingualism. "If they [the Mexican children] are going to live in this area,"
she argues, "they have to learn to communicate."[39] And to her the ability
to communicate is the initial step toward opportunity and the outside

world. She believes the Rio Grande community offers scant opportunity for a cultivated mind. "I want them to leave Redford," she insists.[40] Many accepted her challenge; their achievements attest to the seeds of knowledge planted in the grocery store-library. According to journalist Dan Bodine,

> *what this gray-haired woman with the soft smile and kind eyes has accomplished in her poor community, defies description. The walls of her store say it best perhaps. She calls it her Hall of Fame. There hang pictures of such people as engineers, doctors, teachers, and accountants, a few of the many who've tilled the soil of their minds here within these walls, all former students in the Redford area—from both sides of the river—who've gone on to successful careers away from this tiny town. "It was the Library,"* she says. And her conviction, like truth, shines through.[41]

And so you have them—"the other women" I had been seeing—the women whom I remember so fondly, each so different, yet all so very much alike. In assessing their achievements, one must consider a single but complex question: were they, with their marked individuality, typical of the Big Bend country, or somehow distinctly unique? The answer to that question requires a multi-perspective examination.

Throughout the course of history whenever there occurs widespread poverty and suffering, and where there are no appropriate social agencies, there have always been the few—usually women—who come to the aid of the less privileged. Within this broad context these women were not unique. Like Jane Addams, the social reformer who founded Hull House, a settlement home in Chicago, and Edna Gladney, the guiding spirit of Fort Worth's Edna Gladney Home, these women undoubtedly fall within this general category of social activists.[42]

However, on closer examination, there emerge significant differences. Unlike Addams and Gladney, these women worked in a rural setting. Also, while Addams and Gladney are considered social reformers, Casner and Daniels—and to a lesser degree, Madrid—worked toward specific goals with little or no thought of changing the system. Furthermore, no social organizations or movements bearing their names have sprung up in their wake, and no one has come forward to perpetuate their work. Poverty, ignorance, suffering, and deprivation still exist along the Rio Grande, as well as along the Trinity River and the shores of Lake Michigan. Yet all did, within the scope of their specific objectives, help improve the quality of life of their subjects.

To understand fully Casner's, Daniels's, and Madrid's motivation, one must examine them within the region in which they served. First, the Big Bend country, by its very nature, establishes unyielding parameters that, if the occupants are to survive, must be observed. Two prime factors set the tone for social interaction in the Big Bend country: scarcity and remoteness. People living in semi-isolation need each other; loneliness places a high priority on friendship. Before moving to the Big Bend, Mrs. H. E. Gatlin had lived in Boston, Washington, D.C., and St. Louis. Yet she found in the shadow of the Chisos Mountains a new social climate unlike any she had previously experienced. People were important; isolation drew them together. "You had to go all the way around the mountain to see anyone, clean on down to Hot Springs," she explained. "Everyone cared so much for their neighbors. . . . Whatever happened to you, happened to them. And you began to be that way too."[43]

In beginning "to be that way too," Mrs. Gatlin was assuming the image of her new homeland; unquestionably the *border environment shapes the people*. She had discovered in the remoteness of the Big Bend country a sense of community that did not—and probably could not—exist in a metropolitan area. It was in this setting of need and mutual trust that Maggie Smith, Kathryn Casner, Mary Daniels, and Lucia Rede Madrid performed their services. It was a perfect meshing of need and desire; the enduring scarcity of the Big Bend country, combined with the unrestricted flow of immigrants from Mexico, produces a never-ending body of underprivileged. Therefore, within the scope of their individual value systems, these women found along the Rio Grande the means of personal fulfillment. In offering their services to those in need, they became legends in the Big Bend country.

Rex Ivey, the never-elected mayor of Lajitas, Texas, who has lived along the border for nearly three-quarters of a century, viewed my three friends as unique to both the borderlands and the period in which they served. Speaking specifically of Maggie Smith and Mary Daniels, he said, "They trusted everybody and everybody trusted them. Back then *this country down here was based on mutual trust. We all needed each other to survive.*" Then after a moment of thoughtful reflection, he added, "I guess that's part of our problem now, people don't seem to need each other anymore."[44]

Thus Rex Ivey pronounced a somber benediction to a quality of life that has long since disappeared along the Rio Grande. They—Casner, Daniels, and Madrid—for all the good they achieved, were unique to both the region and the period in which they worked. And while the need for their services remain, no one has taken their places. Regional demographics deem it so. Ranching, farming, and mining have given way to tourism, which has ushered in a new population and a new social climate. Current tenures are brief, and personal relationships casual; regional traditions have dissipated with the changing times. People like Mrs. E. H. Gatlin and those who once "cared so much for their neighbors" have been replaced with an ever-changing population, casually aware of others and caring little for their needs. Indeed, "people don't seem to need each other any-more."[45]

SCENE
II

"A Few Men Are Going to Die"

Conflict is a universal response to personal differences. During the early twentieth century, conflict in the Big Bend country was closely tied to the environment; scarcity prompted disagreement, while remoteness allowed the participants to resolve their differences in the manner of their choice. Mediation was seldom an alternative; most thought in short terms, and violence erupted.

The Big Bend country did not necessarily cause people to be bad any more than it prompted them to be good. For those, either good or bad, the region simply provided them the opportunity to express themselves without restraint. The choices ran the gamut of human behavior; the region simply magnified the extremes.

To better understand this prevalence of Big Bend violence, one must first consider the character of the individual who elected to live there. In the early twentieth century, that region was not a place for the weak or fainthearted. "The ruggedness of the land is matched by the harsh climate," wrote historian Ron Tyler. "The sun scorches down most of the year, and only vegetation adapted to heat and drought flourishes. Big Bend residents endure dry summers, broken only by 15 to 17 inches of rainfall annually.... Simply put, the Big Bend is a desert."[1] Tyler further implies an analogy between Big Bend plant life and the tenacity of those who settled there. "Even the vegetation marks off and defends its living space. 'Each plant in this land is a porcupine.... It is nature armed to the teeth.'"[2]

Man, like the surrounding plant life, also went armed. It was a practical necessity; remoteness made law enforcement a matter of personal responsibility. Elmo Johnson, rancher, farmer, and trading post operator, stated that when he moved to the lower Big Bend in 1927, "the few people there carried the law in a holster or slung over their back."[3] Living some 125 miles from the county seat, Johnson felt this was necessary; he could recall only three times in seventeen years that the Brewster County sheriff visited his trading post. Therefore, the enforcement of law in the Big Bend, whoever's law enforced by whoever carried the guns, was destined to yield an uneven brand of justice. This became another legacy of the Big Bend country.

Another equation in the study of Big Bend violence is the region's close proximity to Mexico. Fugitives from justice could flee south into Mexico, while northbound Mexican immigration—illegal or otherwise—added a multiethnic quality to border life. Racial misunderstanding and discrimination were inevitable. These, combined with poverty and the economic exploitation of a remote international boundary—smuggling—form a peripheral theme in the three chapters that follow.

Scholars and intellectuals are sometimes prone to explain a complex issue in single phrases. Judge Brian Montague, a legal philosopher and former Big Bend resident, viewed the prevalence of violence in that area as "the congenital birthright of rugged individualism."[4] One can conclude that while the region may be a strong contributing factor, it alone is not a prescription for violence. Conflict and violence may occur in any environment—Savannah, Springfield, Cicero, or the South Bronx. And there is a psychological factor that defies regional analysis: *some people are just plain damn mean.*

Time changes everything, especially the deeds wrought by man. It has been more than eighty years since Jim Gillespie encountered Rozell Pulliam in the Alpine post office (chapter 4), seven decades since George Billalba and the Coffman boys engaged in their shootout at Study Butte (chapter 5), and twenty years since the Baiza-Acosta feud eventually spent itself (chapter 6). And while the Big Bend's arid climate remains constant, the region's greatest changes have occurred in its social and economic climate. Fewer permanent residents compete for the region's meager resources, while a large portion of the population is transient, visiting the area to enjoy its natural beauty. Friendships are casual, and while personal differences still arise, organized law enforcement is ever present. Seldom does one now feel an obligation to resolve an issue through violence.

Within the broad scope of Big Bend history, Jim Gillespie, George

Billalba, the Coffman boys, and the elder Baizas and Acostas represent a transitory sequence in time. They all played roles in a tragic drama that is no longer acceptable in contemporary society. They, like the roles they played, were also victims of the changing times. Unknowingly, they left the Big Bend country a better and safer place to live.

CHAPTER

4

"Somebody Has Got To Be Killed"

It had snowed all the way from Balmorhea to Ysleta, and being unaccustomed to severe winter driving, I was particularly fatigued when I arrived in El Paso. After checking in at a motel, my first telephone call did nothing to enliven my spirits. After I had driven some eight hundred miles, Arthur Ekdahl refused to be interviewed about his work with the Chisos Mining Company at Terlingua. (I had just begun researching my book *Quicksilver.*)[1] His silence was understandable. As the company bookkeeper, the two sets of books cited in the mining company bankruptcy litigation were not the subject for polite conversation, even with a struggling graduate student.

At that point it did not appear that December 9, 1967, would be a day I would remember fondly. And then something happened that caused me to feel I was playing a role in the opening scenes of an Agatha Christie mystery novel. My next scheduled call was to George Billalba, the central figure in chapter 5, "Shootout at Study Butte." I opened the telephone book to the B's, ran my finger down the column, and, when I located George Billalba's name, I suddenly had the frightening sensation that someone had been awaiting my arrival. *George Billalba's name had been underlined in pencil*! Almost in shock, I dialed the number; there was no answer. Subsequent attempts to reach Billalba that night also failed. Apparently another person also looking for Billalba had previously occupied that same motel room.

Fearing total failure, I, with some trepidation, dialed the residence of O. C. Dowe. A pleasant female voice answered the telephone. Yes, that was the Dowe residence, but O. C. had already gone to bed. "He's a very old man, you know," she explained. "But I am sure he will want to talk to you. Please call back in the morning." Things were indeed looking brighter; the Sunday morning telephone call yielded an invitation to lunch.

Sunday lunch with the Dowes was indeed a family affair, some three generations, and my fascination with his account of early days of Big Bend law enforcement was shared by the entire family. As a mounted United States customs inspector, his recollections focused on the seamy side of border life, specifically the Gillespie-Pulliam affair. This was both a life-threatening and time-consuming case that remained graphic in O. C.'s memory. As the interview progressed, it was evident he was enjoying re-living the drama, but he also appeared to be tiring. Periodically, he would excuse himself and leave the room for a few minutes. In his absence, his daughter-in-law explained, "O. C. has to take little catnaps nowadays. He tires easily." He would soon return, however, obviously revived and eager to continue his account of conflict and illicit enterprise along the Rio Grande. And so it turned out to be a memorable weekend in El Paso. I am indebted primarily to O. C. Dowe for the account that follows.

From Brownsville, Texas, to a point just west of El Paso, the Rio Grande forms approximately eight hundred miles of the United States-Mexico border. Nowhere else in the Western Hemisphere—and probably the world —does one international boundary separate two nations of greater economic disparity. For more than a century citizens of both nations have, without governmental sanction, attempted to exploit this economic imbalance for personal gain. The process is called smuggling.

The focal point of much of this illicit trade is, and has been, the Big Bend region of Texas; physical geography deems it so. While the fluctuating depth of the Great River facilitates clandestine crossings, the region's rugged remoteness conceals the intruders and makes legal enforcement difficult. The items of this contraband trade vary with the period. Early in this century it was cattle, horses, and liquor; later it was dope, guns, ammunition, and exotic birds. But despite all countermeasures employed, smuggling seems destined to continue. "The government has always kept a lookout along the river," a former Big Bend resident observed. "They can't stop it. There will always be some going across if the rewards equal the risk. And when the rewards are high, a few men are going to die."[2] Death and smuggling go hand in hand. And with armed men functioning beyond the pale of law enforcement, violence has become a metaphor for international larceny. Thus the past holds a tragic lesson for the future.

The cattle industry has long been the mainstay of the Big Bend economy. Beginning in the early 1880s, cattlemen moved into the region and rapidly claimed the watered areas for their herds.[3] With the adjacency of Mexico and its long-established cattle industry, Big Bend cattlemen soon looked to the South to replenish their herds. While much of this international trade was legitimate, some cattlemen attempted to increase their profits by bypassing the customs fee. One such person was Jim Gillespie.

Balanced against Gillespie's liabilities (reportedly he would go to dances and shoot out the lights for fun), his greatest assets were his charm and personality.[4] One former Big Bend resident remembered him as "the cowboy debonair, a Prince Charming of the Range." Dapper and well dressed, "he always rode a good horse, and his saddle, spurs, and chaps were about everything a cowboy could desire. And in a beautiful leather holster on his right hip was a handsome but dangerous looking pearl-handled Colt six-shooter."[5] Gillespie's side arm was far more than a decorative appendage. Other than providing security and projecting a macho self-image, it moreover symbolized man's inhumanity to man in the Big Bend country.

In the spring of 1912, Gillespie decided to import a large herd of cheap Mexican cattle and fatten them on his Big Bend range in the hopes of reaping a good profit on the United States market.[6] In 1912, international transactions required careful preplanning. Not wanting to carry a large amount of cash into Mexico, Gillespie arranged for C. A. Hawley, bookkeeper and store manager with the Chisos Mining Company at Terlingua, Texas, to hold in trust $25,000. Gillespie, in turn, proceeded to Mexico and purchased the cattle by issuing handwritten letters of credit to be drawn against money held by Hawley. The system worked. Within a period of about two weeks Hawley stated he paid out the entire $25,000.[7]

On March 12, Gillespie entered 510 Mexican cattle through the Lajitas port-of-entry, on which he paid the import duty.[8] En route to his range, he and his drovers, accompanied by a young United States customs agent named Gibbs, stopped at the Chisos Store in Terlingua. Gillespie and his men obviously had been drinking, but young Gibbs, according to Hawley, was "the drunkest man I ever saw on his feet."[9] As the agent assigned to clear the herd through customs, Gibbs obviously was in no condition to discharge his responsibilities. Hawley, although suspicious, asked no questions and Gillespie subsequently began moving his herd northward toward Alpine.[10]

Hawley heard nothing more of the incident until about a month later when O. C. Dowe arrived in Terlingua investigating a report of cattle smuggling at Lajitas. The source of Dowe's information was a letter from Rozell Pulliam, a Big Bend cattleman on whose ranch Gillespie had temporarily held his herd. Although admirable, Pulliam's commitment to law enforcement proved to be an ill-advised move.[11]

Dowe's investigation confirmed Hawley's earlier suspicions; the "Prince Charming of the Range" had indeed tarnished his image. After tracking the herd, or herds, from the Lajitas crossing, a new scenario began to emerge. Dowe learned that one portion of the herd on which Gillespie had paid duty crossed the Rio Grande at the Lajitas port-of-entry on March 12, which he trailed to the Pulliam Ranch about twelve miles north of Terlingua. He also discovered that later that night Gillespie's drovers crossed about two hundred head of large Mexican cattle, on which no duty had been paid, upriver from Lajitas.[12] Dowe followed that trail across the mountains and learned that on March 15, the smuggled cattle had been rebranded with Gillespie's *d* brand and mixed with the legal herd on the Pulliam ranch. Dowe continued trailing the cattle and found them

Big Bend rancher Rozell Pulliam, whose report of a cattle smuggling incident led to his death by the smuggler in the Alpine, Texas, post office in 1912.
Courtesy Junior Historian Files, Marfa Public Library

pastured on the Lockhausen Ranch near Marathon.[13] He took legal possession of the herd on May 13, rented an area east of Marathon known as the McFarland pasture, and assigned mounted customs men to hold them pending litigation. Dowe, in turn, filed suit to enforce the forfeiture of 603 of the animals because of unlawful importation.[14] Gillespie, of course, was furious.

Traditionally, cattlemen live by two sets of law, those enacted by state legislatures and the self-imposed moral customs adapted to life on the range. It was the latter that commanded the higher respect. In driving the two hundred head of smuggled cattle across the mountains, Gillespie's drovers violated an unwritten law among cattlemen: they cut Rozell Pulliam's fence and failed to repair it. "Everyone carried clippers to pull staples out of three of the posts," Dowe explained. "You took down the wire, tied it, moved the cattle, and replaced the [wire with the] staples. If Gillespie had done this, I would never have heard about it. But that was just too much [for Pulliam] to swallow. Roselle [*sic*] Pulliam was a lawman's friend," Dowe explained further. "He had given me quite a bit of information on law breakers, but fence cutting made him mad."[15]

Dowe also had to contend with Gillespie's anger. In losing possession of his herd, the young cowboy had to face two critical issues. Between February 21 and May 31, 1912, Gillespie had executed three notes totaling $13,600 payable to the El Paso Bank and Trust Company and offered the seized herd as collateral. The notes matured on August 12 and October 1, 1912.[16] With his cattle impounded, Gillespie stood little chance of meeting these obligations. He confronted Dowe, "'O. C., I think you ought to tell me who gave me away. If I find out I will shoot the son-of-a-bitch in the back, and I think I know who he is.'" Dowe, of course, remained noncommittal.[17] The growing probability of conflict over the smuggling issue, however, became a frequent topic of Big Bend conversation. "Jim was on the warpath," Hawley wrote, "and Roselle [*sic*] Pulliam was the special object of his wrath. Again I heard the remark, 'Somebody has got to be killed.'"[18]

Some three weeks following Dowe's May 13 seizure of the herd, United States district attorney Charles A. Boyington presented the government's case in federal court in El Paso. He pleaded for the forfeiture of Gillespie's herd; the case was set for hearing on the first Monday in October. This decision, in essence, destroyed Gillespie financially. By October, his herd would have been impounded, and unmarketable, for five months, while, in the meantime, his three notes would have matured, leaving him with no means of repayment. This obviously was not a matter that Gillespie would take lightly; those familiar with the case, including Rozell Pulliam, could foresee trouble.

Events of the summer of 1912 remain largely undocumented, but Pulliam, for reasons unknown, made an auspicious decision. He purchased a ranch near Hachita, New Mexico, and moved his family to that location. O. C. Dowe believed he made the move primarily to avoid a showdown with Gillespie, which, by then, appeared inevitable. "He didn't want to have any trouble," Dowe explained. "That's why Rozell left the Bend."[19] Prior to leaving Brewster County, Pulliam turned his cattle over to his father, William M. Pulliam, and found a buyer for his Big Bend ranch. The closing was scheduled for mid-September, and Rozell Pulliam returned to Alpine for the final transaction. It proved to be exactly that.

It is not known if Pulliam anticipated meeting Gillespie, but should that occur, he came prepared carrying a Colt .45 pistol in a belt holster. It also remains unclear if Gillespie knew that Pulliam was returning to Alpine. Either by plan or act of fate, Gillespie left his Marathon residence on September 16 and arrived in Alpine sometime later that day. He too came armed, carrying an automatic pistol. Alpine insurance agent G. B. Crawford believed that sometime that afternoon Gillespie learned of Pulliam's presence in Alpine. He recalled seeing Gillespie standing outside of Kirkeys' open air theater that night. "He kept on the outside," Crawford remembered. "Never went in. I could tell he was looking for somebody. He had that mean look in his face."[20]

If Gillespie was searching for Pulliam, he did not find him. Instead, he spent the night drinking and gambling, Mrs. Robert Pulliam learned later. "He had lost heavily," she explained, "and had been the target of supposedly good-natured kidding about his impending trial."[21] Gillespie arrived early the following morning at a downtown restaurant and joined Louis Starnes, Southern Pacific Railroad agent, for breakfast.[22] Wayne Cartledge remembered that Starnes left the restaurant around 8:30 that morning, before Gillespie, and as he walked down North Railroad Avenue (now West Holland Avenue), he saw Pulliam enter the post office. "He then saw Gillespie coming from across the railroad tracks," Cartledge explained. "He [Gillespie] crossed the street and headed for the post office." Starnes was not sure if Gillespie had seen Pulliam, "but he knew he was armed and if the two met there would be a killing."[23]

As Gillespie entered the post office, Starnes's first impulse was to intervene, but by then it was too late. Gillespie had already stepped up on the plank sidewalk in front of the post office; in four strides he disappeared inside the building. Starnes counted six shots. The delivery boy driving Richey's Grocery hack jumped to the ground to restrain the frightened animal.[24] It was over almost as soon as it had begun. According to eyewitnesses, Gillespie entered the crowded post office as Pulliam was leaving. Recognizing Pulliam, "Gillespie took two or three rapid steps forward to where Pulliam was standing and commenced shooting" at point-blank range. After four shots Pulliam fell backward mortally wounded; Gillespie then stepped forward and fired two more shots into the prone body. "When the body was removed," the *Alpine Avalanche* reported, "two bullet holes were found in the floor where he had fallen."[25]

Either premeditated or the result of quick thinking, Gillespie's next move stood him well in the forthcoming trials. He "walked over to the body and took Pulliam's pistol," the *Avalanche* reported. Without speaking to anyone, he left the post office and entered Huddleston's store next door, where he met L. B. Caruthers. When Caruthers asked for the gun, Gillespie replied, "'I will give it to you *if you will protect me.*'"[26] Caruthers took the gun, and the two began walking toward the Brewster County courthouse. The following day Gillespie stated in his jail cell that he shot Pulliam in self-defense and had retained Wigfall Van Sickle as his attorney. Van Sickle represented his client well; bail was set at $10,000, and on September 26 the "cowboy debonair" was released from jail.

Thus the moral code of the cattleman's frontier—"somebody has got to be killed"—had been upheld.[27] Murder, however, seemed like a high price to pay for silencing a witness in a cattle smuggling case. Yet Gillespie's motivation—fear, hatred, or retribution—would never be known. History is frequently punctuated with periods of gnawing silence; such was the case of James W. Gillespie.

The paths of justice frequently follow circuitous routes. During the next three years litigation became a way of life for Gillespie. Immediately following his release from jail he appeared in El Paso where he and the El Paso Bank and Trust Company filed a joint plea of intervention in *Cause 375*. They denied any of the cattle were fraudulently imported into the United States and claimed the government had no right to dispose of the herd. Attorney R. E. Thomason successfully pleaded their case. On December 19, 1912, the court ordered the United States marshal to deliver to the claimants the 603 head of cattle upon their giving bond in the sum of $12,500, the appraised value of the herd.[28]

With the herd dispersed and the bond still in force, Gillespie returned to El Paso on April 15, 1913, when a twelve-man jury heard evidence in the smuggling case. No quick decision was forthcoming; the court ordered meals and lodging for the jury while they deliberated into the second day. They finally agreed that "probable cause had not been shown for the prosecution" and voted in behalf of the claimant.[29] Although the verdict was a tentative victory for Gillespie, a troubled future still awaited the "Prince Charming of the Range." During the next two years the justice system appeared to collapse in the process of assessing penalty for the murder of Rozell Pulliam. Many believed that Gillespie was a contributing factor.

Immediately following the murder, the Brewster County court, assuming that Gillespie could not receive a fair trial in Alpine, ordered a change of venue and transferred the case to Jeff Davis County. That trial ended in a hung jury, and on January 20, 1913, the case was transferred next to Presidio County. The judge postponed this trial because four of the defendant's important witnesses were absent. "Judge Douglas fined the absent witnesses $500 each," the Avalanche reported, "and had an attachment issued for them."[30]

The case was transferred next to Maverick County, where a special venire of sixty names was drawn and ordered to appear on November 26, 1913. Two days later the trial began. Gillespie, as usual, pleaded not guilty, and on December 6 the members of the jury stated they could not reach a verdict and asked to be discharged. They voted six for conviction and six for acquittal. The judge, in turn, ordered the case transferred from Maverick County to Wilson County.[31] Thus the pattern was destined to continue.

The third and final trial was held in Floresville on January 8, 1915, and also ended in a hung jury.[32] The fact that the three murder trials, in which the evidence was so incriminating, ended in hung juries did not go unnoticed. O. C. Dowe, who testified for the prosecution at all three trials, suspected that Gillespie had, in some clandestine manner, influenced the indecisions. "It was an open-and-shut case," Dowe believed. Gillespie had threatened to "shoot the son of a bitch in the back" that gave him away, and "I had to testify to that. There was bound to have been a payoff [to some of the jurors], but it was never proven," Dowe explained. "Gillespie was a big spender; got next to a lot of people. . . . He would go ahead of the trial, put on parties. A real smooth talker and a ladies' man. He must have found people to cause the mistrials." The parties Gillespie hosted were lusty affairs. "He was quite a cut-up," Dowe continued, "and a heavy drinker. [He] would pull off his boots and play the piano with his feet. Got in with the best families where the trial would be held. You couldn't help liking Jim."[33]

Dowe, however, was the exception. He purposely tried to avoid any contact with the defendant during the trials; the single confrontation occurred in Floresville. After testifying that Gillespie had threatened to kill Pulliam, the two met unexpectedly in the lobby of a hotel. Dowe entered the hotel and, not noticing who was sitting on the opposite side of the stove, seated himself. When he looked up he found himself staring Gillespie squarely in the eye. Neither spoke; both felt committed to stare the other down. "There was no talking, just looking," Dowe recalled. "I knew he was armed all during the trial. People told me I was next on his list. I kept my eye on him; watched him all the time. Nothing happened, but with him, you could never be sure."[34]

With a fourth trial pending, Gillespie moved to New Mexico and established residence near Corona. If his motive was self-preservation, he made a bad decision; his charm and masculine appeal proved to be his undoing. Gillespie became attracted to the wife of one Paschal Luttrell, and while the latter was away, he visited Mrs. Luttrell in her home and allegedly insulted her. Two days later, on Saturday, July 24, 1920, he and Luttrell met at the Corona post office. Luttrell asked Gillespie to sit down on the porch of the post office building; he said he wanted to discuss the matter. An argument ensued and Gillespie leaped to his feet, cursed Luttrell and stated that "he would kill him if anything further was said upon the subject." Whereupon Luttrell drew his pistol and "with the barrel of said pistol 6 to 12 inches from the face [of Gillespie] . . . shot him . . . almost between the eyes." Luttrell claimed self-defense. His trial began at Carrizozo, Lincoln County, New Mexico, on November 15, 1920, and the jury returned a guilty verdict on November 20. The sentence was not less than twenty years nor more than twenty-five years in the state penitentiary. Luttrell's subsequent appeal was denied.[35]

When the news of Gillespie's death reached Alpine, Brewster County sheriff E. E. Townsend went to the home of Mrs. Pearl Pulliam, Rozell's widow, and told her, "Well, Pearl, they finally got him." She was delighted, but when she learned that Luttrell was in prison, she, with Townsend's help, circulated a petition to gain his release, which apparently was successful. "When he got out he came here to Alpine to thank me for helping get him out," she recalled. "I told him I was glad he did it. It needed to be done."[36]

The Pulliam-Gillespie affair was a multifaceted tragedy. Two men died, a family was destroyed, two men lost their jobs, and the state invested a lot of money in purposeless litigation. And that was but a single incident in a century-long drama that is still being played out in the Big Bend country. While some aspects of the international cat-and-mouse game are in constant flux, others never seem to change. Clandestine border penetrations still occur with discouraging frequency, challenging the law enforcement agencies to rely on ever-changing technology to seal the ever-widening cracks along the international border. Today helicopters and light civilian aircraft piloted by patrol inspectors of the United States Immigration and Naturalization Service watch over the same forbidding landscape O. C. Dowe once traversed on horseback.[37]

The 1980s initiated a new phase in Big Bend history. As the war on drugs escalated, so did the rewards to those who ran the risks of smuggling the illegal substances into the United States.[38] And with the lure of unprecedented profits, it became increasingly difficult to distinguish between the good guys and the bad guys. On May 8, 1992, federal judge Jerry Buchmeyer sentenced Presidio County sheriff Rick Thompson to a life sentence without parole for smuggling 2,400 pounds of 93 percent pure Columbian cocaine through the Ojinaga corridor, valued at 50 million dollars.

In retrospect, when considering the current technical innovations employed in border law enforcement, the Pulliam-Gillespie episode appears as just another tragic interlude in the history of the border wars in the Big Bend country. Will it ever end? "¿Quien sabe?"

CHAPTER

5

Shootout at Study Butte

~

I learned early on that much of Big Bend social and cultural history lacked specific documentation. If a matter was not reported in the newspapers or settled in court, the only remaining source of information was oral. That meant meeting people—lots of people—and meeting Big Bend people meant friendships.

One friendship begot another, and over the years my circle of friends continued to grow. For example, it was through Ross Maxwell that I met Bob Cartledge, and Bob, in turn, referred me to other longtime Big Bend citizens who referred me to others, ad infinitum. Thanks to their thoughtfulness, their recollections enabled me to record many events that otherwise would have been lost to history. Such was the case of the Billalba-Coffman shootout at Study Butte.

Although Cartledge had been involved in that tragic episode as justice of the peace, he insisted that I contact other sources. Brian Montague, he advised, had prosecuted the case in Brewster County and could be a great help in providing additional data. Following an interview with Elmo Johnson in Sonora, Texas, I called Montague in Del Rio. I introduced myself, mentioned Bob Cartledge's name, and explained my mission. "The Billalba-Coffman case. My, that was a long time ago," he reminisced. "Never worked so hard in a losing effort. I tried to win 'em all, but that one got away." And then, after a long pause, he continued, "I suppose there was a lesson to be learned there; never try to prosecute a man you think is innocent." I could see my patience was yielding results; he then asked the key question, "How can I help you, Mr. Ragsdale?" I requested an interview the following morning. He agreed and suggested that I be in his office at nine o'clock. Although his calendar was full, he would try to work me in.

When I arrived at Montague's Del Rio law office the following morning, it was "standing room only." Anticipating a lengthy wait, I introduced myself to the receptionist, who responded with some surprise, "Oh, Mr. Ragsdale! Mr. Montague said for *you* to come right in." He welcomed me warmly and immediately began discussing the case. Although it was, for him, a failed undertaking, he, like many of my other interview subjects, seemed to relish the opportunity to relive their earlier years along the border. But Montague was different in one respect; through training and experience, he could delineate the social and cultural background of an event, in addition to providing the more pertinent details. And while I kept many of Brian Montague's paying clients waiting that June morning in 1966, I feel greatly indebted to them, as well as the man who told the stories. His recollections filled many vacant gaps in documenting the Billalba-Coffman affair.

Traditionally, one of the distinguishing features of the Big Bend country has been its divided society. Politically, economically, educationally, and ethnically, the community falls into two distinct social groups—Hispanic and Anglo. Both societies bear their individual identities; the extremes further dramatize the region's social diversity. This is a region of haves and have-nots, of considerable wealth and abject poverty, where the illiterate far outnumber the literate, and where political decisions traditionally had been made by the few. Translated into the regional vernacular, this is—or was—a *white man's country.*

Although the late twentieth century brought an amelioration of racial prejudice and social imbalance, such was not the case a half century previous. Some of the region's less responsible citizens found in Anglo enthnocentrism the license to dominate and sometimes abuse the less fortunate, specifically the Mexicans. And when some exceeded the authority vested in them by local custom, they discovered there were limits of scurrility to which that society, be it Mexican or Anglo, would tolerate. Such was the tragic story of Jack and Winslow Coffman.

In the post–World War I era when the price of quicksilver dropped, several operators in the Terlingua area terminated production.[1] At Study Butte, a mining village located some five miles east of Terlingua, the owners of the Texas Almaden Mining Company closed that facility and engaged Dan G. Coffman as watchman, with J. B. Huntley as his assistant.[2] Coffman lived in the mining village and continued operating the company store while guarding the abandoned complex. He began this assignment in March of 1921, and remained there for about one year. Seeing little future in guarding an abandoned mine, he left Study Butte in early 1922 to work on his farm near Shafter, Texas. Before leaving, however, Coffman introduced his son, Aubrey (Jack), age twenty-one, to Edgar Gleim, one of the mine owners, who engaged him as his father's replacement. Not wishing to live alone at an abandoned mine, Jack induced his younger brother, Winslow, age nineteen, to join him at Study Butte. Leaving his two free-spirited and undisciplined sons at Study Butte was a decision Dan Coffman should have considered more carefully.

With Dan Coffman's departure, trouble began immediately. Jack's first brush with the law and clash with the local Mexican community occurred just west of Study Butte near Terlingua Creek. Becoming embroiled in an argument with a Mexican, he resolved the matter by "pistol whipping" the defenseless farmer. When Justice of the Peace Robert L. Cartledge learned of the incident, he summoned Jack to his office. Cartledge could not recall the nature of the encounter, but when questioned about carrying a prohibited weapon, young Coffman explained that, because of his watchman's duties, Brewster County sheriff E. E. Townsend authorized him to carry the weapon. Cartledge assessed no fine in the matter but warned Jack about his personal conduct, plus the dangers and responsibilities of going armed.[3]

Disregarding Cartledge's advice, both Jack and Winslow soon gained well-deserved reputations as drunks and troublemakers at the Mexican *bailes*. H. C. Hernandez, a Terlingua resident at that time, remembered them well. They frequented the Mexican dances "always looking for girls and trouble," he recalled, "and always trying to pick a fight with someone, especially Mexicans."[4] The combination of sotol, girls, and weapons was a certain prescription for trouble.[5] And trouble was soon forthcoming, but this time with Winslow as the instigator.

It occurred on a Saturday night following a Mexican dance in Terlingua. A messenger reported the matter to Robert Cartledge; Winslow Coffman had been stabbed and was taken to the Carmen Casteneda residence in Terlingua's Mexican section. Cartledge called Dr. R. A. Wilson, the Chisos Mining Company doctor, and together they went to the Castenedas where young Coffman lay unattended. The justice of the peace was the last person Winslow wanted to see, and when the two men entered the room he greeted them with a barrage of profanity. Forgetting momentarily the obligations of his Hippocratic oath, Dr. Wilson exclaimed as he left the room: "'Let the ungrateful ———— lie there and bleed to death.'"[6] Cartledge, not knowing the extent of Winslow's injuries and feeling a sense of duty to the boy's father, prevailed upon the doctor to aid the bleeding man. Together they returned to the room, and while Cartledge held young Coffman in the bed the doctor surveyed the extent of his injuries—an open knife wound just below the left shoulder blade. Using some of Winslow's remaining sotol, Dr. Wilson disinfected the wound, which he closed with some eight or ten stitches.[7] Winslow returned to Study Butte the following day, and some two weeks later sent Cartledge the following letter:

> *Study Butte, Texas Jan. 22, 1923*
>
> *Mr. R. L. Carledge* [sic],
> *Dear Mr. Carledge* [sic]. *About this trouble, I wish you would keep this quite* [sic] *and not say anything to my father. It would be trouble sure enough. I am going to stay away from those dances. Am not going to any more of them.*
> *W. O. Coffman*
> *P.S. Getting along fine.*[8]

Cartledge never reported the incident to Dan Coffman. It was not necessary; Coffman was well aware of his sons' predilection for liquor and the good times. In a letter written on October 15, 1922, some three months before Winslow's injury, Coffman urged his sons to "take care of things the best you can and *cut all drinking*."[9] The admonition went unheeded. During the next four months Coffman corresponded frequently with his sons, discussing various matters of mutual concern: personal finances, farm conditions, his dependency upon them, their relationship with the Fredrico Billalba family, and their uncertain future at Study Butte. And while the correspondence focused primarily on personal business, also implied is a father's deep affection for his sons, mixed with an uncharacteristic measure of masculine tenderness. Each letter ends with "Love, Dad." Jack and Winslow were the Coffmans' only children.

On March 5, 1923, Coffman wrote his sons that he was "sure busy [on the farm], [I] need one of you boys awfully bad to help me. . . . I hope Winslow is on the road, am looking for him every day. Have had some land cleared. Am going to plant corn next week—Let me hear from you."[10] In the same letter Coffman urged his sons to terminate their business relations with Fredrico Billalba, a highly respected Mexican rancher in the Study Butte area, and his son, George. "Jack, tell Geo[rge] Villalba to pay for that truck or turn it back," he wrote. "And also, get the type writer [*sic*] from George V. . . . Tell old Fred Villalba to get busy and pay his acc[ount], and [also] get after old Sam Nail."[11]

In subsequent correspondence there appears a growing concern for his sons' future at Study Butte and George Billalba's role in their feared dismissal. Dan Coffman wrote:

> *Jack, old E.M.G. [Edgar M. Gleim] ran over this morning. Says*
> *G. W. Gleim wanted me to go over to Ft. Davis. He wanted to see me. . . .*
> *I sure believe they are going to take that store or do something. Some one*
> *[sic] is telling or writing us up, I guess. So we had better get all we can*
> *up here [Shafter], in the land line. Reasons for me trading for this place.*
> *Let them have the job if they want it. We can make more here, my way.*
> *. . . Yes, Jack, I raised $300.00 in Alpine on the cows, for six months time.*
> *Am having a Devil [of a time] getting by, at present. Has old George*
> *Villalba paid for that truck or not? He was to pay the 15th this month.*
> *No mor [sic] news. I sent your ck to Marfa State Bank. Love, Dad.*[12]

In the final letter in this exchange, it appears that Coffman assumes that their tenure at Study Butte is nearing an end and George Billalba is the culprit. He believes that Billalba wants to replace them as mine watchman. Coffman writes:

> *Also found out something else on the road to Alpine. Old Geo.*
> *Villalba has been writing Gleimes about something and there is no*
> *telling what it was. He wants that job down there, of course. Now the*
> *thing is, watch them. Make old George [Billalba] pay for that truck by*
> *the 15th. I think it is $60.00 he owes. It is entered on back of note. If he*
> *don't pay, take truck. I saw Bob C[artledge] on road. You see him and*
> *he will help you out. And when you get even [apparently with the*
> *Billalbas] let them go. I made the loan, all right. Got $300 from Alpine*
> *State Bank. I hope that old woman leaves there, if you need any help get*
> *old Simmons. And keep every thing locked up good. . . . Getting late.*
> *Love, Dad.*[13]

Their worst fears were soon realized. In late May, 1923, Edgar Gleim went to Study Butte, discharged the Coffmans, engaged George Billalba as their replacement, and instructed them to surrender the keys to Billalba.[14] Assuming, and with good reason, that Billalba had engineered their dismissal, the Coffmans were furious. And following their father's recent advice to see Bob Cartledge—"he will help you out"—they first went to Terlingua to confer with the justice of the peace. Venting their anger to Cartledge, they proposed an immediate showdown with Billalba. Cartledge advised otherwise, suggesting instead that they leave at once for Shafter. Jack, however, hesitated, explaining that his car was not roadworthy; he had broken a leaf in a rear spring. Cartledge quietly pondered the matter. Convinced that if the Coffmans remained in Terlingua a confrontation with Billalba was inevitable, he felt he had two choices: either place them in jail in protective custody, or repair the car himself so they could leave town. He chose the latter, instructing them to take the car to the mining company shops for the necessary repairs. The company would bear the expense.[15]

Cartledge thought the matter was settled; he was wrong. Instead of going to the company shops, they drove east toward the Mexican section of Terlingua where they picked up the sister of a Mexican girl with whom Jack had been living, and a blind musician named Florentino, who played guitar and sang Mexican love songs. With a fresh supply of sotol, they headed for Study Butte for one last fling before leaving for their father's farm at Shafter. They partied until midafternoon the following day. Still bolstered by the liquor, they decided to look for George Billalba in the abandoned mining village and punish him for taking their job. Accompanied by their two girlfriends, they first searched an empty bunkhouse. Finding no one there, they methodically knocked over furniture, scattered the contents, and took random shots with their pistols.[16]

Next they drove to a dwelling behind the store building, parked their car, and called to Billalba. He was there, asleep on the front porch. Awakened, he got up from his cot and, not realizing the purpose of their mission, began walking toward the car. As Billalba approached the vehicle, both Jack and Winslow opened fire at point-blank range. "It was unbelievable they didn't hit him as he made his way back to his house," attorney and former judge Brian Montague explained. Once inside the house Billalba grabbed a .30-30 rifle, returned to the front door, and attempted to talk to his assailants. Ignoring Billalba, they continued their barrage of pistol fire. "Awakened by the shooting, his three-year-old daughter came up behind him," Montague continued. "That scared him as he was afraid she would be killed. I think that was when he made his decision. Remember, up to now he hadn't fired a single shot and they were still shooting." Assuming that Billalba was not armed, the two gunmen followed him to the house and started up the front steps. It will never be known whether they heard the shattering of the broken window pane or saw the barrel of a rifle pointed unexpectedly in their direction. Billalba shot twice. Almost simultaneously Jack and Winslow Coffman collapsed as they fell forward, face down. Both died instantly, each with a loaded pistol in his hand.[17]

Although Billalba shot in self-defense, he knew he was in deep trouble. A Mexican had killed two Anglos, and there were no witnesses. Obviously in a state of emotional stress, he, however, acted wisely. He loaded his family in the Coffmans' old Buick, drove to Terlingua, and surrendered to Justice of the Peace Robert Cartledge. He and Billalba left immediately for Alpine where Cartledge placed him in the custody of Brewster County sheriff E. E. Townsend. Before departing, however, Billalba insisted that he keep his rifle for his own protection. Cartledge agreed, realizing that in this emotionally charged community Billalba's life was in danger. Cartledge recalled that while driving north to Alpine, as each automobile approached, Billalba, fearing it might be Dan Coffman, would reach in the back seat for his rifle. On one occasion when he thought he recognized Coffman, Cartledge stopped the car and ordered Billalba to hide behind a rock ledge until the car passed.[18] After accepting the prisoner in Alpine, Townsend also recognized Billalba's vulnerability and quickly "hurried him out of the country as a precautionary measure."[19]

The double murder attracted wide attention. The *Alpine Avalanche* reported the event as follows:

> *Immediately after the news of the killing was received, Dr. R. A. Wilson and Mr. T. M. Newton hurried to the scene with the hope that the boys or one of them might still be alive. They were both dead, shot through the breast and lying side by side, their pistols also by them. They were near the door on Billaba's [sic] porch as he said. Beyond this nothing is known of the fight or the cause, except there is a rumor that the affair came up over a reported change in management of the mining company business or store. One of the Coffman boys was in charge of the store which is near the Billaba [sic] home.[20]*

Later that night the bodies of the two young men were delivered to the Livingston Funeral Company in Alpine. The following day their unusual visibility attracted many local sightseers. Hattie Grace Elliott, a former Terlingua schoolteacher, still has vivid memories of that occasion. "When the bodies were brought in here [Alpine] to the Livingston undertaking parlor," she recalled, "I went over there [with a friend] who had known the boys.... That was the first time I ever looked at a dead person and I almost went into fits. I was just horrified at the way they looked.... I was sorry I went, because now, I don't even have to close my eyes to see those two boys laid out on wooden tables, out under a shed."[21]

The Coffmans were buried at Marathon in the same grave; the double entombment attracted both mourners and the inquisitive. "I didn't know the boys, but I was there," recalled Hallie Stillwell. "In fact, everybody from around there came to the funeral. It was real sad, burying those two young boys in the same grave like that. I cried my eyes out. Roy [her husband] was friendly with Dan [Coffman]. They didn't seem to be bad folks. I thought they were respected people."[22] On May 31, 1923, an *Alpine Avalanche Supplement* contained the Coffmans' obituary. Both the length and the emotional overtones reflect the wide public interest generated by the double tragedy:

> *Like all children they were the apple of their parents' eyes.... At one fell sweep all that they hold dear is gone. They had hopes and aspirations for their boys like all parents.... [They] took them to San Antonio where they were given a business course. But some way, the Providence that rules the lives of men has decided otherwise and the boys have finished their race here on earth.... Although men in stature and size they were but boys, Winslow being 21 and Jack 19, almost twenty. They were boys that feared no danger and possibly therein lay their fate.... It seems a pity, a pity that they should be cut off right in the bloom of life, but He who rules the destinies of men knows why these things must be. Help us to understand.[23]*

The law enforcement agencies accorded the case high priority. On Monday night following the Thursday afternoon shooting, Deputy Sheriff T. I. Morgan arrested and placed in jail Jacob [Jake] Billalba, brother of George Billalba. He was "charged by complaint and complicity.... alleged to have been at his brother George's house when the killing occurred. The officers are still working on the case."[24] With two sons charged with murder, Fredrico Billalba sought the best legal defense available, the well-known Marfa law firm, Mead and Metcalfe. Their services were not cheap; Fredrico Billalba signed a $3,000 note and later deeded his Big Bend ranch, about thirty sections, to the law partners.[25] They, nevertheless, served their client well. When the Grand Jury returned the indictment on August 14, 1923, charging George Billalba with the murder of Winslow Coffman, the attorneys moved for an immediate trial. Brian Montague, the prosecuting attorney, did not understand their reasoning unless they were confident of acquittal. Montague discussed the case with Sheriff Townsend, who agreed acquittal appeared imminent, "but he was certain that if Billalba was tried and freed now, Dan Coffman would kill Billalba in the courtroom." Montague and the sheriff met with the defense attorneys; they agreed on a six months continuance.[26]

In the interim, however, Metcalfe began gathering evidence for his defense of Billalba; he soon discovered one key item in a most unlikely place. Billalba told him that just prior to the shooting, he received a letter from the Coffman boys in which they referred to him "in vulgar and uncomplimentary terms ... and after reading it, [he] wadded it up and threw it in an open [outhouse] toilet."[27] Realizing the importance of this evidence, Metcalfe went immediately to Study Butte where he retrieved the letter from its ignoble depository. It met his fullest expectations; upon those inflammatory statements rested the foundation of his defense. He knew full well that ethnic slurs issued prior to attempted murder would play well before an all-male, all-Anglo jury.

The three-day trial began in Alpine on February 28, 1924; thirty-two witnesses were called, eighteen specifically for the defense. These included Gregornia and Fredrico Billalba, the defendant's parents; his two brothers, Fred and Jacob; Justice of the Peace Robert L. Cartledge; Brewster County sheriff E. E. Townsend; W. D. Burcham, a mining engineer closely associated with the Study Butte quicksilver mines; and Florentino, the blind Mexican musician. Cartledge; E. M. Gleim, the Coffman's employer at Study Butte; and Dr. R. A. Wilson were additional witnesses called by the state.[28] C. E. Mead represented the defendant in court, District Attorney Brian Montague and County Attorney John Perkins represented the state; and C. R. Sutton, Judge, 83rd Judicial District of Texas, presided. The trial's preparation, the assemblage of personnel, the extended testimony, and the attorneys' emotional oratory, all stood in marked contrast to the jury's brief deliberation. In just fifteen minutes they announced a not guilty verdict. To District Attorney Montague, even this seemed unnecessarily long.

During the trial Montague and Arch Allen, one of the jurors, lived in the Karnes Rooming House on the south side of the railroad tracks in Alpine. Both carefully avoided discussing the case. However, following the verdict Allen asked Montague, who prosecuted an obviously weak case, "'Why did you take so much time with your closing speech when you didn't have a chance of winning?'" Embarrassed and slightly amused, Montague responded, "'Oh, I guess I just had to get it out of my system. But tell me something, Arch, why did it take you so long to reach a verdict?'" "'Why Monty,'" Allen answered, "'it took us just one minute to reach the not guilty verdict, but we spent the other fifteen minutes hoping Dan Coffman and his friends would get out of the courtroom and avoid trouble.'" Montague paused, slowly shook his head, and added, "Several times we almost had a killing in that courtroom."[29]

Long before the trial began, Montague realized there was little chance of winning a guilty verdict. Even in a class-conscious society, the evidence clearly favored the defendant; Billalba unquestionably acted in self-defense. During the pretrial investigation at Study Butte, Sheriff E. E. Townsend, on learning the circumstances of the shooting, attempted to prepare Montague for the inevitable. "'As a D. A., Monty,'" Townsend stated, "'you haven't got as much as a crooked stick to lean on in this case.'" Montague agreed, "That was the darndest case of suicide two boys ever committed. They were two dangerous men. Neither ever saw a 'bugger' in his life." And therein lay the tragedy of Jack and Winslow Coffman. Within their frames of reference offensive violence—specifically, skill with firearms—was their only means of establishing supremacy over others, especially Mexicans. In this case, however, they became the victims of their own aggression, a fact their father could never accept. According to Montague, who knew Dan Coffman well, "He was never convinced that they shot first. When I discussed the case with him, he just shook his head in disbelief and kept repeating, 'My boys never missed a shot in their lives . . . never missed a shot in their lives.'"[30]

The Coffmans' accuracy with firearms raises a question that can be resolved only by conjecture. With their continued barrage of point-blank pistol fire aimed at George Billalba, why did they consistently fail to hit their target? Considering their reputed marksmanship in the light of their record of racial hatred and abuse, one can suspect that they were either trying to frighten Billalba as punishment for their dismissal or to force him to leave Study Butte in the hopes of regaining their job at the mine. Even under the influence of sotol and firing repeatedly at close range, had they intended killing Billalba, which was unlikely, there would have been little chance of his surviving. In retrospect it appears they fell victim to their own devious scheme, whatever that may have been.

Dan Coffman also was forced to bear the weight of the tragedy. Childless and alone he returned to his farm in Shafter. Faced with disposing of his possessions left at Study Butte, he turned to Robert Cartledge for assistance. On March 28, 1924, approximately one month following the Billalba trial, he wrote Cartledge:

> As I forgot to ask you about the things we have there, when I saw you in Alpine, now if you want to buy those bedstead springs and mattresses, please let me know. I priced them to Author [Arthur Ekdahl] at $40.00 for the two.
>
> And the horse you had there at $60.00, and the cows at $20.00 a head, the calves throwed [sic] in. I think this is about as reasonable as you can get that stuff any where [sic], and the rest of those things, will get them as soon as posibl [sic]. You know how many of those cows you have in your place, and the rest of them you can pay for as you gather them.
>
> Am very buisy [sic] with my farm at present, hope to make something out of it this year, have every thing looking nice at present, and if nothing unfore seen [sic] happens will make some money this year, if pricez [sic] holds up.[31]

Obviously not wanting to return to Study Butte, Dan Coffman was attempting to close one sad chapter in his life while viewing the future with guarded optimism. I could learn nothing more about Dan Coffman, but considering the failure rate of dry land farmers in the Big Bend country, it is doubtful that he ever achieved the optimistic future he envisioned.

6

The Anatomy of a Family Feud

PART 1: A SUNDAY AFTERNOON AT ESPINO'S TAVERN

When an author begins researching a new topic, various unexpected sub-topics begin to emerge, which may or may not be relevant to the primary subject. Such was the case in the initial stage of my *Quicksilver* research.[1] Reading some thirty years of the *Alpine Avalanche* on microfilm provided a broad overview of the Big Bend region. Frequent news items included the weather, range conditions, school news, social activities, and illegal immigration. Also weekly reports of violence and personal conflict— murder, robbery, theft, assault, and smuggling—documented another topic of major concern. From this survey I realized that any comprehensive history of that region must address the prevalence of violence, its causes, and the casual disregard for law and order as well as human life.

In the published accounts of violence there appeared with noticeable regularity one name—Baiza. The Baizas were a large Mexican family that lived variously on both sides of the Rio Grande in the lower Big Bend country. Their name became synonymous with trouble. According to former court reporter Edith Hopson, "During each term of court there was always a Baiza on trial for something."[2]

I first heard Nona Baiza's name mentioned in connection with an ongoing feud between the Baiza and Acosta families. The trouble apparently began in the early 1950s when the Acosta brothers allegedly killed Nona's son, Adolpho Baiza, in Mexico. By 1967, three men had died and

*Pablo Baiza, astride a burro, moving his household furnishings across the
Rio Grande to Mexico. Because of their frequent encounter with Big Bend
law enforcement, the Baizas enjoyed the protection afforded by that remote
section of the international boundary. Courtesy Smithers Collection, Harry
Ransom Humanities Research Center, University of Texas at Austin*

the growing tension between the two families indicated more violence lay
ahead. Since Nona Baiza was the family's surviving matriarch and bilingual, I wanted to meet her. She apparently was the key person from whom
I could gain some insight into this tragic conflict.

Hart Johnson, a Fort Stockton attorney and judge with an interest in
local history, had aided me previously in arranging interviews in that area.
On the morning of December 8, 1967, I called Hart from Alpine and asked
if he could arrange a meeting with Nona Baiza. He said it was possible. I
was to drive to Fort Stockton, check into a motel, and await his call. His
response came in a most unexpected manner. I should point out here
that the law in Fort Stockton worked in strange and mysterious ways.

Soon after registering at the Sands Motel, I was surprised by a knock
on the door. Other than Hart Johnson, no one knew I was in Fort Stockton. Opening the door, I was even more surprised to be confronted by a

uniformed deputy sheriff. Dispensing with initial pleasantries, the verbal exchange was brief and to the point:

"You Ken Ragsdale?"

"Yes."

"Understand you want to see Nona Baiza."

"I do."

"Drove by where she stays. She wasn't there. Said she'll be back. I'll pick 'er up in the morning and have her in the sheriff's office at ten o'clock. You be there."

"Thank you. I will."

Without further conversation, the deputy returned to the patrol car and quickly departed.

This marked a new experience in historical research. Never before had an officer of the law offered to apprehend a resource person and deliver them at my convenience for an interview. Hart Johnson obviously had connections; his thoughtfulness would yield a prime source of information on a volatile subject not casually discussed by family members. But what bothered me most was that this old woman, whom I had never met, would probably be frightened when the deputy arrived the following morning to drive her to the sheriff's office. Unknown to me, however, Nona was not easily frightened, and an escorted trip to Pecos County sheriff C. S. (Pete) Ten Eyck's office was not without precedence.

Meeting Nona Baiza the next morning was an unforgettable experience. Speaking without hesitation, she gave an appalling account of her son's murder, the subsequent killings, and her view of the ongoing vendetta. Her manner and appearance were as dramatic as her oral recollections. After the interview, I returned to my motel to write a quick summary of our meeting. For fear of intimidation, I avoided using a tape recorder. The account is as follows.

On learning that she was wanted in the sheriff's office, Nona feared the summons meant more family trouble. Not waiting for the deputy, she walked alone to the courthouse on that cold December morning. When I first saw her she was sitting in Sheriff Ten Eyck's office waiting for me. She sat alone in an oak chair across from the sheriff's secretary's desk. Her head was bowed. I could not see her face; it was hidden by an old-fashioned splint bonnet. The secretary introduced us. As Nona raised her head her features became visible for the first time. Age, trouble, the sun, and deprivation had etched deep lines across her face. She did not know her age, but time had clearly marked its passing. She had no teeth; her right eye was kept squinted in an effort to compensate for partial blindness.

Her faded blue print dress had silver buttons; only two matched. The collar, closed with a safety pin, held a short length of what appeared to be a gold watch chain. That was her only attempt at adornment. She held an old paper sack that contained something of value to her; several times she removed a tax notice that she did not understand. I noticed she wore two pairs of hose. The inner pair was coarse and dark blue; the outer pair was lighter and filled with runners and holes. She obviously had dressed to face the cold winter morning.

As Nona recounted Adolpho's murder, her head weaved slowly in response to her emotions. Several times tears filled her faded eyes that had seen so much trouble. She squinted as if trying to hold back tears that told more than any words Nona could articulate. "They [the Acostas] killed my boy for his cows," she claimed. "They hung him up. Shot him. Cut out his tongue. Stuck their old knives in him. Tore off all his clothes. Then the buzzards and wild dogs ate him. We only brought back some of his bones."

I could see her frail body gradually tense as the two gnarled old hands grasped the paper sack tighter and tighter. Then she turned toward me, her right eye squinted tighter as if to see me better. "My boys have killed two of those Acostas," she explained. "Only one is left; they'll get him." Then she paused and seemed to relax. After several seconds of silence she raised her head. The tears were gone. "I know it's wrong to kill," she continued. "God will punish us. But what they did to my boy. What they did to my boy." Again there was silence. She seemed to stare out the window as if at nothing. Then she bowed her head, staring at her fingers as she fondled the frayed edges of the old paper sack. All I could see was the silhouette of an old woman whose shoulders appeared bent by nearly a century of trouble, strife, and disappointment. Life along the border in the Big Bend country had taken its toll.

Nona Baiza was, unquestionably, a product of her environment. In the early twentieth century the Big Bend region, with its remoteness, aridity, scarcity, and isolation, placed an indelible imprint on its occupants. These factors became especially visible in its residents' relations with one another. Life at best was a struggle for survival, and when matters of personal disagreement arose, violence was the usual order of business. In the absence of organized law enforcement, fists, clubs, guns, or knives were used to resolve individual differences. And with sanctuary only a stone's throw across the Rio Grande, the survivors, guilty or otherwise, were seldom brought to justice. It was in this desert fastness where only the strongest (or the best armed) prevailed, that Nona Baiza raised her family, three boys and three girls. Little is known of the girls. For the boys, appearances in the courtroom and county jail became an accepted way of life, and in the end one died, two survived, and two Acostas were laid to rest. Be it life or death, there were no winners in this borderland drama.

From subsequent records I learned that Nona Dodson was born on March 3, 1881, on a ranch near Globe, Arizona, the daughter of Harve and Minnie Dodson.[3] The family began a circuitous trek: ranching near Pecos, Texas, a two-year stint in Alpine, three years on Terlingua Creek, and in 1904 the family moved further south nearer the Rio Grande and remained there some two years until their house burned. Leaving the river country, the family sought refuge high in the Chisos Mountains, establishing a permanent residence at a location known later as Dodson Springs. Dr. Ross A. Maxwell, former superintendent, Big Bend National Park, described that remote site as

> approximately five straight-line miles from the nearest wagon road and several miles farther by trail. All supplies were packed in. The only improvement around the house was a watering trough for goats that doubled as a dipping vat. Dodson [served] as a guide for early visitors [to that area]. On one early trip to the South Rim [of the Chisos Mountains], he showed a visitor his home below the rim. Looking over the very rugged terrain, some 1,500 feet below, the visitor asked, "Mr. Dodson, how did you move the family into the ranch?" He replied, "Me and the old woman walked in, the kids was born here."[4]

Dodson, of course, exaggerated about the family's origin. The residence, however, when compared to later living standards, almost defies description. A 1937 photograph shows a one-room rock structure, probably not more than twenty feet long and approximately twelve feet wide. (The National Park Service demolished the structure in the 1940s.) It had what appears to be a shingle roof, three small windows on one side, a dirt floor, and a single front door. The windows, which had no glass, were covered with wooden panels made from Arbuckle Coffee cases. This was home to *fourteen people*: the parents, five boys, and seven girls.

Goats and cattle were Harve Dodson's primary source of income. He maintained a goat camp some two or three miles south of the homeplace. In the wintertime when bear depredations increased, Dodson assigned two or three of his teenage daughters, including Nona, to live at the camp and protect the goats from the wild animals. The girls lived in a primitive shelter constructed of willow logs with a dirt floor and roof. According to contemporary accounts, the bears apparently were more frightened of the girls than they were of the bears. Goat losses were noticeably few.[5]

Nona Dodson lived her teenage years virtually isolated from the outside world. Twice a year Harve Dodson embarked alone on a two-day horseback ride to Marathon to purchase household supplies. Later the boys were allowed to accompany their father on these trips to the "outside." William Dodson was about ten years old when he made his first trip to Marathon. His sisters were not so fortunate; most were in their late teens before they were allowed to leave the ranch and go to town, either Marathon or Alpine.[6]

The amenities at Dodson Springs were few, and opportunities for social and cultural enlightenment, including school, highly circumscribed by isolation. The school at Dugout Wells, established around 1911, was located some twelve miles from the Dodson residence. For the school-age children, travel was difficult, attendance intermittent. When Nona's brother William was about five he entered Dugout School where he remained about two years. Nona received no schooling, but with her mother's tutoring developed limited reading and writing skills.[7]

Illiteracy was the norm for many Big Bend children, both Anglo and Mexican. Ramon Franco, who lived on the west side of the Chisos near Terlingua Creek, attended Molinar School, located about a mile and a half from his home. What literary skills he gained from his two and a half years of schooling soon disappeared. He considered himself typical. "Many Mexican children living along the Rio never went to school," according to Franco. "Just as soon as they could walk, they went to work. Pretty hard life." When Franco was drafted for military service in 1942, he could neither read nor write.[8]

The Dodson family, however, faced problems other than schooling. Twelve people, obviously, could not exist permanently in this primitive setting. Minnie Dodson, Nona's mother, was probably the first to go; her parents separated in 1918. Sometime prior to 1920, her younger brother Del married and established a separate residence some eight miles south of the Dodson home near the eastern end of Puenta de la Sierra. Del Dodson emerged as another tragic figure in the Dodson family. A victim of some mental disorder, he subsequently took his own life, with his wife reportedly assisting in the suicide.[9]

Although no records of Nona's marriage are extant, she early on chose a life apart from the Dodson homestead. Sometime shortly after the family settled in the Big Bend, Nona, sixteen, eloped with Pablo Baiza, a Mexican from Santa Elena, Mexico, who was fifteen years her senior.[10] Upset over the marriage, Harve Dodson unsuccessfully prevailed upon his daughter to return home.[11] Her first child, Francisca, was born in Mexico; her second child, Adolpho, was born three years later. Although only six children appear on the 1920 United States census, a former neighbor stated that Pablo and Nona ultimately had eight children. The Baizas eventually returned to Brewster County and established residence some ten miles downriver from Castolon.

If Nona had hoped to improve her lot in life by eloping with Pablo Baiza, such was not the case. Although her struggle with poverty and deprivation continued, the family continued to grow. Edith Hopson of Alpine recalled visiting their home in the mid-1920s. She was appalled by the large number of small children and the abject poverty in which they lived. "They had a flock of little naked children that scattered like quail when we drove up," she explained. She discovered one of the children had a broken arm; the broken portion "dangled" by the flesh of the child's arm. It appeared to have been broken several days, and no attempt had been made either to set the break or take the child to a doctor. Hopson explained that her husband attempted to set the break with an improvised cast made of sticks.[12]

Hopson was particularly vague about what Pablo did for a living. She noted, however, that the family had some goats and Nona made goat cheese, which she sold to customers across the Rio Grande in Santa Elena, Mexico. W. D. Smithers, who knew the family well, was also unsure of Pablo's primary source of income. "He might have done a little smuggling of cattle and horses," Smithers explained. "He was just like old Candelario Baiza [his brother], he led a shady life. You couldn't find out what they were doing."[13]

Such was the world of Nona Baiza and hundreds of others, mainly Mexicans, who ranched and farmed—and most likely smuggled—along the Rio Grande. Living between two countries, they simply followed the green grass along both sides of the river. Regardless of the side on which one chose to reside, they lived in an essentially free society; political and judicial restraints existed in name only; law enforcement was a myth. Left with no alternative, individuals enforced their own brand of justice. Inequities were bound to arise.

For many, this was a land of perennial poverty. Scarcity became an accepted way of life as all competed for the region's scant resources. Within this social setting poverty and generosity were seldom synonymous; when one's estate was threatened by another, they yielded no quarter. Brave and desperate men frequently died defending what they thought was rightly theirs; that was the unwritten law of the Big Bend country.

The Baizas added a new equation to Nona's already troubled life—murder. Apparently the key perpetrator was Pablo's brother, Candelario, who, according to one source, was "one of the worst men on the border. He killed a lot of people just to see them die."[14] That Candelario Baiza was a violent man cannot be doubted, but what actually occurred at the Pablo Baiza residence on January 29, 1930—and the family's involvement—will remain forever a mystery. According to an eyewitness account during the drinking-gambling soiree at the Baizas, one of the two Garcia men (they were brothers-in-law) became embroiled in an argument with Candelario Baiza's teenage son, Valentin. In the ensuing struggle, Garcia cut young Baiza with a knife. Although the injury was not serious, Nona reported the incident to Candelario, who was then living across the river in Mexico. Enraged over the injury to his oldest son, Candelario arrived shortly at the Baiza residence, confronted the Garcias, and began a methodical massacre of the two young men. After Candelario shot the first man with his rifle, the other ran for safety toward the Rio Grande. Reaching the river's edge, he fell forward into the cane break where Candelario shot him in the back. At that point Pablo Baiza, Sr., became involved in the fray. He chased the wounded man on a mule, roped him, and drug him back to the house where Candelario applied the coup de grâce.[15] The *Alpine Avalanche* reported that the encounter "*is believed to have been the culmination of a family feud.*"[16]

After the bodies were found in an abandoned goat pen in Mexico, Sheriff W. O. Hale arrested Pablo Baiza and his oldest son, Adolpho, for the double murder and placed them in the Brewster County jail in Alpine. A few days later he arrested another son, Pablo, Jr., for the same crime. Two other suspects, Candelario Baiza and Harcola (Jake) Billalba, were also indicted for the same crime but not apprehended. They were reportedly hiding in Mexico.

For the impoverished Mexican family this was a devastating blow. Nona took charge in the matter and engaged the Marfa attorneys, Mead and Metcalfe, to represent the family. (Mead and Metcalfe had previously defended George Billalba. See chapter 5.) Nona signed her name; Pablo and Adolpho made their marks. In order for a bondsman to post the bonds and advance the $600 retainer, Pablo and Nona transferred to him one hundred head of cattle, plus their lease rights to two large parcels of Big Bend grazing land. They made the latter transfer on March 26, 1930.[17]

Adolpho's trial began on September 3, 1930, with Nona playing a key role in the courtroom drama. She undoubtedly tipped the scales of justice in her son's behalf. Court reporter Edith Hopson remembered

> *a young Mexican had told the officers about what had happened—that the Baisa's [sic] had roped them [the two Garcia men] and dragged them to death behind their horses—back and forth before those assembled—a regular Roman Holiday! The young Mexican . . . asked to be placed in protective custody and was kept in jail for some time before the trial, since he said he was sure he would be killed if he did not stay there. During the trial I do remember that he was very frightened, and would not sit down in the witness chair, but asked permission of the judge to remain standing. When the District Attorney would ask him a question, Nona, who was seated in the back of the Court room, would rise to her feet and stare at the witness, and he then could not remember anything. This happened not once, but several times during the trial, and the prosecuting witness' testimony was practically worthless.[18]*

During the three-day trial defense attorneys Mead and Metcalfe apparently served their client well. After deliberating only five minutes, the jury returned a not guilty verdict on the first ballot.[19] Although the court released Adolpho Baiza from the murder indictment and eventually dropped additional charges against Pablo, the family, nevertheless, was forced to bear the onerous burden of the prosecution. Their legal defense had cost them both money and property they could ill afford. They did, however, survive the crisis. This encounter with the law dominated their struggle through the early 1930s, and they would find no relief with the advent of the 1940s. This decade brought great changes to the Big Bend country that would eventually destroy their traditional way of life. The opening of the Big Bend National Park and the purchase of thousands of acres of farm and ranch land would launch a great exodus from an area that for generations had been their home. Forced to emigrate to a different and unfamiliar environment, they carried with them their social and cultural values formed over decades by the stringent life they had known along the Great River. These values were destined to clash with those of others who had no comprehension of border culture. In the end it would be the Baizas and other traditional Mexican families who would suffer most from this great displacement.

In the early 1940s the trek began. One by one the Baiza children abandoned their riverside home in search of a new life. For a time Nona and Pablo remained behind, but following Pablo's fatal heart attack, Nona also bid farewell to her home of over a half century. Reluctantly she joined her children who had found work on farms and ranches near McCamey, Big Lake, and Fort Stockton. It was in Fort Stockton on that cold December morning in 1967 that I first met Nona Baiza.

The peace and security that Nona sought in her later years were never forthcoming. The specter of conflict and violence that for ages had shadowed the Big Bend country was destined to follow in her footsteps; there would be no escape. Although the family settled in a semiurban environment, the self-imposed law of the Rio Grande frontier would inevitably set the pattern for their relationships with others. Matters of disagreement would be settled one-on-one; they could see no alternative. Thus the Baizas would become all too familiar figures in the Pecos County courthouse.

Sometime in the summer of 1958 (the exact date could not be confirmed), news reached the family in Fort Stockton that Adolpho Baiza, Nona's oldest son, had been savagely tortured and murdered in Mexico. The body was not found until some three weeks later, "tied to a tree with his hands tied behind him," his uncle, Valentin Baiza reported, "castrated, teeth pulled, cut up," and completely dismembered.[20] The family expected immediate action; there was none. Law enforcement officers in both the United States and Mexico claimed the matter was outside their jurisdiction.[21] Making funeral arrangements at that remote site in Mexico posed an additional family burden. They purchased a casket from a Fort Stockton funeral home, carried it to Mexico, where they performed the interment themselves.

When the authorities failed to act, four brothers of the dead man, Pablo, Augustin, Carlos, and Vallerino Baiza, launched their own murder investigation. Traveling on horseback, they crossed the Rio Grande at Santa Elena and headed south toward La Panthera, near where Adolpho ranched. The remoteness of this location increased the difficulty of their mission. Adolpho had purposely chosen this site because of a previous encounter with the law. Apprehended for illegally crossing cattle infected with the blackleg, he moved his herd to La Panthera to keep the government agents from destroying the contaminated animals. This decision proved to be Adolpho's undoing. "Many things can happen there," Valentin Baiza explained later, "and no one ever knows it."[22] The Baizas' investigation, however, yielded few leads. They returned to Texas to continue their search.

Again tragedy struck the Baiza family. Augustin Baiza was killed in an automobile accident while "trying to find out about Adolpho's death," Claudio Baiza explained. "He was trying to find the right people to kill. He always wore a gun." Although the Baizas could find no hard evidence to identify the killers, they came to the conclusion, rightly or wrongly, that it was a gang reportedly led by Cornelio Acosta and accompanied by his brother Eulalio.[23] This view was also shared by other members of the Fort Stockton Mexican community.[24]

By the autumn of 1958, the Acostas were, unknowingly, marked men. Time, however, was in their favor; at that point the Baizas were not absolutely sure who were the "right people to kill." A casual remark made in an Odessa cantina, however, clarified the matter, at least to the Baizas' satisfaction. One Juan Garcia told Claudio Baiza that he "overheard the Acostas talking about how they killed Adolpho—they tied his hands and legs, twisted a rope around his neck, shot him repeatedly, and broke many bones."[25] At last, to the Baizas' satisfaction, they knew the "right people to kill."

In the minds of its practitioners, borderland justice is a flexible matter. When that system fails, responsibility for final adjudication falls to the individual who has been wronged. An Acosta had killed a Baiza, and now it was a Baiza's turn to act; Pablo assumed the responsibility for evening the score. He chose the site with care and foreknowledge. On Sunday afternoons Cornelio Acosta frequently met his friends at Espino's Tavern, a typical West Texas beer joint located on the Imperial Highway just north of Fort Stockton's city limits, where Sunday beer sales were legal. There the customers drank beer and socialized usually until near closing time. There would be witnesses and possibly retaliation. Pablo discounted these; he had a personal mission to fulfill.

Late on Sunday afternoon, October 5, 1958, Pablo left the McDonald ranch near Girvin, Texas, where he was employed, and drove south on Highway 67 in his pickup truck. He arrived in Fort Stockton some forty-five minutes later and turned right on the Imperial Highway and continued north some three and a half miles, where he turned into Espino's Tavern parking lot. His plan was well conceived; he found Cornelio Acosta standing outside the tavern talking to some friends. Cornelio apparently never saw Pablo get out of his pickup and raise his 30.06 Savage rifle. "One shot was fired," the *Fort Stockton Pioneer* reported, "striking Acosta in the chest and coming out his back. He died instantly." Pablo stepped back into his pickup and drove away.[26]

Shortly after the 7:30 shooting he voluntarily surrendered to city patrolman Frank Clark. Pablo later told Sheriff Ten Eyck and Deputy Buck Luttrell that he " 'didn't care what happened to him [self],' and that he made the trip from Girvin for the expressed purpose of killing Acosta." In his confession to the sheriff, Pablo accused Cornelio Acosta of "being one of five men who recently robbed, tortured and killed his brother in Mexico. . . . He claimed three of the men were still in Mexico and two of them escaped to this country." He added that "he [Baiza] had been in Mexico to investigate the case on his own in the past two weeks and claimed officials there said they could do nothing about anybody in the United States. He added that he had been advised [apparently by the Mexican officials] to 'go shoot him [Cornelio Acosta].' "[27]

After being formally charged with murder in Justice of the Peace O. T. Jernigan's court, Pablo posted a $5,000 bond on November 5, 1958. The sheriff signed the document for Pablo, who was then free to return to his duties at the McDonald ranch. Travis Crumpton, a prominent West Texas attorney, agreed to represent Pablo in the forthcoming trial. In the interim, however, he admonished his client, as well as other members of the Baiza family, to avoid any further contact with the Acostas. They apparently heeded his advice. No further incidents had been reported when Judge Hart Johnson called *Cause No. 577,* the *State of Texas vs. Pablo Baisa* [*sic*], for trial on January 5, 1959, in the 112th Judicial District Court of Pecos County, Texas. Crumpton and prosecuting attorney Connell Ashley chose the jurors with great care. Crumpton indicated that the argument would be based on self-defense. By noon only eight jurors had been chosen.[28]

Questioning of witnesses began in the afternoon of January 5; the prosecution called only five witnesses, the defense fourteen.[29] Nona Baiza testified for the defense. She, however, was more conspicuous in the gallery than on the witness stand. According to Sheriff Ten Eyck, she assumed complete control of the situation, telling every member of the family where to sit and what to say when called to testify. And while Nona appeared consistently on the opposite side of the law, she at least exhibited great respect for Ten Eyck and the position he held. Once when he stopped to speak to a family member during the trial, Nona interrupted him, addressing the young Baiza in Spanish: "'Take off your hat! You are speaking to the *alto sherif* [high sheriff].'" Ten Eyck also expressed compassion for Nona and the tragedy she endured. "During the last ten years," he explained, "Nona has broken fast. Adolpho's death seems to be always on her mind. You know, Adolpho's death was what started it all. The feud, you know."[30]

Although Pablo Baiza was on trial for his life, Travis Crumpton evolved as the real "star" of the proceeding. Joe Primera, a Fort Stockton High School history teacher and one of two Hispanics on the jury, recalled that Crumpton would "go through a lot of motions like an actor in a theater," using his sunglasses like a theatrical prop. Attempting to solicit the jury's sympathy, he apologized, explaining that he was a diabetic, and since the bright light impaired his vision he was forced to wear the glasses indoors. But probably the most convincing evidence presented in the trial was actually disallowed by Judge Johnson. Crumpton kept waving before the jury—although the jury never saw them—what he claimed were photographs of the Adolpho Baiza murder scene. He hoped to cite Adolpho's murder as justification for Pablo's retaliation, to which Judge Johnson objected. He wrote: "I did not permit the story [of Adolpho's murder] to be placed in evidence, because nobody could testify to the facts except by hearsay, and there was no real proof offered of what they [the photographs] were. . . . The Defendant Pablo Baisa [*sic*] in our case could only testify that he had always understood that an Acosta would kill a Baisa [*sic*] on sight. The 'on site' in the case was that Baisa [*sic*] saw Acosta first in a beer hall and shot him without any warning."[31]

The judge's reference to Pablo's testimony that "an Acosta would kill a Baisa [*sic*] on sight," added a new dimension to the interfamily conflict. All the evidence leading up to the Espino's Tavern slaying indicated that the trouble began with Adolpho's slaying. Some of the older members of the Mexican community, however, thought otherwise. The consensus was the family feud had been brewing for years; it began in Mexico. Ramon Franco believed Candelario Baiza was the catalyst: "Candelario Baiza killed Satarino Acosta from the back. My family, my mother, and my uncles used to tell me he killed him over there in Santa Elena. They got mad [in an argument] over [the ownership of] a rope. Satarino was riding a horse and Candelario hid in some bushes and shot him in the back as he rode by. [And to add insult to injury], he [Candelario] then took Satarino's hat and rode away. That was the beginning of the family feud."[32]

Following two days of testimony Judge Johnson gave his charge to the jury, which deliberated more than five hours before returning a verdict. Crumpton apparently had made a convincing argument with his self-defense plea. And while Judge Johnson challenged the jury to base their verdict solely on the evidence presented in the courtroom, as members of the community they could not overlook other overriding facts to which they apparently gave careful consideration. They viewed this murder as another episode in the ongoing family conflict; at least three men had died and most likely there would be others before the matter ran its course. They also recognized that blood feuds are deep personal and ethnical issues whose arbitrary rules are promulgated outside the perimeters of legal adjudication. Juryman Joe Primera explained:

> They started to feud in Mexico. We knew that. One Acosta killed a Baiza, another Baiza killed an Acosta, and an Acosta, a Baiza, and so on. We knew he was guilty because he said he [Pablo] had killed him [Cornelio]. . . . And he knew he was guilty and was ready to go to prison. He knew he had broken the law. But most members of the jury felt that if he went to prison we would lose another citizen. He spoke no English and would not be able to follow instructions, and most likely would get into more trouble there. The substance was to find him guilty and give him a five-year probated sentence.[33]

On January 6, the jury returned a guilty verdict and recommended a five-year term of confinement. "We further find that the defendant Pablo Baisa [sic] has never before been convicted of a felony," wrote jury foreman Cecil Mitchell, "and we recommend a suspension of his sentence of good behavior."[34] Judge Johnson concurred. In assessing the punishment, the sympathetic jury obviously tempered justice with mercy—their justice and their mercy—setting free a man who had admitted committing premeditated murder. In probating Pablo's minimal sentence, the jury obviously looked beyond the evidence and the code of laws that encompass such crimes and based their verdict on regional and ethnical considerations that probably would not apply elsewhere. Two Mexican families were engaged in a feud. That was essentially an interfamily matter, they reasoned, and would be so dealt with. This was essentially borderland adjudication enacted in an urban setting; perimeters of justice are sometimes not easily defined west of the Pecos.

The end of Pablo's trial marked the beginning of a tenuous era of peace between the Baiza and Acosta families. Pablo continued working at the McDonald ranch and reported once a month to Probation Officer Eugene Upshaw at the Pecos County courthouse. But matters of such intense hatred could not lie dormant forever. And so the mantle of family pride would ultimately be passed to another.

7

The Anatomy
of a Family Feud

PART 2: ANOTHER BEER JOINT KILLING

Valentin Baiza was born in Terlingua Abajo on May 21, 1907, the son of Candelario and Alvina Baiza. The oldest of ten children and nephew of Pablo Baiza, Sr., Valentin became accustomed to the adversities of the river country at an early age. Like other members of that remote Mexican community, he learned to accept the region's meager amenities; life was primarily a struggle for survival. Some farmed, others ranched, yet despite the inherent hardships, most felt it was a far better life than they had once known in Mexico.[1]

Valentin never attended school, never learned to read or write. When he was twelve years old he found employment on the Fredrico Billalba ranch. For fifty cents a day he herded cattle on the unfenced range that extended from the Rio Grande to the Chisos Mountains. Ranch work became Valentin's lifelong occupation, one in which he took great pride. In the finest tradition of the American West, he viewed himself as one of the "Noblemen of the Plains" who pursued his profession only on horseback. He disliked urban life, preferring to remain permanently at the *rancho*. "I'm in my glory when I'm outside of town," he explained later.[2] After leaving the river country in the early 1950s, Valentin moved first to Marathon and later found permanent work on the J. C. Montgomery ranch near Fort Stockton. "The Baizas are the only remaining old-time cowboys in this region," Fort Stockton attorney Shelby Blades explained. "Every rancher feels that if he can hire a Baiza he is lucky because a Baiza knows how to take care of stock. They have that reputation."[3]

Had Valentin remained permanently at the *rancho* his encounter with the Acostas might have been averted, but that was not to be. Too much had occurred, too many men had died, and within Valentin's frame of reference, family loyalty had forced the matter to the point of no return. Valentin had carried with him to that West Texas village a value system born of the Big Bend frontier. Lacking education and positive role models, and believing the simplistic teachings of the Bible (an eye for an eye, a tooth for a tooth), he, like his cousin Pablo, viewed the family conflict in its most basic terms: carry a gun, protect yourself first, and never mediate. Strike without warning, never considering the results of your act. The Acostas also shared this primitive perspective; vindication was the only solution. And so members of both families found themselves trapped in that crucible from which only violence could provide an escape. That was one rule of borderland justice: "somebody's got to be killed."

In the interim preceding the next encounter, all evidence in the family vendetta appeared to brand the Acostas as the aggressors. When the jury gave Pablo Baiza what they considered a token sentence for killing Cornelio, the Acostas felt violated. And while their animosity was directed at all Baizas, Valentin appears to have been their primary target. "That's why they were after Valentin Baiza," Shelby Blades explained, "because they weren't satisfied when they [the jury] turned Pablo Baiza loose with a five-year suspended sentence."[4] Also, Valentin had housed all the family members who came to Fort Stockton to attend Pablo's trial. Although he never appeared at the courthouse, the Acostas felt that he, only a cousin of the accused, was providing unnecessary comfort to their enemy. Valentin soon became aware of his vulnerability. His son, Roy Baiza, explained that "when Pablo shot Cornelio [Acosta], one of the other Acostas said they would kill another Baiza. My father knew he was in danger and always carried a .38 in his boot."[5] Valentin regarded that as his margin of safety.

There would be, however, other interfamily confrontations before the bloodletting began anew. In the late autumn of 1965, Juan Acosta, the son of Cornelio Acosta, whom Pablo Baiza had killed, became embroiled in a barroom argument with Augustin Baiza, Valentin's nephew. During the verbal exchange Juan threatened to kill Augustin, *or any Baiza,* on sight. Augustin reported the incident to Valentin, warning him that his life was in danger and to "look out for trouble."[6]

Trouble was not long in coming. About one month later Valentin encountered Eulalio Acosta in Joe's Place, a bar located at 216 West First Street in Fort Stockton. During the course of the evening Eulalio followed Valentin into the rest room where he told him he was going to kill him. Valentin said "just let me know when and where." At that point two other men entered the rest room and Valentin returned to his table and began drinking his beer. Shortly thereafter, Eulalio and Valentin got into a fight and Eulalio hit Valentin in the head with a full bottle of beer. According to Roy Baiza, Valentin's son, they "really tore up the place," and the police placed Valentin in jail.[7]

In retaliation for Cornelio's death, an Acosta had struck a blow for family honor. Blood was drawn, Valentin was hurt and humiliated, and the stage was set for more violence. This was a family feud; the point of reason and calm mediation was long past. With the momentum of hatred and violence out of control, members of both families would now view the others with guarded suspicion. Someone else, they assumed, was going to die. That was the rule of the game.

Other than pursuing the feud, the Baizas and Acostas were considered responsible members of the Fort Stockton community. According to their neighbors, they went to work, attended church, paid their bills, and educated their children. Excepting family, school, and religious activities, the typical West Texas Mexican family functioned within a somewhat limited social milieu. There was, however, one exception. Most Mexican males enjoyed membership in an informal, men-only fraternity that met frequently in that well-known public emporium, the barroom, sometimes known as a beer joint. And while this center for masculine recreation did not exist solely for that purpose, these all-male gatherings frequently led to conflicts.

And so it was on Sunday afternoon, February 20, 1966, that Valentin Baiza entered Bueno's Drive-In, a beer joint located on the Imperial Highway just north of the Fort Stockton city limits. He and two friends seated themselves at the bar and ordered beer. Valentin was not seeking trouble. "He obviously did not go to Bueno's to kill a man," defense attorney Shelby Blades explained later. "He went out there to drink a few beers and visit with his friends before returning to the ranch."[8] He was, however, armed. Less than one month before Eulalio Acosta had told him he was going to kill him. That fact was well established; only the time and location were left to question. Valentin, therefore, carried his protection inside his right bootleg.

Some thirty minutes later Valentin noticed two men enter the room through the west door. One was Eulalio Acosta; the other was Manuel Ramirez. He knew both of them. They seated themselves at the bar near Valentin and began talking. Valentin quickly recognized the potential for trouble; Eulalio had threatened him, and this could be the time and place. "From then on he [Valentin] looked straight ahead," Blades recalled. "He didn't move. He didn't know what [his two friends] were saying to him. . . . He was paying strict attention . . . every nerve in his body was [directed] toward Eulalio." Above the usual barroom sounds—talking, laughter, beer bottles clinking, and music from the jukebox—Eulalio spoke to Ramirez in a manner calculated to gain Valentin's attention. "'Is that a Baiza?' Ramirez answered, 'Yeah, that's a Baiza.' Eulalio continued, 'I'm not afraid of any of the sons o' bitches. I can kill 'em on sight.'" To Valentin, this was the fulfillment of Eulalio's threat.[9]

Circumstances sometimes force quick decisions. From Valentin's standpoint, he was facing a situation of either kill or be killed. Without speaking to either of his companions, Valentin whirled around on his bar stool and faced Eulalio for the first time. Drawing his pistol from his boot, he fired two quick shots at Eulalio. Both hit their mark. Eulalio was able to get to his feet, and seeing Valentin's gun still drawn, stated, "'You've already shot me,' whereupon Valentin shot him again as he fell right at his feet." Before leaving the bar, Valentin reportedly looked down at his victim and said, "That's the way I wanted to see him."[10]

It should be noted that events surrounding the murders of both Cornelio and Eulalio Acosta—the time, the location, the subsequent arrest, and adjudication—bear marked similarities. Both occurred on Sunday afternoons at bars located immediately north of the Fort Stockton city limits, and following the shootings both Valentin Baiza and Pablo Baiza drove directly to Sheriff Ten Eyck's residence and surrendered voluntarily. Valentin stated he had killed a man and handed the sheriff the murder weapon, a Colt .38 automatic pistol, whereupon the sheriff placed him in jail.

On March 26, 1966, the Baiza family engaged Fort Stockton attorney Shelby Blades to defend Valentin. He foresaw the challenge of defending the murderer of an unarmed man. His fee was five thousand dollars. Blades first arranged bail for Valentin. Planning to enter evidence at the trial of the ongoing family feud, he and Roy Baiza, Valentin's son, left immediately for Mexico. They hoped to gather information on what had occurred there to ignite the conflict, but their effort yielded nothing. Realizing that time was his greatest ally, Blades next pleaded for a continuance beyond the original September, 1966, trial date, which Judge C. E. Patterson granted.

Faced with the charge that his client did "unlawfully and voluntarily and with malice afterthought kill Eulalio Acosta," Blades began carefully planning Valentin's defense. First, he submitted to the court a list of fourteen character witnesses, reputable members of the local business and ranching community. Other than the occurrence in Bueno's Drive-In, these men would testify that Valentin Baiza was a dependable and responsible citizen and not a threat to society. Second, Blades knew from experience that his only hope for either an acquittal or a light or probated sentence was to present his case before a sympathetic jury. Juries, he knew, were unpredictable, but a carefully chosen panel could greatly reduce the margin of chance. Before entering this procedure, Blades turned to Percy Foreman, whom he considered "one of Houston's top criminal lawyers." During "the longest long distance telephone call I ever made," Blades took copious notes on the technique of jury selection in a murder indictment, a process that he dutifully followed when Judge Patterson called the case for trial on April 17, 1967.[11]

Jury selection began at 10:00 A.M. on April 18, and continued throughout the day and into the night. At 10:30 P.M. Judge Patterson called for adjournment. Blades was leaving no room for error; he had learned his lesson well. Questioning of prospective jurors began the following morning at nine o'clock, and finally ended at 3:45 P.M. Testimony for the prosecution, led by District Attorney William H. Earney and Special Prosecutor R. D. Burleson, began at 4:20 P.M. At 5:30 P.M. Judge Patterson again recessed the court until nine o'clock the following morning.[12]

When court resumed, the prosecution attempted to discredit the self-defense plea entered by the defense. Both Earney and Burleson hammered away at the theory that Valentin was "out looking for an Acosta," and further attempted to "rule out the possibility of self-defense due to the location of the fatal wound in Acosta's body." Earney emphasized that since Eulalio Acosta was wounded on his right side nearer to his back than to his chest, "he was shot by surprise, somewhat from the rear, and was not moving toward the defendant." Earney believed that if he could convince the jury that Acosta was shot in the back, that would negate Blades's claim of self-defense. But that was not to be. Under cross-examination Earney asked Valentin "how could he claim self-defense if the man was shot in the back. As I recall the answer to that was, 'I guess the bullet went around him.' The pathetic part about that was, I guess the jury believed that. I am sure some of them laughed, but when they got down to the gist of the matter, they believed him."[13]

The state rested its case at 11:40 A.M., and the defense began testimony at 1:35 P.M. Blades built his defense around a plea of justifiable homicide for reasons of self-defense. He attempted to convince the jury "that Baiza shot Acosta after the victim [who was unarmed] made a threatening gesture toward his pocket and that the defendant had been 'in fear of death or serious bodily injury' for several months."[14] Blades then called Valentin to the witness stand in his own defense. The defendant told the jury "that he had carried a pistol for self-defense for several months prior to the shooting. He related that on the day of the slaying, Acosta had allegedly driven by him on a local street and 'spit' out of a car window in Baiza's direction." In addition to basing his defense on the law of communicated threat, Blades, in questioning the witness, focused heavily on the ongoing family feud. Earney objected, but the judge allowed the testimony to stand. By 1966, with the Baiza-Acosta conflict well established in community awareness, Blades believed correctly that the jury, comprised of local citizens, would understand and respond sympathetically to the mores of regional culture. News coverage of the trial reflected that local awareness. "The 1966 tragedy was the third slaying involving the two families— Acostas and Baizas," the item stated. "Directly involved in both cases [Pablo's and Valentin's] is a widely-circulated, but unsubstantiated story which indicates that relatives of both slain Acostas aided in a 1958 kidnapping and killing of a Baiza relative [Adolpho] in Mexico."[15]

At 8:30 on the morning of April 20, Judge Patterson met with the attorneys to hear their exceptions to the court's charges. Since there were none, jury arguments began immediately, with each side allocated one hour to summarize their pleas. Deliberations began at 11:29 A.M. The judge recessed the court at 12:30 P.M., and the jury returned to the jury room at 1:30 P.M. Those who expected a quick verdict, especially the prosecution, were soon disappointed. At three o'clock jury foreman Gene Day sent the following note to the judge: "Sir, could we have the testimony of Sra. Francisca Acosta, the wife of the deceased. Also the testimony of the defendant, Valentin Baiza." Other notes followed. The foreman next requested a ruling on "the new law concerning adult probation and the option of the defendant to select jury or court sentencing." The foreman later asked "if the defendant is found guilty of murder without malice, will the court accept a recommendation from the jury for a five year probated sentence?"[16]

By then the prosecuting attorney had a premonition of defeat. "When they started sending notes down like they were, I could see what they were trying to do," Earney recalled. "They were trying to find him guilty and give him a light sentence, or find him not guilty altogether. It looked like we were going to lose everything right there, as far as the state was concerned."[17] Late in the afternoon the jury returned its verdict: "Guilty of murder without malice, and hereby assess punishment at confinement in the State Penitentiary for a term of five years. We recommend that the sentence be probated."[18] Before adjourning the court, Judge Patterson accepted both the verdict and the recommendation.

Shades of the Pablo Baiza trial—a five-year probated sentence for murder. Blades and the Baizas were elated; Earney felt defeated by a jury that apparently placed personal and regional values above the right of law. He explained his frustration: "When a jury gets in a room like that, they start weighing equities. They don't necessarily follow the evidence. Many times [when] the jury votes their personal values, they are putting equity into the criminal court," and that violates the purpose of trial by jury. Earney also cited the murder scene, Bueno's Drive-In, as another factor in what he considered a breach of justice. "There is nothing more exasperating than a beer-joint killing," he argued. "There can be fourteen people crowded into one rest room that is six-by-six and they didn't see a damn thing that went on." Earney argued further that if the defendant shoots the unarmed victim in the back and the jury elects to "give him five years, it certainly shouldn't be probated." Then assessing his court-room loss in view of the circumstances, Earney could at least partly ratio-nalize the verdict: "I kinda felt, in the light of the feud and everything, they [the jury] felt like that [the killing] was a job well done and things were evened out."[19]

Scoring the results of family feuds depends solely on one's statistical knowledge, and in drawing his conclusion, Earney was noticeably deficient. Counting from Adolpho's death, the score was one Baiza and two Acostas dead. However, beginning with Candelario Baiza's alleged murder of Satarino Acosta, the results give the Baizas an even greater margin of vic-tory. But discounting the statistics, there are no winners in these family contests of blood; the Acostas were unmistakably the losers. The three shots fired in Bueno's Drive-In not only killed another man but launched his survivors on a life of sorrow and deprivation. Francisca Acosta was left with ten children; only two were married. As the family's sole sup-port, she found work as a cleaning woman at the El Rancho Motel in Fort

Stockton. Mrs. Acosta was forty years old; her salary was thirty dollars a week.[20]

For the Baiza family, life returned to normal. The day following the verdict, Blades accompanied Valentin to the probation office where they met his employer, rancher J. C. Montgomery. A probation officer was assigned to the case, a visitation schedule established, and Valentin returned to the ranch with Montgomery where he resumed his duties. Actually, and legally, Valentin's probated sentence was merely a threat of imprisonment. By not violating the terms of his probation, he would remain a free man; according to the court record, Valentin was an exemplary client.[21]

Valentin's period of freedom was relatively brief. He alone deemed it so. In early December 1972, Valentin was found beside a wrecked pickup truck with a bullet wound in his forehead. He died the following day. Although many believed this was a feudal matter, an investigation by the Pecos County Sheriff's Department concluded that "Mr. Baiza accidentally turned over his pick-up, escaped without injury, found his twenty-two rifle in the wreck, sat down by the pick-up, put the rifle between his legs, and fired a bullet to his forehead. All of this happened on the ranch where he worked."[22] Roy Baiza, Valentin's son, who found his father still alive, rationalized the tragic scenario. He concluded that since his father was drunk and wrecked the ranch owner's truck, "he was certain he would be fired. Having to leave the ranch was just too much for him, I guess. And he just decided to end it there." And following a moment of silent reflection, Roy concluded, "He just loved life on the ranch. In fact, he said, 'I will die on the *rancho*.' And he did."[23]

And thus Valentin Baiza removed himself voluntarily from the inter-family conflict. With one less Baiza, another Acosta still walked the streets of Fort Stockton. Nona Baiza, however, remained the family's ultimate scorekeeper. Less than six months after the jury convicted Valentin for the murder of Eulalio Acosta, she stated with fierce vindictiveness: "My boys have killed two of those Acostas. Only one is left; they'll get him."[24] The next target was Manuel Acosta, the youngest brother of Cornelio and Eulalio Acosta. He was the only member of the Acosta family still living in the United States. (The others were reportedly living in Mexico.) But Manuel soon removed himself, involuntarily, as a potential target. Federal authorities arrested him in Terlingua, Texas, and charged him with drug trafficking, for which he was sent to the minimum-security federal corrections institution at Big Spring, Texas. The minimum-security concept favored a reduced sentence; Manuel subsequently escaped and returned to Mexico.

Manuel Acosta was the last of the Acosta family members reportedly involved in the kidnapping and murder of Adolpho Baiza. Most local observers believed his departure would terminate the interfamily conflict. But that was not to be. The confrontation between Luis Granado Baiza and Florentino Acosta Garcia added a new dimension to the conflict. Florentino, Luis Baiza's adversary, was *both* a cousin to Cornelio and Eulalio Acosta as well as the son-in-law of Pablo Baiza, Sr., and brother-in-law of Adolpho Baiza, whose murder had started it all. Also, Florentino's wife and Luis Baiza, were first cousins, and Florentino was a first cousin to Valentin Baiza, as well as a cousin of Luis Baiza, the man whom he would subsequently kill. Although relationships within the Acosta and Baiza families were sometimes blurred, the hatreds engendered by the killings were well defined. Be it uncle, cousin, brother, or aunt, the name of the game was still family honor—the Baizas versus the Acostas. And thus more blood was destined to be shed.

Luis Granado Baiza, the son of Candelario Baiza and brother of Valentin, was born at Terlingua, Texas, on September 27, 1928. Like his father, brothers, and uncles, he emigrated to the Fort Stockton area in the late 1940s and soon found work as a ranch laborer—a cowboy. He pursued his equestrian occupation with a physical handicap. Later fitted with a wooden prosthesis, he became successful both as a ranch hand and as a popular rodeo performer. "He was a great horseman," his nephew Roy Baiza explained. "On one occasion he was thrown from a horse and broke his wooden leg. Not to be outdone, he got up, placed the broken limb over his shoulder, and limped off the arena, much to the amusement of the crowd."[25] Luis's handicap, however, may have been a factor in his subsequent demise.

In early December, 1976, Luis Baiza and Florentino Acosta Garcia became embroiled in a heated argument at Joe's Place, that popular Mexican bar where Valentin Baiza and Eulalio Acosta had had their fight. During this altercation Florentino drew a knife and attempted to stab Luis, who grabbed the blade and broke it. In the ensuing struggle, Florentino stabbed Luis in the stomach with the stub blade, which opened a severe gash but did not penetrate the stomach cavity. Bar owner Joe Espino called the police, who apprehended both men and placed them in the Pecos County Jail.

The two men would indeed finish what they started, and again in Joe's Place. The final encounter occurred there on Sunday, December 26, 1976. Several of the Baizas, including Roy, were there drinking beer. So were two of Florentino's sons, but the two groups encountered no difficulties. However, following some two hours of family visitation, Roy announced he was leaving and suggested the others accompany him. Only Luis remained; he wanted another beer. At approximately 8:50 in the evening, bar owner Joe Espino saw Florentino enter the bar through the front door. Apparently there was no verbal exchange between him and Luis. "I then heard a gun shot," Espino stated. "I looked at Florentino and he had a pistol in his right hand. At that time I saw Luis Baiza, who was sitting at a table, fall to the floor. . . . Florentino Garcia then placed this pistol [an IMA .38 revolver] on the bar and asked me to call the police."[26] Florentino was sixty-four; Luis was forty-eight. Both were married and had families.

Florentino was indicted on January 10, 1977. On July 19, 1978, in Cause No. 1089, a jury in the 112th District Court found him guilty of voluntary manslaughter. He was sentenced to eight years in the state penitentiary at Huntsville, where he died on July 14, 1979.

In evaluating this tragedy within the context of the Baiza-Acosta feud, local observers differ. According to Fort Stockton attorney (and later district judge) Alex Gonzalez, this final encounter between the two men stemmed partly from the embarrassment Florentino suffered at the hands of his friends, "who kidded him about being bested by a cripple. In the macho world of the Mexican male, this was a matter hard to live with." Gonzalez believed that the hatred Florentino harbored from this embarrassment probably overpowered any desire to strike a blow for the Acosta family.[27] Ramon Franco, a respected member of the Fort Stockton Mexican community, disagreed. He viewed this latest beer-joint killing as a continuation of the family feud, extended to the next plateau of family relations.[28] Roy Baiza agreed but was more forthright in his appraisal: "Two Acostas were dead, and now two Baizas. I think this evened the score."[29]

Family feuds in their various forms are endemic to the human race and transcend period, region, race, and motivation. It is only incidental that the Baizas and Acostas were Hispanic and grew up in the Big Bend country of Texas, and that the Hatfields and McCoys, America's best-known feudists, were Anglo and lived in the Tug River Valley of West Virginia and Kentucky. There are, however, social, cultural, economic, and regional factors that relate these warring factions other than the alleged murder of a family member and the theft of a hog.

Isolation, both political and geographic, be it in Texas, Kentucky, or West Virginia, appears as one condition conducive to feuding. In the last half of the nineteenth century the Tug River Valley in which the Hatfields and McCoys lived constituted a pocket of primitive culture "shut off from the progress of the world and touched but lightly by civilization."[30] According to most scholars of the feud, cultural restrictions imposed by physical isolation became a breeding ground for violence. "The feud and the culture from which it emerged were anachronisms of modern society," writes Altina Waller. The participants, therefore, "represented a primitive way of life which had somehow been preserved in much the same way that prehistoric fossils are preserved."[31]

The universal lack of organized law enforcement in the areas of isolation where the feuds erupted, comprises another piece of this complex mosaic. In this regard Texas, Kentucky, and West Virginia share a marked commonality. Virgil Carrington Jones, in his study of the Hatfield-McCoy feud, explains that "there was virtually no police authority. . . . The mountaineer of that day, keen-eyed, hard-bitten, courageous, felt that he was a law unto himself. His life was primitive and so was his passions."[32] Likewise, the Baizas felt justified in enacting their own brand of justice since law enforcement officers in both Mexico and the United States claimed the matter of Adolpho's death was outside their jurisdiction.

Aside from the climate and physical terrain, the Tug Valley in the late nineteenth century differed little politically and culturally from the Big Bend country in the early twentieth century. Both regions were virtually devoid of the amenities of enlightened society. Few inhabitants attended either school or church. Both Anderson (Devil Anse) Hatfield and Randolph McCoy were illiterate, as were the elder Baizas and Acostas. Valentin Baiza viewed this cultural deficiency as a contributing factor in the feud. "Ignorant people are the ones who go armed defending themselves," he explained. "Life is difficult for one that does not have education. That's why the feud has gone on because a lot of ignorant and uneducated people" are at war.[33]

Another commonality of most feuds is exceedingly large families. Anderson (Devil Anse) Hatfield was one of ten children; he and Levicy Chafin had thirteen; Randolph McCoy, his neighbor and enemy, sired sixteen offsprings; while Pablo and Nona Baiza produced eight. Family size alone is not a prescription for aggression, but once the family unit is threatened, especially when the adult members lack positive moral and ethical values, or confidence in legal redress, the results can be regrettable. In both settings, men took the law in their own hands, initiating their own method of adjudication. Justice in blood feuds is simply a matter of evening the score.

Commenting on this self-perpetuating cycle of violence, Ricardo Romo, professor of Mexican-American history at the University of Texas at Austin, placed the interfamily conflict in the context of the Big Bend environment. "This is obviously a situation of a frontier society," he explained. "The frontier is not closed in the Big Bend. These folks lived in that era, and in that society you carry a gun, you use superior weapons when you can, you protect yourself first, and you worry only about solving that problem then and now. They never thought about the consequences. This is the shortcoming of a person who has a poor education. They think in short terms instead of long terms."[34]

Valentin Baiza obviously thought in short terms, but once the death of Adolpho had been avenged, at least to his satisfaction, he apparently felt a deep sense of remorse. He seemed to realize that the death of Eulalio Acosta solved nothing; his single act of violence simply transmitted to another family the burden of loss endured by the Baizas. According to Adan Acosta, Eulalio's son, Valentin made repeated offers to help support Adan's widowed mother and her ten children. The offers were rejected. There may have been another factor in Valentin's sudden generosity—the relationship between the Baizas and the Acostas. Adan Acosta recalled that his grandmother told him that once when Valentin's mother was ill, she, the mother of Eulalio Acosta, breast-fed the infant Valentin.[35] Having nursed at the breast of the enemy may have prompted Valentin to ponder the consequence of his vengeance.

Exploring further the root causes of feuding, Professor Romo removed ethnicity as a factor, while focusing on the environment. Drawing an analogy between my own family and the two families about whom I am writing, he reasoned that "if the Ragsdales had lived in the Big Bend country with similar kinds of education, with several generations of being poorly educated and learning the simple notions of what the Bible teaches you, I don't care if it's Ragsdale, or Romo, or Baiza, or the Acostas, it's that region, it's that environment that's affecting you."[36] In further support of Romo's rationale, it should be noted that it was an Anglo, Nona Dodson Baiza, not a Mexican, who had blatantly fanned the flames of violence:

"My boys have killed two of those Acostas. Only one is left; they'll get him."[37]

Fortunately for Manuel Acosta, his incarceration and ultimate escape to Mexico removed him as a Baiza target. His departure, however, was only one factor in his survival. Folk singer Bob Dylan offered a musical interpretation: "The Times They are A-Changin'." Change, both social and economic, was creating a new environment in which family feuding no longer flourished. While expanded law enforcement ended most of the late-nineteenth-century Texas feuds, some scholars credit industrialization in Appalachia as a major force in ending the Hatfield and McCoy troubles. Other factors hastened the demise of the Baiza-Acosta feud. With the time gap separating the elder Baizas and Acostas from the children of the next generation came a new enlightenment and a new social awareness that rejected violence as a solution for interpersonal problems. They, unlike their parents, could see alternatives.

One key factor in this transformation was that education and urbanization had diluted the strength and importance of the family unit. "Much of the family pride died with the current generation," explained Fort Stockton attorney Alex Gonzalez. "The lack of these family values that were treasured by that generation—Valentin and Pablo Baiza—has surfaced in the young men, especially as more peace-loving people. They no longer want to fight the battles of their forbears."[38] Fort Stockton businessman Pete Terrazas viewed this change from the perspective of the older generation. He regarded the Baizas and Acostas as "very responsible, hardworking people who paid their bills and educated their children. These people had a lot of pride, were very courageous, and not afraid—as typified by this ordeal. Their bloodline was valued." Terrazas, however, emphasized the expanded educational opportunities that the community afforded (and the reason both families emigrated to Fort Stockton) as the major turning point in the feud. He continued: "The younger generation didn't feel it was in their interest to risk their lives for something they really didn't understand. And education and enlightenment has [at last] come into it."[39] With the broader perspective of life that education and urban living afforded, the children of the feudists no longer felt the constraints of earlier family customs.

And so ended what came to be known throughout the Big Bend country as the Baiza-Acosta Feud. Following almost two decades of conflict and the death of four men (five, if Satarino Acosta is included), members of both families could again walk in peace without fear of assassination. A new generation of Baizas and Acostas meet socially at picnics, fiestas, and school and church functions with no thought of reprisal. Baizas bear no animosity toward the Acostas; Acostas bear no animosity toward the Baizas.[40] Members of both families could at last find peace; the hatred and malice generated by the preceding generations were finally laid to rest.

Elizabeth Taylor, Hallie Stillwell, and Other Big Bend Treasures

No matter where a person lives, be it New York, Los Angeles, the Nebraska corn belt, or the piney woods of North Carolina, environment is the primary conditioner of human life. Each setting attracts a certain type of individual who, in turn, adjusts to that environment and builds a lifestyle within the parameters imposed by the region. Nowhere is this truer than in the Big Bend country of Texas. A distinct type of people elected to live and work there, and the product of their effort bears the region's unmistakable imprint. Be they ranchers, treasure hunters, photographers, or filmmakers, all for different reasons had to compromise with the region in order to fulfill their individual objectives.

Throughout her life as a Big Bend ranch woman, Hallie Stillwell had to come to terms with capricious weather cycles in order to survive. In dry times she sold cattle, in wet times she bought cattle, and when that failed, she sought temporary employment elsewhere. She, therefore, compromised and survived when others left. Lacking darkroom facilities and having to fabricate his own equipment, photographer W. D. Smithers compromised with the elements and produced an incomparable pictorial record of the region. George Stevens moved a 250-member film crew from

Hollywood to Marfa, which lacked studio facilities, support personnel, adequate housing, and food services. And in addition, he brought with him a cast that had to be taught "how to talk Texas." He compromised with the region and produced an epic film. The ones who probably compromised the greatest were the treasure hunters. They were seeking treasure that in all probability did not exist in the first place. Yet they discovered a treasure more enduring than any gold or silver they had hoped to recover.

Each in his or her own way came to terms with the environment and made a significant contribution to the history and culture of the Big Bend country. They all compromised; their stories follow.

8

"Hallie Stillwell Is What This Country Is All About"

As with many of my Big Bend friends, I met Hallie Stillwell (1897–1997) while researching *Quicksilver*. She also contributed to *Wings Over the Mexican Border*. When I began gathering material for this book, Hallie, of course, was high on my list of people to interview. In September, 1989, while en route to Alpine, I stopped in Fort Stockton to continue researching the Baiza-Acosta feud. I had planned to interview Hallie the following Monday in Alpine. However, when I completed my Fort Stockton assignment earlier than planned, I called Hallie to see if I could move that interview up to Sunday afternoon. Her response was pleasant but firm: "No Ken, it just won't work out. I go to church Sunday morning and play poker all Sunday afternoon. It'll just have to be Monday." And Monday it was.

During the ensuing thirty years Hallie and I met on many occasions for both business and pleasure. And each time when it was business, the meetings were always a pleasure. I once arrived in Alpine by train and, because I was unable to rent an automobile, Hallie provided a pickup-and-delivery service, carrying me from one interview to the next. Then she accompanied me that evening to a delightful dinner with humorist H. Allen Smith and his wife in their charming mountainside home. It is friendships such as this that endear me to the people of the Big Bend country.

People throughout Texas either knew, claim they knew, or wanted to know Hallie Stillwell. She was a most remarkable lady, her honorary titles manifold. She had been recognized by the Texas senate, honored by Texas governors, and designated a Texas *Grande Dame* by *Texas Monthly*. In 1992, she was inducted into the National Cowgirl Hall of Fame, and two years later Texas governor Ann Richards welcomed her as a member of the Texas Women's Hall of Fame. Local honors include "Sweetheart of the Terlingua Chili Cookoff" and Alpine's "Bicentennial Queen." In addition, Hallie lived within sight of several geographic landmarks that bear the family name—Stillwell Canyon, Stillwell Crossing, and Stillwell Mountain. Not surprising, she had emerged as one of Texas's most notable personalities.

Such honors come only to the deserving. She had driven covered wagons, punched cattle, taught school within pistol-shot of a Mexican revolution, owned and managed a ranch for some seven decades, survived drought and the Depression, faced charging bulls and foreclosure-prone bankers, served as justice of the peace, jailed lawbreakers, and married eloping couples. She was a popular newspaper columnist, wrote books, delivered fascinating lectures, and operated a bustling trailer park and a popular trading post. All the while she remained a lady of great eloquence, class, and charm. To her statewide cadre of friends and admirers Hallie Stillwell was a living legend; she preferred the more straightforward designation, ranch woman.

Hallie Stillwell would have been a unique phenomenon in any setting, but in the Big Bend country she emerged as someone very special, a pragmatist who assessed the options and compromised with natural forces over which she exercised no control. Thus, she struggled and prospered in a hostile environment where the defeated far outnumber the survivors. And Hallie Stillwell was, above all else, a survivor.

She made her unceremonious entry into the Big Bend country seated on the spring seat of a covered wagon driving a span of ornery, trail-weary horses. She was thirteen years old; the year was 1910. It had been a circuitous journey. Born near Waco, Texas, on October 20, 1897, the third child of Guy and Nancy Montgomery Crawford, she and her family began moving as soon as the mother and baby could endure wagon travel. Their destination—the West.

Following several intermediate stops in Texas, the family reached New Mexico's Estancia Valley area, located some forty miles southeast of Albuquerque, in 1907.[1] Guy Crawford soon discovered the educational opportunities for his children failed to meet his expectations. Again the

*Hallie Stillwell seated in front of "Hallie's Hall of Fame," a museum
portraying the life and times of the Big Bend's most famous citizen.
School teacher, author, journalist, lecturer, jurist, and "arguably the most
famous rancher in West Texas," Hallie Stillwell survived and prospered
in the Big Bend when others failed. Courtesy Mike Leggett*

wagons were loaded and the family embarked on the twenty-four-day
trek back to Texas. Their destination, Alpine. Guy Crawford had a dual
purpose in choosing that site: relatives and good schools. "Alpine had the
reputation of being a good school town," Hallie explained. "And so many
moves were made for schooling."

This would be their final move; the Crawfords had at last found a
permanent home. The opportunities in the vast Big Bend country would
fulfill their greatest expectations. There was cheap land, generous hardworking people, and good schools. New businesses were opening, and
new settlers were arriving daily. Guy Crawford believed the town had a
future and the future was now. But there was something more. As the
Crawford wagons descended into the Alpine basin from the northwest,
even the thirteen-year-old Hallie was awe-struck by the area's natural
beauty. She recalled her feelings as she counted the purplish blue mountains that ringed the valley, and viewed the rolling expanse that seemed to
stretch endlessly beyond the farthest horizon. This would be her home;
she would never be happy anywhere else.

For the next decade, schools dominated Hallie's life, and she fulfilled her father's highest expectations. She loved school, the people she met, and the things she learned. That Monday morning in September, 1910, when she entered the sixth grade in Alpine, remained clear in her recollections. The day began with assembly; the first person to speak was the principal, J. Frank Dobie. Although Dobie would become the state's preeminent man of letters, the wellspring of Hallie's literary aspirations came not from him but from her history teacher, Jessie Gourley. She evolved as the greatest single force in shaping Hallie Crawford's professional life. "She was a big influence on me," Hallie explained. "She stimulated my interest in history."

By the time Hallie graduated from Alpine High School, her career plans were complete. She wanted to write, and she wanted to be a teacher. But since teaching offered greater opportunities for employment, that became her immediate goal. Fortunately, teacher preparation in 1916 was a comparatively simple process. By the time she received her high school diploma, she had earned a first-grade teacher's certificate. The Presidio schools offered her a contract for seventy-five dollars a month, which she accepted. That assignment, however, carried two noticeable drawbacks. First, her schoolroom was located within a pistol shot of Pancho Villa's revolutionaries; and second, she faced a room filled with Mexican students who spoke no English, and one Anglo student who spoke no Spanish.

Following one year at Presidio, Hallie acceded to her father's entreaties and accepted a similar, and considerably safer, assignment at Marathon. There were other marginal benefits: no gunfire in the background, a five-dollar-a-month salary increase—and she would meet Roy Stillwell, her future husband. Theirs was a whirlwind courtship, a romantic scenario that has been repeated thousands of times in romantic fiction. It followed a time-tested formula: the cowboy meets the new schoolmarm at a dance, sweeps her off her feet (literally); they get married and live happily ever after. Although her knight in shining armor was twenty years her senior, Hallie's feelings for him were sincere and deeply felt. And while she may not have heard violins or seen rockets exploding in the air, she held a deep affection for Roy Stillwell. Some seven decades later, attempting to recapture her thoughts on that occasion, she admitted that "it's just hard to say [what] my true feelings [were]. . . . Roy was a good man, he was honest, and he had high principles. He was fun-loving and I felt like it would be security, that I would have a good husband. And after all, that's what a lot of young girls were thinking about in those days. . . . But I thought of security, of home life, and [the desire] to settle down."

Hallie Crawford and Roy Stillwell were married on August 27, 1918, in Alpine, Texas. Following a brief honeymoon in San Antonio, they returned to Marathon, loaded their few possessions in Roy's Hudson Super-Six, and embarked for the Maravillas Creek ranch and a new life together. When the newlyweds arrived at the ranch late that afternoon, Hallie was startled by her discovery: the Stillwell "ranch house" was a one-room twelve-by-fifteen-feet cabin that they were to share with two cowboys.[2] Hallie had accepted Roy for better or worse, and what she saw was much worse than expected, but from Hallie's point of view, it had to get better.

While the transition from schoolteacher to ranch wife may appear minimal, Hallie learned early on that neither tradition nor personality qualified her for housework. The "womanly woman" model prescribed by Victorian society somehow had excluded individuals of her independent bearing. She was educated, opinionated, bored by light conversation, and eager to be part of Roy's life on the ranch.[3] Although Roy fulfilled the "manly man" role in the Anglo male-directed frontier society, he, nevertheless, had accepted Hallie as his all-encompassing partner in life. If she chose to break tradition and ride the range with him, that was just fine. And break tradition she did, with Roy as her mentor. A teacher never had a more ardent pupil. Hallie learned about cow tracks, yearling tracks, cattle brands, panther tracks, and signs of coyotes. She learned to watch buzzards circle as a sign of trouble and to check baby calves for screw worms. "I learned everything I know about ranching from Roy," she acknowledged. "He knew his business and I worked right by his side. . . . And I learned a lot from the cowboys. You know, *I got involved.*"

While Hallie's role in ranch affairs was a matter of choice, she was, in her own way, forging a break with both the past and the present. Traditionally, women of the West, especially ladies of class and refinement, seldom involved themselves with business, and more especially with ranching and the direct management of livestock. She did both with Roy's approval. And as the range work expanded, so did her responsibilities. She kept books, did the banking, managed the money, paid the taxes, and solicited cattle buyers to market the herd. She seemed to recognize, as few other ranch wives did, that she had a commitment to her husband that extended beyond companionship, motherhood, and maid service.

Although Hallie never attempted to be different without purpose, she soon realized that she was, nevertheless, socially out of step with other Big Bend ranch wives. She eventually discovered, however, that her involvement in ranch work as a young bride was preparing her for a career she neither wanted nor otherwise would have chosen. But who can predict the future? And in the short term the future looked bright.

The 1920s were halcyon years for the Stillwells. The family grew from two to five,[4] cattle prices increased steadily throughout the decade,[5] while their family income stabilized at approximately $12,000 annually. Hallie considered that "an awful lot of money at that time . . . [and] we had a good time. We didn't think about saving money." And therein lay the problem; while enjoying the good life, they failed to heed the signs of impending change. Even in the late 1920s, Big Bend ranchers still felt isolated from the mainstream of American economic life. Understandably, the initial news of the 1929 stock market collapse caused slight concern in the region.

Ultimately, the economic dip did reach the Big Bend country with stunning impact.[6] In addition to the depressed cattle market, there came into play another negative factor that further ravaged the Big Bend cattle industry—drought! In five of the six years between 1930 and 1935, the region received below average rainfall.[7] With cattle prices in decline and the drought worsening, the Stillwells' future looked bleak. They had entered an era that came to be known as the Great Depression.

Desperation bred desperation. In addition to the drought and diminishing ranch income, their longtime source of funding came to an unexpected halt; the Marathon State Bank ceased operations. The Stillwells suddenly found themselves in an economic vacuum. "We owed a $999 grocery bill, plus taxes and a land payment," Hallie remembered. With no savings, deeply in debt, and without a money source, the Stillwells turned to the lender of last resort, the federal government. They applied to the Rural Agricultural Credit Corporation (RACC) for an emergency loan. Much to their surprise and satisfaction, the drought relief service of the United States Department of Agriculture proved responsive to their needs. On January 31, 1933, they received an $8,000 emergency loan at 6 ½ percent interest with repayment due in one year. One year later, unable to repay the note, they executed a second note in the amount of $10,000, secured by 875 head of stock. Still unable to pay the previous notes, they executed a third instrument in the amount of $8,038.34, due to mature on October 31, 1935.[8]

The federal loan proved to be the Stillwells' economic salvation during the mid-1930s. "It was difficult for a family of five to live on fifty dollars a month [the RACC's monthly stipend] and still try to run a ranch," Hallie explained. "But we did it." Maintaining a posture of fierce independence, she emphasized, "It wasn't relief! It was a help. We paid back all of that loan. Every dime with interest. *It wasn't welfare.*" The program continued as long as the drought lasted.

Big Bend ranchers remember well the year 1936. In addition to being the state's one hundredth anniversary, that was the year that the rains came. Cattle prices also began a slow ascent that continued for another decade.[9] Good rains meant good grass and the end of expensive supplementary feeding. "I can remember this so very well," Hallie pointed out. "We didn't have to feed our cattle from thirty-seven to forty-seven. We had ten years that we didn't have to feed."

The Big Bend economy may be calibrated by wet and dry cycles. Experienced ranchers learned early on to compromise with the elements; in dry years they sell cattle to reduce inventories and cut expenses; in wet years they buy cattle to boost their income and resolve the indebtedness incurred during the dry years. This is an ongoing way of life to which Big Bend survivors have learned to adjust.

As the 1930s gave way to the 1940s, the Big Bend ranching community could at last look to the future optimistically. The rains continued; the region recorded 17.95 inches in 1940; the 33.09 inches that fell the following year remain a Big Bend record.[10] With the ranges restocked, the future looked bright. And then came that fateful Sunday in December, 1941. The United States' entry into World War II touched the lives of all Americans, including those living in the remotest corners of civilization. In the Big Bend the escalating conflict created an ever-growing demand for higher-priced beef, but with fewer people on the ranches to produce it.

Hallie responded to the emergency with a deep sense of patriotism. She participated in war bond drives, collected scrap metal for defense, and helped entertain troops stationed in the lower Big Bend, while serving as president of the Marathon school board. And still there was ranch work. "I did a man's work in those days," Hallie explained. "I would ride miles and miles on horseback, and I did my share [of work] in the branding pen."[11]

And then on August 6, 1945, the world entered the atomic age and a period of tenuous peace. The euphoria that followed the end of World War II eventually spent itself as the country reentered the business-as-usual mode. In the Big Bend country business as usual meant raising beef, but beef needs grass and grass needs rain. According to some local wit, the reason Big Bend ranchers have tanned faces is because they spend so much time looking at the sky for signs of rain. Based on this assumption, by the time the 1940s played out, all Big Bend ranchers had sunburned faces. During the summer of 1947 they saw nothing but cloudless skies; worsening conditions the following year confirmed the beginning of another dry cycle. Hallie remembered how in late April she and Roy "had gone down to see how the cattle were doing. We found the water was starting to dry up in the surface tanks. . . . We saw we were going to have to either move 'em, feed 'em, or sell 'em." They had already begun dispersing the herd and were down to about 600 head. Hoping that the fall rains would carry them through to the late winter sales, they decided to hold on a little longer. This meant buying hay to supplement the little remaining range grass. Roy left the ranch around noon for Marathon to purchase a load of hay. That was an important date—April 28, 1948—which Hallie circled on the calendar. From that day forward feed costs would begin eroding away any remaining profits.

There occur in everyone's life certain identifiable dates and events that alter the course of things to come. In Hallie's case, it was already circled on her calendar. Sometime late in the afternoon, just before sunset, she received the news. A passerby came to tell her that Roy had been injured in a truck accident and was taken to an Alpine hospital. The family left immediately for Alpine. The doctor explained that, in addition to internal injuries, Roy had sustained a severe concussion. The prognosis was not encouraging. Hallie spent the night at Roy's bedside. He never regained consciousness and died about noon the following day.

Shock gave way to sorrow, sorrow to remorse, and eventually Hallie had to face the numbing reality of the future alone. There were decisions to be made, and her first ran counter to the well-meaning advice of friends. No, she would not sell the ranch; that was her home, her life, and her children's birthright. Somehow she would hang on until conditions improved. It had always rained, and she knew it would rain again. But Hallie had assets in addition to her determined optimism. "I knew exactly where we stood," she explained. "In fact, I probably knew better than he [Roy] did about finances." During the war years and even before, with Roy preoccupied with labor shortages and range conditions, Hallie managed the day-to-day ranching operations. "I had experience [working with Roy]," she continued. "I knew how to market cattle, I knew prices, I knew weights, and that was a big help."

Hallie possessed another negotiable asset, one she inherited from Roy: "Always tell the truth, pay your debts, and keep your credit good. You can't operate without good credit." And now in the midst of a prolonged drought with diminishing resources, good credit would be essential to her survival.

These were her big pluses, but there also were larger-than-life minuses. First, although Roy left Hallie an estate valued at $34,999.78, those were not negotiable dollars. This included 7,352.3 acres of dry, unwatered ranchland valued at $2 per acre, on which ran cattle valued $14,162.50, which, in their present condition were not marketable. In addition, Hallie inherited a $7,796.99 indebtedness, and only $2,132.68 in cash reserves.[12] Second, she was a woman assuming a man's role in a region and in an industry traditionally dominated by the "manly man." Since the beginning of the range cattle industry, big men wearing big hats and making big talk symbolized the industry and the region that produced the beef. Growing up in the West, Hallie had become acutely aware of the gender delineation that pervaded the cattle culture. If the prospect of competing on the range, in the commission houses, and in the auction barns bothered her, she didn't show it. She had other priorities; her energies would be spent trying to survive while searching the skies for signs of rain.

If the elements ever conspired to test one's character to the limit, they undoubtedly did so for Hallie Stillwell. Her search for salvation in the skies yielded nothing that year, nor for several years to come. The seasons had again come full circle; the Big Bend country, and most of America's heartland, was again locked in the throes of prolonged drought. According to the U.S. Department of Commerce, 1948 was "the driest year since 1924. . . . That year [1948] the Big Bend region recorded only 12.36 inches of precipitation, 5.38 inches below normal. In 1950, conditions improved somewhat, but declined in 1951 with a 4.24-inch deficit. Searing heat combined with increased aridity further devastated the parched ranch lands. The following year the Boquillas Ranger Station, located some thirty-five miles south of the Stillwell ranch, reported the lowest precipitation in the state, only 4.09 inches. That station also recorded the state's highest temperature, 115°.[13]

During the next five years the region continued to register rainfall deficits. The 8.38 inches of rainfall in 1954 was the lowest since 1934, when only 7.72 inches was recorded. The year 1955 produced a 6.51-inch deficit; only three months—June, July, and October—exceeded one inch of precipitation. The following year brought no improvement. The U.S. Department of Commerce reported in July that "many cattlemen ... struggled desperately to survive one of the worst droughts of record. They faced the hard decision of holding on in hopes of rain or liquidating their herds."[14]

Facing an unpredictable future and hoping for an ever-elusive miracle, Hallie refused to give in. Liquidation was not an option; no experienced rancher wants to sell poor, underweight cattle. So she began to look for greener pastures, literally, and Colorado beckoned. George Benson, an old friend and Big Bend rancher, had already taken refuge from the drought in Colorado. He suggested that Hallie do likewise. She liked the idea and with his help rented a summer pasture near his in the Colorado Springs area. Around mid-May, 1948, she gave the order and the roundup began. That day remained graphic in her memory. For the first time in her life she was leaving the Big Bend country in search of survival.

When the trucks arrived and began loading the cattle, Hallie's thoughts were drawn inevitably to the recent tragedy of Roy's death. Now she was experiencing another loss—a symbolic loss. The cattle she and Roy had raised together were being taken from their home range. This herd was their own creation. Now it was being removed to a place she had never been, where she would be working with people she had never met. But she was left no choice. The tail gates slammed shut, and the trucks began rolling north toward Alpine.

As Hallie watched the cattle being herded into the Santa Fe cattle cars, she had, for the first time in weeks, a feeling of optimism; things were going to get better. Wrong. New problems lay ahead. At Sweetwater, Texas, where the railroad unloaded the cattle for feed and water, a cold, driving rain was falling. In reloading, the workmen made a fatal error. By not providing fresh bedding hay in the cattle cars to absorb the body moisture, the cattle became chilled in transit and many developed pneumonia. When the herd was unloaded in Colorado Springs three days behind schedule, some thirty-five animals were dead.

The railroad denied responsibility for the loss, and Hallie sued the Santa Fe. Not wanting to go to trial, the company dispatched a staff of lawyers to discuss a settlement. They arrived at the ranch bearing stacks of documentation to defend their position. For the first time in her life Hallie felt totally intimidated; she had neither legal representation nor any personal records of the disaster. "They talked and talked and I felt smaller and smaller," she explained. "I didn't think I was going to get a dime. They finally asked me what I wanted and I said I just want what the cattle was worth." At that point the attorneys then left the room apparently to discuss a settlement. When they returned one said they would settle for the actual market value of the dead animals. Hallie accepted the offer; the company check accorded her at least a temporary feeling of solvency.

The Colorado venture proved to be a wise decision. The cattle prospered on the lush Colorado grass, and in late September, Hallie sold some 350 fat beefs to the Campbell Soup Company at an unexpected profit. There remained, however, almost a trainload of drought-stricken cattle with baby calves that had to be moved before the harsh Colorado winter set in. Again George Benson offered a solution. He had purchased a ranch in Oregon with year-round grazing and had located a similar property, which he advised Hallie to consider. She flew up to Oregon, liked what she saw, and gave the owner $1,000 in earnest money until she could arrange a loan for the down payment. This necessitated a long-distance telephone call to George Baines, president of the First National Bank in Alpine. There was much difficulty in completing the call, and, when Baines finally answered, the service was so poor that he could barely hear Hallie. She remembers the conversation went something like this:

Hallie shouting: "Mr. Baines, I need a $10,000."
Baines shouting: "Hallie, what do you need $10,000 for?"
Hallie shouting: "I'm going to buy a ranch."
Baines shouting: "Hallie, do you know what you are doing?"
Hallie shouting: "Yes. I think I do."
Baines shouting: "Well, write a check. I'll send you a note to sign."

On receiving Baines's approval of the loan, Hallie was reminded of Roy Stillwell's earlier admonition: "'Always tell the truth, pay your debts, and keep your credit good. You can't operate without good credit.'" Even in the face of mounting indebtedness, Baines still respected Hallie's ability to pay her debts.

Hallie remained in Oregon to close the deal, which she hoped would bridge the gap to solvency. For the $10,000 down payment, plus $10,000 annual increments, she received title to four sections of ranch land, two in a watered valley and two in the high country. "It was a perfect arrangement," she explained. "We could winter the cattle in the valley around the hay stacks, and then drive them to the high country where the grass stayed green all summer. You couldn't ask for a better arrangement."

The arrangement, however, had its flaws; maintaining two operations, one in Texas and one in Oregon, duplicated some costs and separated the family. While Son supervised the Oregon property, Guy ran the Big Bend operation, and Hallie commuted between the two properties. She, how-ever, maintained her base on the Maravillas with a singular objective in mind—curbing the mounting indebtedness while attempting to develop an alternate income. For the first time in her life she would be forced to look beyond the land and the cattle to survive. Hallie would soon learn the true meaning of the word *diversify.*

During a subsequent visit to the recently opened Big Bend National Park, an employee mentioned to her that, since they were forbidden to cut timber in the Park, he was facing a real problem with finding a fuel source for heating and cooking. Suddenly Hallie saw opportunity; she could sell him all the wood he could use. The two parties entered into a verbal contract; eighteen dollars a cord cut in eighteen-inch lengths. "Eigh-teen dollars a cord sounded like a lot of money, pure profit," she recalled. But there was only one problem; being desert bred, Hallie didn't know what constituted a cord of wood.[15]

She subsequently learned the woodland terminology, as well as de-veloping a strategy for harvesting the timber. At last fate seemed to be turning in her favor. The following day a group of Mexicans came to the ranch looking for work. Hallie struck another deal; for $1.50 per cord, they would cut the timber and deliver it to the ranch. There still remained the matter of cutting it into eighteen-inch lengths. In seeking a solution to this problem, she gave new meaning to the old adage, "necessity is the mother of invention." "We borrowed a saw from a man in Marathon," she explained, "and put it on the back wheel of the truck. We jacked up the truck and let the wheel turn the saw and cut the wood up in eighteen-inch lengths, stacked it, and they came and hauled it back to the park."

For some three years the sale of wood to the park provided a minimal but much needed flow of cash into the Stillwell coffers. She carefully di-vided this between living expenses and debt service to the First National Bank in Alpine. With the mounting interest, little was left for the princi-pal, but George Baines remained patient. This financial windfall, how-ever, soon ran its course; when the National Park Concessions installed oil-burning stoves, they no longer needed Hallie's wood. Again, she had to seek an alternative income, and she, like some of her drought-stricken neighbors, was forced to turn to one of the region's last remaining natu-ral resources, the *candelilla* plant. Through a fairly simple boiling pro-cess, the outer waxen layer of this plant is recovered and marketed for a variety of industrial uses.[16] During the early 1950s the market remained strong as wax buyers canvased the region for the raw product.

Hallie and Guy engaged about forty Mexican nationals to gather and process the plants at five different "wax camps." The Mexican workers, who either built their own primitive living quarters—*jacals*—or lived in caves, harvested the weed with huge machetes, which they loaded on burros for transportation back to the "wax camps." "When I started making wax I paid fifteen cents a pound to the men," she explained. "I furnished the acid, which didn't cost much. I furnished the burros, which didn't cost much, and the pack saddles. Then I got all the way from forty-five cents . . . to about sixty-five cents [a pound for the raw wax]. . . . I could make money."[17]

At the outset of this operation, demand was high, as were the profits. Hallie remembered that during their first year of operation profits reached some $30,000, and orders for floor and chewing gum wax went unfilled. By the third year, however, the same factor that crippled the ranching business—the lack of water—also began cutting into their wax profits. According to one Big Bend historian, "because the water supply [for the boiling vats] diminished and it was too expensive to haul water over the rough terrain," profits were cut in half. And the following year cheap imported wax from South America forecast the end of Hallie's wax venture. When the price of native wax dropped fifteen cents in one day, she realized the end was near.[18] "When you find you are simply swappin' dollars, there is really no reason to continue fighting a losing battle. So we called a halt."

Although Hallie was able to temporarily appease George Baines with her various enterprises, the interest clock at the First National Bank continued ticking away. It was not yet high noon, but her options were fast running out. In the early 1950s, women's employment opportunities in the Big Bend country were limited primarily to clerking and teaching school. A clerk's salary would scarcely dent Hallie's loan balance, and "I just didn't feel like I had the time and money to spare to renew my teacher's certificate." But when things appeared the bleakest, fate again seemed to rescue Hallie from the brink of bankruptcy.

This time opportunity came from a most unexpected source. When Glen C. Wilson, a San Antonio architect and longtime friend of the family, learned of Hallie's financial struggle, he introduced her to Frank Ackerman, who booked lecture tours throughout the eastern United States. Wilson convinced both Ackerman and Hallie that, with her natural charm, poise, and knowledge of ranching, she would be successful on the lecture circuit. In late September, 1951, dressed in the regional attire of a Texas ranch woman, Hallie embarked for Kentucky, carrying a briefcase filled with lecture notes and an emotional burden of apprehension and uncertainty.

When she mounted the lecture platform the first time and began to speak, Hallie quickly realized her preoccupation with failure was unfounded. She fulfilled Glen Wilson's expectations in abundance; Hallie was a hit. For the next six weeks she traveled throughout Kentucky, lecturing at schools, colleges, universities, ladies clubs, and service clubs. While the pay was good—$200 an appearance plus expenses—she also acquired some marginal benefits of enduring value. In addition to developing her communication skills, Hallie discovered there existed a wide interest in Texas ranching and a marked appreciation of her role as a working ranch woman. She found this new awareness richly rewarding, especially at a time when her self-esteem had reached low ebb. Ackerman also recognized in Hallie a valuable property. "He wanted me to follow that schedule again the following year," she recalled, "but it was a lonely life and I felt like I was needed at the ranch."

The joy of homecoming was suddenly tempered with her first visit to the bank. Dick Rogers had replaced George Baines as bank president, a move that boded ill for Hallie and her $65,000 unpaid note. "He did not understand me and my ranch operation," she explained. "He was hard at times and soft at times; he blew hot and cold. He gave me a hard time." Rogers was, nevertheless, firm but flexible in defining the bank's role in Hallie's future ranching operations: "I'll feed your cattle, but I won't feed your family." Roger's ultimatum set in motion a chain of events that would completely alter the Stillwell's lifestyle. These were changes that Hallie had hoped to forestall, but Rogers left her no choice. Her objectives were twofold: resolve her indebtedness and save the ranch. The overriding question was how. As she rode horseback alone along Maravillas Creek and surveyed the ravages of the drought, she reluctantly eliminated one option. The ranch alone could not save itself; the negatives far outweighed the positives. With no rain there was no grass, and without grass the remaining herd was still unmarketable. And to further complicate that issue, the value of the cattle continued to decline; between 1952 and 1955, cattle prices dropped from $22.00 to $12.50 per 100 pounds.[19]

Hallie finally had to face the inevitable; the family could not remain at the ranch and survive. The solution to her problem, if there was one, lay elsewhere. In essence, this meant dispersing the family; members would have to go their separate way and market their skills as best they could.

This was Dick Rogers's prescription to forestall foreclosure. "Son [Roy Walker] was still in Oregon, so Guy gets a job in the [Big Bend National] park," Hallie explained. "My daughter-in-law [Guy's wife, Diane] gets a job teaching school, and of course, I'd been sitting in the saddle for thirty years and had lost all my skills. And I had to come to town and get a job. . . . I had to make my own living."

Hallie established residence in Alpine and embarked on another new experience—job hunting. To many Big Bend ranchers whose fierce independence was their badge of honor, this would have been a humiliating experience. Hallie, however, assumed a different perspective; she was not alone in her financial dilemma. The drought itself had had a leveling effect on the ranching community; many others like herself were also struggling to survive. If job hunting was the solution, then so be it.

Jobs were indeed forthcoming; the city of Alpine became her first employer. The assignment: going door-to-door explaining to taxpaying citizens the cost of the new street-paving program. Her success terminated that job in a few weeks. She next worked for the Alpine Chamber of Commerce in public relations and later found employment in a flower shop. When offered that position she hesitated: "I told 'em I could tie a calf down but I couldn't tie a bow! So they let me answer the phone and deliver flowers." While still working for the flower shop, she was offered the manager's position at the Holland Hotel Coffee Shop. She found the offer attractive: $100 a month, plus a room and meals. After some hesitation she accepted the position and remained there for almost a decade. This became her primary interim income source.

Meanwhile, Hallie and Guy continued to be weekend ranchers, meeting at the Maravillas Creek property, and with the help of the Mexican residents, working their remaining herd. This taxing routine led to more changes in Hallie's life. She subsequently sold both her home in Marathon and the ranch in Oregon, which had become another financial liability. Eventually having to sell cattle to make the third annual $10,000 note payment, she leased the property to one Oscar Burnside, an Oregon rancher, who later purchased the ranch "at a nice profit," which Hallie applied to the bank note. "I made my credit good," she added. In retrospect, "I thought that I had better get my eggs in one basket and devote my time down where I had my friends and knew people." Hallie's financial eggs ultimately found their way into Dick Rogers's basket. He emerged as Hallie's chronic but necessary irritant. "I left the bank many times in tears after a session with Dick Rogers," she explained.

Life continued to be a day-to-day struggle, but Hallie, unknowingly, was approaching a watershed period of her life. Now in her midfifties, two ensuing events would change her lifestyle completely and eventually launch her on the road to solvency. But most important, Hallie Stillwell would emerge as one of the best-known and most respected persons in the Big Bend country.

A chance meeting with Jean Glasscock, wife of *Alpine Avalanche* publisher Jim Glasscock, ushered her into the world of professional journalism. Hallie learned from Jean that Jim wanted to see her, and when she entered his office he came right to the point: "'I want you to write a column.'" When asked about a specific topic, he said, "'You just write something our readers will read.'" Hallie found the offer appealing but was not sure she could fulfill his expectations. She pondered the offer for several days and decided "I would just write about what I observed and what I know. . . . I imagine I haven't missed over a dozen times [in some forty years] without getting a column written."[20] Although the compensation was minimal—about $10 a week—her real reward was the joy of writing what other people wanted to read. As Hallie explained, "I thrive on praise of my column."

The things Hallie knew best were people and ranching; these two themes emerge as part-and-parcel of her column and, understandably, were what interested those living in the Big Bend country. In addition to reports on who was seen in town, who sold cattle at what price, range conditions, and the weather, there also emerged the following sequential subtopics: predators, government regulations, screw worm eradication, interest rates, and soil conservation. The first column appeared on October 28, 1955, with Hallie's byline. It set the style and content for the future. Some excerpts follow:

> *Speaking of these "Flying Ranchers" brings to mind the George Skevingtons who ranch on the Arnold Ranch. . . . [They] commute from El Paso to Fort Stockton by Trans-Texas Airways. They have a car at the airport in Fort Stockton and drive out to the ranch. . . . [George reports they] have good grass and the prospects for winter look mighty good. . . . Enjoyed a short chat with Martha (Mrs. Guy) Combs. She brings her two boys from the ranch in to Marathon to school. They ranch at The Gap about 23 miles south of Marathon. Quite a daily chore but Martha is happy about it all. During the heavy rains in September they had to leave the car parked on this side of the Maravillas. Their house happens*

*to be on the "other" side of the creek and they would wade the creek to
this side where the car was left, and off to school they went.*

    *Mr. [Courtney] Mellard shipped five cars of steers and heifers on
the 14th to Mr. Hobert in Washington, Iowa. One carload consisted of
steers purchased from Perry Cartwright with the average weight at 501
lbs. Perry cut back his heaviest heifers to keep on the ranch "as we have
to restock as we go along." . . . W. H. Terry, retired rancher, has been
confined to his home for quite some time due to illness. At the time of
this writing he is feeling some better. He sure is missed down town—
particularly around the [Holland] Hotel Lobby. . . . Don't forget . . . that
next week is "Texans Eat Beef Week." Let's all eat more meat—it's
mighty good food. What makes tall Texans tall? MEAT!"[21]*

By the November 4, 1955 issue, Glasscock had designed an appropriate logo for Hallie's column—"Ranch News." In a region of vast distances
and sometimes poor communications, "Ranch News" emerged as a public forum for all matters of interest. Avoiding gossip and social trivia, Hallie
wrote with humor and insight, and the region embraced her as their composite cheerleader and den mother. Nothing of importance escaped her
scrutiny. And while she seldom editorialized (exceptions: predators and
government regulations), she nonetheless became the region's most respected chronicler. Hallie was, in essence, compiling a week-by-week contemporary history of the Big Bend country. Names especially made news,
and if they came to town, strangers or neighbors, Hallie knew it and alerted
the countryside:

    *Ranchmen who are interested in putting up a fight against eagles are
meeting at the Holland Hotel Saturday morning at 10 o'clock. Eagles are
getting thick in the Big Bend and that means the loss of many little
lambs, kids, calves, deer and antelope. . . . Had a visit with Tommy
Leary, of Marathon, he is tuning up his tractor to do some sub-soiling
work. Tommy is real enthusiastic about soil conservation. Sorry to hear
that his father, Spud Leary, of San Angelo is under the weather. . . .
Nights are still cold and early mornings frosty, days are clear with bright
sunshine. Weeds are making a slow appearance but with a warm spell
they should really pop up. (1/19/61). . . .*

    *Charley Blakeley came in from Kentucky Monday on his way to Big
Bend Park. He said the sunshine here looked mighty fine to him. (1/5/61).
. . . Sunday was a big day in Alpine—Big Bend Stock Show—and a*

meeting of ranchers about the eagle problem. 4-H boys and girls were out at the crack of dawn getting their stock in readiness for the show. (1/26/61). . . . The snow that fell Sunday and Monday over the Big Bend was good and wet. On top of the already wet ground it was just about the best thing that has happened to the range in a long time. . . . Around town this week: I saw Punch Roberts, who is feeling fine now since he recovered from a bad experience of being out all night, in the cold, after his pickup got stuck in a badger hole. (2/23/61). . . . Rex Ivey of Lajitas brought in the first blue bonnets that I have seen this year. Rex says they are blooming in places, mostly near the Rio Grande. . . . Asa A. Jones has completed 20 acres of root plowing. (3/2/61). . . .

Texas Ranger Arthur Hill is carrying a broken arm, and of all things, caused by a fall from a wheelbarrow. Everyone naturally thinks he got it from a fight with outlaws, but not so. (1/4/62). . . . Joe Lane, president of the Highland Hereford Association, is highly pleased with the Screwworm Eradication Program. The program is about two years ahead of schedule. (3/13/62). . . . I am happy to report that the Pollard Ranch got a good well of water on top of a big high mountain at something over 400 feet. That will open up a lot of new pasture land for them. (4/5/62). . . . A big thrill for those who saw Harry James and his orchestra in Alpine Monday. The group had lunch at the Holland House Coffee Shop, then spent some time on main street. They were en route from Mexico to San Antonio. (3/9/61). . . . Watch this space for a report of rain. It's the same song—second verse. (3/30/61). . . . Mr. and Mrs. Ollie Cox in town Monday, are still unhappy about losing to thieves most everything on their ranch except the house and land. (4/6/61). . . .

Murphy Bennett of Marfa and Alpine last Thursday reported that a grass fire started by lightning on Wednesday night, burned off two sections of the M. D. Bryant country. Ranchmen fighting all night put the fire out before it spread further. (4/26/63). . . . The busiest place in the Big Bend for the past month is the Santa Fe Stock pens. Cattle by the hundreds are being weighed and shipped out of these pens. Their weights are slightly under last year's, prices have held strong. (10/25/62). . . . The first snow of the season to fall in Big Bend came Monday night. It was about the wettest snow I ever saw and four inches in depth. Couldn't have been better. (11/22/62). . . . Hunting season on black tail deer will get off to a big start on Saturday. Hunting is big business in the Big Bend and the Sportsman's Club does a good job in welcoming and assisting the hunters. (11/29/62). . . . Merry Christmas, everybody. It should be a good

Christmas, beautiful warm days for the past week should change and
bring in a nice snow for the holidays. That would be mighty fine.[22]

With pen and pad in place of her old Woodstock typewriter, Hallie continued to communicate with loyal readers far and wide. Gerald Raun reported that shortly after he acquired the *Alpine Avalanche* in 1990, Hallie took a vacation; the response was immediate. He "received a number of phone calls and letters, from as far as New Jersey, asking if we had dropped the column—and complaining if that were to be the case" to cancel their subscriptions.[23] While Jim Glasscock probably exaggerated when he claimed that Hallie's column doubled his circulation, her good friend Inda Benson, obviously prejudiced, appears to confirm Raun's statement: "Hallie's column is the only reason many of us take the *Avalanche.*"[24]

Hallie's success with "Ranch News" prompted her to explore other journalistic opportunities. She felt the major Texas dailies needed Big Bend representation. Although the *Fort Worth Star-Telegram* became the first recipient of her freelance coverage, she views her initial effort as on-the-job-training.

Hallie knew she had a good story; a young hunter went berserk and killed a lot of wild game—deer and antelope—out of season. While he was still being held in jail, she called in her story to Pressley Bryant, state editor for the *Star-Telegram.* She remembered the ensuing dialogue as follows:

Bryant: "Hallie, how many did he kill in Jeff Davis County?"

Hallie: "Well, I don't know. A whole bunch."

Bryant: "Who was the judge who reported it to you?"

Hallie: "I don't know."

Bryant: "How much fine did he have to pay?"

Hallie: "I don't know that either."

Bryant: "Hallie, you don't have a story. You get out now and get me a story."

"I had to go out and get all the details," she recalled. "So I guess if you want to know who really influenced me, it was Pressley Bryant. He taught me how to write a news story." Success bred success, and subsequently the *El Paso Times, San Antonio Express,* and *San Angelo Standard-Times,* as well as the Associated Press and United Press International all solicited her services. On June 23, 1990, in recognition of her fifty years in journalism, the Texas Press Association presented Hallie with its Golden 50 Award.

Hallie had always wanted to write a book; it fell to Big Bend historian

Virginia Madison to lead the way. The two met while Virginia was re-searching *The Big Bend Country of Texas*. She had gone to the Maravillas Creek ranch to interview Roy Stillwell and was equally impressed with Hallie's knowledge of the region. The two became close friends, and fol-lowing the publication of *Big Bend Country* in 1955, they began discussing a joint project on that region. Later, while visiting the Big Bend National Park an idea began to take form; members of the park staff kept asking the two writers about the origin of various place names in that region. Their recurring questions articulated in the regional vernacular—"how come it's called that?"—set the theme, as well as the title, for the coopera-tive venture. According to Hallie, they "decided that since the park was interested in something like that, that we would put together a book. So that's really how come." *How Come It's Called That?: Place Names in the Big Bend Country* was an immediate success; the first edition quickly sold out, as did a second and a third edition. Having long since recouped their original investment, Hallie explained, "what we get now is all gravy."[25]

Gravy, in this context, is a relative term, and what there was of it came too late to benefit Hallie when she needed it the most. Her combined income from the hotel coffee shop, writing the "Ranch News" column, plus her infrequent "stringer" news stories, fulfilled only her immediate needs. There was nothing left for the bank, which mandated Hallie's peri-odic visits with Dick Rogers. In retrospect, she viewed Rogers with mixed emotion: "He stayed with me . . . [but] he was *hard*. He and I didn't see eye-to-eye on a lot of things. I really had a hard time, but he stayed with me." Hallie recalled the deep anxiety that preceded her meetings with Rogers and the emotional trauma that ensued: "Dick was a good banker but I left his office in tears many times. . . . He scared me. Well, he didn't scare me so much, but he did scare Guy. It got to the point when we would have to renew our notes, Guy would get sick. And I finally told him, 'I'll take care of it.' Many times I would go in and sign the notes and then take them down to the ranch for Guy to sign, because I didn't want him to come to town and face Dick Rogers."

While Rogers had confidence in Hallie, her delinquent note remained a matter of concern. With her renewal date set for December 1, he would call her in early October to ask if she had contracted her calves for the fall sale. "So I would have to go contract my calves," she explained. Winter sales, however, worked to her disadvantage, which she finally explained to Rogers: "Look, Mr. Rogers, we have a different country down where I am. It's lower. We have good winters and we winter good. Our summers are hot and my calves don't weigh much in the fall and that's really no time to sell 'em. If you will make my note to come due on the first of May, and let me sell my calves in the spring, after they'd been wintered, I'll do better. He said, 'I hadn't thought about it like that.' And I said, that's the way it is. So he changed my renewal date to May 1."

The drought continued, as did Hallie's inability to resolve her indebtedness, a matter that still weighed heavily in Rogers's calculations. Sometime later, prior to a renewal date, he called her at the hotel coffee shop and asked her to come in for a conference. The sound of his voice contained an ominous overtone; she walked to the bank expecting the worse; Rogers fulfilled her darkest premonitions. She remembered the ensuing dialogue as follows:

Rogers: "Hallie, why don't you sell that ranch and get that burden off your back? You could go and travel and have a good time. Now, Nellie Mae McElroy has sold her ranch and you could sell yours."

Hallie: "Well, no. I just can't sell mine."

Rogers: "I guess you think that you have a better ranch than she has."

Hallie: "I do. And beside that, Nellie Mae didn't have any children. I can't sell my ranch and sell my childrens' birthright. I just can't do it."

Rogers: "You can't grow any grass."

Hallie: "We've been in a drought ever since you've been here [at the bank] and you have never seen this country when we have had rain."

Rogers: "With all the rain in the world, you'd never have any grass; you'd never have anything but a little fuzz."

Hallie: "You just wait and see. It will rain one of these days and things will change."

Following a brief reflective pause, Hallie added, "That was one of the times I left out in tears." Rogers, however, once again renewed Hallie's note. In evaluating their confrontation, emotional and traumatic as it may have been, she at least considered herself the temporary winner. In the face of the ongoing drought and her inability to pay on her note, she continued to hold title to the ranch. All was not lost, but life always appeared bleakest as she pondered her future in the aftermath of those sessions with Dick Rogers. It was on just such an occasion that Hallie was unexpectedly elevated to the second plateau of her watershed period.

Brewster County sheriff Jim Skinner entered the Holland Hotel Coffee Shop that morning in 1964 and took his usual seat at the counter. When Hallie served him his morning coffee he dropped an emotional bombshell; Justice of the Peace Jim Parker had just died of a heart attack and he thought she should apply for the position. Both flattered and frightened, she hesitated, but after considering her present position in the light of her economic future, she decided to discuss the matter with her old friend, County Judge Felix McGaughey. The judge encouraged her to file a formal application with the Brewster County Commissioners' Court, which, in March, 1964, appointed Hallie Stillwell Justice of the Peace, Precinct 1.

Hallie had just taken the biggest professional leap of her life. During her initial days in office, while questioning her qualifications and debating the wisdom of her decision, she received State Senator Dorsey B. Hardeman's much appreciated letter of encouragement: "While your technical training and background, as related to the fictions of the law, may leave something to be desired in an appellate judge, nevertheless, your experience, education, ability, energy, good looks and good common sense qualify you far and away beyond some of those in judicial positions who cover their ignorance and shroud their pomposity in mantles of ebony hue."[26]

Senator Hardeman's letter gave Hallie the confidence to face an unpredictable future in a critical and as yet untried role. The senator was indeed prophetic in evaluating her credentials, as well as in his prognosis for success. Had the senator bothered to check her ensuing judicial record, he would have discovered that legally Judge Hallie Stillwell was a strict constructionist. In the courtroom, both plaintiff and defendant, irrespective of their identity, received equal consideration under "Hallie's Law." Family and friends were no exception. She fined her grandson for speeding, the mayor of Alpine $200 for driving while intoxicated, and her best friend, Inda Benson, $25 for speeding.

Performing traditional men's roles was nothing new to Hallie; the judiciary was no exception. But on occasion when courtroom exchanges became unnecessarily volatile, Sheriff Jim Skinner would intervene verbally: "'The judge is a lady. Watch your language.'" But when a negative ruling prompted a similar response, Hallie stood firm. "She'd say, 'This is the way it is and the way it's going to be,'" explained Judge Sam Thomas. "'If you don't like it, I can't help it. Just pay up and move on.'"[27] Although firm, she nevertheless dispensed justice with mercy. Many sentenced to jail terms bore no grudge. "I befriended a lot of old winos that I had to keep in jail.... And when they got out they would come and ask me for a dollar." When asked if they got it, she responded emphatically, "Oh, of course."

Every four years Hallie ran for reelection and won every race. In 1970, however, she received her stiffest challenge from an African American, Lewis B. Gordon. With the approach of the May Democratic primary, Hallie realized she could be in trouble. With a black man as her opponent, race inevitably emerged as an issue. This she could not understand. Three days before the election, she placed an unusually large two-column ad in the *Alpine Avalanche,* stating, "I have tried to be fair and just . . . [to all, and] . . . I am taking this means of asking for your support."[28] She received the support she sought, but by a dangerously thin margin—only fifty votes.[29] After the election she asked Gordon, a longtime friend, why he ran against her. "'You know, the LULACS [League of United Latin American Citizens] came out and told me to get an office,' he explained, 'and I couldn't think of any office except your office. So I just ran for that.'"[30]

Hallie would stand for reelection one more time. In 1974, she faced LULAC-sponsored Johnny Sotello, whom she defeated by seventy-four votes.[31] Four years later, at age eighty-one, Hallie decided to end her political career. Her unexpected departure from the bench prompted an areawide outpouring of public approbation. On December 17, 1978, two weeks before her official retirement, Brewster County honored her with a standing-room-only surprise party. The gifts were exceptional. Local friends and courthouse colleagues gave her a round-trip ticket to anywhere in the world, and Texas governor Dolph Briscoe commissioned her "The Yellow Rose of Texas." On February 28, 1979, the Texas senate passed Senate Resolution No. 171, honoring Hallie Stillwell, who "began her public service career at age 67, after devoting her life to teaching, writing, and ranching." The resolution also cites "her invaluable contribution to the history, growth and strength of Texas and Texans."[32]

Hallie's decision not to seek reelection was not an easy one. She enjoyed the work, religiously attending annual seminars to broaden her knowledge of the law. "If I had been younger I might have pursued the law," she explained later. Age was an obvious factor, but there were other considerations. Although each election brought increased LULAC opposition, probably the greatest underlying factor, other than age, was economic.

In the meantime, conditions at the ranch had improved. Despite Dick Rogers's negative view of her Maravillas Creek property, Hallie never lost confidence. Rain, the eternal giver of life and the ranchers' ultimate salvation, was bound to come again to the Big Bend country. In 1957, after a decade-long dry sequence, the rains came, ending "the worst drought on record. . . . The average rainfall over most of Texas exceeded longterm means," the United States Weather Bureau reported. That year the Big Bend region received 13.62 inches of precipitation, a 2.04 deficit, which increased the following year to 22.98 inches, a 7.32 inch overage. By May, 1959, continued "rain brought about ideal soil conditions to most of the state." During the following two years, 1960 and 1961, the Big Bend posted overages of 1.44 and 3.92 inches respectively.[33]

Another wet-dry-wet weather cycle had again come full circle. While still working at the Holland Hotel Coffee Shop, Hallie's subsequent visits with Dick Rogers became more frequent and the conversation upbeat. She now had grass—not just "a little fuzz"—and needed more cattle. And with improved prospects of repayment, Rogers had money to lend. Thus Hallie began a replay of that regional dictum: "In dry times I sold cattle; in wet times I bought cattle. That's how you survive in the Big Bend country." And once again she entered the buying mode.

Then there occurred a totally unexpected event that made retirement more palatable. In 1965, when the Texas Highway Department improved FM 2677 between Persimmon Gap and La Linda, they severed a portion of the Stillwell Ranch that was too small on which to run cattle. When vacationing travelers began camping on the unoccupied land, opportunity beckoned. "I decided to put in a few [recreational vehicle] hookups and hire somebody to stay there and watch the ranch," Hallie explained. "People were infringing on me anyway." The infringing people lay the groundwork for another Stillwell enterprise; four years later she established the Stillwell Store and Trailer Park.

Both businesses flourished; at the height of tourist season some 200 to 300 people receive daily accommodations at the trailer park. Not one to dwell on statistics, Hallie estimated the annual gross income from the trailer park and store at "around $200,000," which exceeds the ranch income in most years.

Prosperity was something Hallie had not experienced since the early postwar years. She had been poor and in debt; now she was solvent. And affluence was a source of great pride, especially when considering her long-standing indebtedness to the First National Bank. "I don't owe that bank a dime," she explained. "I paid them off sometime in the late 1970s, soon after Dick Rogers died." She had, however, long since made her peace with Rogers. So one by one the Stillwells returned to the Maravillas; together they formed the working mosaic that became the Stillwell enterprise. Hallie, however, continued to oversee the combined operations, lamenting all the while that she could no longer ride a horse, tie down a calf, or wield a branding iron.

There were, however, compensations. She had more time to lecture, write, and travel. Her weekly "Ranch News" column continued to appear in the *Avalanche,* and in 1991 Texas A&M University Press published her highly popular recollections, *I'll Gather My Geese.* At age eighty-two, when most of her contemporaries were, at best, immobile, she traveled alone to London. "I wanted to go and couldn't get anybody to go with me," she said. "I had a good time. I like to visit cities for the shows and museums. . . . [but] for living, I want to live here. I want to live in the country."[34] Once asked if she didn't get lonely living in that remote section of Texas, she replied: "Lonely, heavens no. I'm never lonely as long as I can see the mountains." There was little chance of Hallie ever being lonely. On October 20, 1991, the family celebrated her ninety-fourth birthday at the ranch with the dedication of "Hallie's Hall of Fame" museum. That event drew hundreds of celebrants from all over the state.[35]

A regional celebrity and a designated Texas *Grande Dame,* Hallie bore the title with dignity, humility, and good humor. Journalists, historians, folklorists, television news crews, sundry filmmakers, and autograph seekers all find their way to the Stillwell Store, where Hallie, "seated on a wooden chair like a wise old queen . . . entertains visitors with stories about her early days of ranching. . . . People stare at her, mesmerized by her vast antiquity and the ease with which she plays her role as the mother of West Texas."[36] Another journalist wrote, "She can talk for hours in the first-person without coming across as an egomanic. Hallie has taken the scenic route through the first 92 years of her life, and she has made a point of remembering every graceful curve. . . . She paints pictures with words, and every story is a masterpiece."[37]

Hallie's appeal was multifaceted: author, lecturer, journalist, ex-jurist, regional cheerleader, unique personality, and, according to *Texas Monthly,* "arguably the most famous rancher in West Texas."[38] Every comment, regardless of the topic, was a quotable quote. The serious scholar, however, views Hallie Stillwell within the more limited scope of regional culture. She not only was the product of the environment, a living symbol of a regional experience, she possessed the capacity to interpret that experience for others. Yet the visitor quickly discovered within Hallie Stillwell a perplexing regional dichotomy: a charming lady of class and culture who survived and ultimately prospered in one of the nation's most inhospitable regions. She was, at the same time, unquestionably the antithesis of an accepted regional philosophical concept: "Man does not modify this country; it transforms him deeply."[39] While Hallie may not have changed the country per se, she had nevertheless survived, her body and mind absorbing all the shocks and blows the region could inflict with no visible scars or damage. She stayed when others left; she succeeded when others failed; she would never say it had been easy: "I've been so hot I could have died. I have been so cold I thought I'd freeze. I've been so tired I thought I'd drop. But you just go on. In fact, I haven't been a failure. I don't know if I have accomplished great things, but I haven't been a failure."[40]

Failure and determination seldom coexist, and Hallie's will to survive meant preserving the ranch, the family, and a way of life that took precedence over all other considerations. Unlike others expelled from the region by drought, economic depression, hardship, scarcity, and isolation, she, through determination and diversification, found a solution for survival. She simply learned to compromise with the forces over which she exercised no control. And within that limited context she did indeed submit to the dictates of the region. "Ranchers have had a pretty hard time, prices have fluctuated and we've had our droughts," she explained. "It's just hard to make a go. . . . So, I learned to diversify and do things other than raising cattle." The ranch, however, remained paramount in her scheme of things. "There's something about ranch life you don't give up," she concluded. "Everything I ever did was for the ranch. I can't imagine life without it."

A million words have been written about Hallie Stillwell, with millions more yet to come, but her old friend Tom Henderson, a master of brevity, paid this great lady an appropriate tribute: "Hallie Stillwell is what this country is all about. She's a legend here, an institution whose story would take a month of *Avalanches* to tell."[41]

CHAPTER

9

Dobie's Children

DISCOVERING THE TREASURE
OF THE IMAGINATION

When my Uncle Arthur Norman loaned me his copy of J. Frank Dobie's *Coronado's Children*, he had no intention of jeopardizing my future. That was in May, 1934, when I was studying for finals in my sophomore year in Troup High School. But instead of reading Washington Irving, Henry Wadsworth Longfellow, and John Greenleaf Whittier, I read Dobie. I read Dobie on the way to school, in the study hall, in math class, in the science lab, on the way home from school, and at night when I should have been studying for finals. And then after I turned out the light, I lay awake thinking about buried treasure and fantasizing exciting explorations to all the romantic sites Dobie describes in *Coronado's Children*.[1] But in spite of my Uncle Arthur's generosity and my total preoccupation with that fascinating book, I passed my finals by the narrowest of margins.

But treasure hunting was never far from my thoughts. Uncle Arthur and I frequently visited some of the older people in the community to talk about buried treasure. "Old money hunters," he called them. They all told similar stories; they knew where vast sums of money were buried, and when on the verge of recovering the treasure, some unexpected catastrophe occurred, denying them a life of abundance. One old gentleman even loaned me his "divining rod" to aid me in my search for local treasures.[2] I still have that accursed device hanging on the wall of my office as a reminder of my teenage naïveté. I, like so many, tried and failed; *the damn thing just didn't work*!

One of the high points of my teenage treasure hunting fantasies occurred when Uncle Arthur discovered that Lee J. Bertillion was living near Mineola, Texas, just a short drive from our home. Bertillion is the key figure in "The Fateful Opals" episode in *Coronado's Children*. When we arrived at his home, the old gentleman greeted us warmly and immediately launched into an endless diatribe about the $37,500 treasure that lay hidden somewhere along the Pecos River. Understandably, I found Bertillion fascinating; he was the first person I ever met whose name appeared in a history book (I thought all of those people were dead); and he was present at the deathbed confession of Dirk Pacer (I love that name), who gave the location of the $37,500 cache of silver and opals. When our visit ended later that day, Uncle Arthur and I were determined to join Bertillion in his ongoing search for the Pecos River treasure. At that point I became a true believer.

The excitement continued to grow. A high school chum named Marshall Rooks moved me one step closer to that $37,500. At least, I thought so at the time. Marshall was a "radio nut," and after I confided to him our projected venture, he said he might be able to help. Remember, this was 1934. Marshall had just read in a radio journal about a recently developed device that would locate metal underground. (Those are now marketed commercially as metal detectors.) Marshall said he could build such a device, and with that in hand, he saw no reason why we couldn't locate the $37,500. That did it! I foresaw how I could broker the treasure hunt; I would bring the interested parties together and off we would go to the Pecos.

But it just didn't happen that way. There was the reality of poverty, a prolonged illness, and the prospects of a college education. The dream, however, persisted. When I enrolled in Tyler Junior College in September, 1937, I explained to Dean H. E. Jenkins that it was possible that I would be absent from school for about two weeks in October. I was going on a "scientific exploration." I didn't explain; he didn't ask, but I am sure when I left his office he erupted in uncontrollable laughter.

Ultimately, I was forced to face reality. The turning point came when another radio repairman explained to me that, because of the inherent limitations of the device Marshall Rooks had described, we would be wasting our time, effort, and money. He convinced me that the sum total of our recovery would be nails, railroad spikes, horseshoes, soda water bottle tops, and tin cans. And so the years have passed, as did both Lee Bertillion and my Uncle Arthur, carrying with them their dreams of buried treasure. Some six decades later I can still recall the excitement of that visit with Lee Bertillion and the high hopes we had of recovering that $37,500 trove. That figure, $37,500, is still indelibly inscribed somewhere on the backside of my psyche; Frank Dobie and his wonderful book had registered their mark. And so I remain one of Dobie's children; I had discovered the treasure of the imagination. This was an enduring image that I would ultimately carry with me to the Big Bend country where I would find others of a similar persuasion.

But contrary to what some people may believe, J. Frank Dobie did not invent buried treasure. Instead, he publicized it, popularized it, institutionalized it, and inflamed the public mind with the possibilities of finding untold amounts of hidden and unlabored wealth. It was Dobie, however, who found the treasure. After six decades of steady sales, royalties from *Coronado's Children* undoubtedly exceed in dollar value all of the buried treasure ever recovered from Texas's crusty soil.[3] And yet the search goes on.

When Dallas-based Southwest Press published *Coronado's Children* in 1931, that event touched off unexpected reverberations throughout the literary world. The choice of Dobie's book as the Literary Guild's February selection marked a literary milestone. This was the first time any book club chose a book from a publisher doing business west of the Hudson River. Yet the book's inherent regionalism—Texas and the Southwest— failed to prejudice the literary critics. From the East Coast, West Coast, Middle America, and the Southeast, came a unanimous verdict: *Coronado's Children* represented unique literary achievement.

R. L. Duffus, writing in the *New York Times,* claimed that Dobie produced a book that is "as entrancing a volume as one is likely to pick up in a month of Sundays." George Currie, literary editor of the *Brooklyn Eagle,* congratulated the Literary Guild for "going to Dallas for its book of the month of February. If there is a more fascinating volume of the stuff that dreams are made of . . . [it is] unknown to this reviewer. . . . For the reader it is a mine in itself of breathless and exciting moments."[4] In the *New York World,* Harry Hansen focused on the book's romance and glamour and proposed embarking immediately on a treasure hunt. "It's a lively book," he wrote, "full of all sorts of tales, enough to make any cynical reviewer buy a spade and yell for time tables of trains to Texas."[5]

No previous book by a Texas author had so fired the imagination of expectant treasure hunters. Many of those who ultimately succumbed to the dream were people who seldom read books, who cared little for Dobie's literary skill, or appreciated the insight with which he assembled this collection of folk tales. While Dobie appropriately characterized his informants—the true believers—as Coronado's children, there would emerge a cadre of new believers who apparently read the book and succumbed to the same malady. Eschewing critical insight, they believed the treasure stories with implicit reverence. They would ultimately join a new throng of treasure seekers guided by the same blind vision as those who told Dobie the stories in the first place. These were not Coronado's children; these were Dobie's.

Dobie was the proper father figure; he had told them the stories and shown them the way. But of even greater importance, he had provided that one essential ingredient for locating buried treasure—*a map.* There it is, sketched in the endpapers of *Coronado's Children,* "Lost Mines and Buried Treasures of the Southwest." From Oklahoma to the Rio Grande, from the Mississippi to the Colorado, there is identified enough buried treasure and lost mines that if recovered would amount to untold millions. This was the dream of Dobie's children. With pick and shovel and visions of success, many headed for the hills. These are the ones who dug the holes, tunneled beneath mountains, moved earth and stone, drained lakes, and changed the course of streams in search of their own El Dorado. These were the true believers. And the search goes on.

Within the broad span of Dobie's map, only two sites fall within the Big Bend country. One, "The Lost Nigger Mine," is in the very heart of the Bend; the other, the "Monterrey stuff," is reportedly stashed near El Muerto Springs in the foothills of the Davis Mountains. Both sites are well documented in *Coronado's Children,* chapters 8 and 10 respectively, and both sites have been and are still attracting the interest of a host of Dobie's children. Their search has left its mark on the landscape.

The legend of "The Lost Nigger Mine" does indeed possess a modicum of regional and scientific validity. The Big Bend country has long been the source of both rare and precious metals, yet evidence supporting the existence of "The Lost Nigger Mine" described by Dobie is somewhat more elusive.[6] According to the account in *Coronado's Children,* the key figure in the episode was Bill Kelly, a black Seminole horse wrangler employed by the Reagan brothers, prominent Big Bend cattlemen. The Reagans were moving a herd of cattle out of Mexico, crossing the Rio Grande near the mouth of a canyon that would later bear their name. (Reagan Canyon figures prominently in the story that follows). Kelly's responsibility was to search both sides of the river for loose stock. Returning to the headquarters camp late one evening, he announced that he had found a gold mine and offered some ore samples as proof. His employer's response was less than enthusiastic; he was hired to hunt horses, not gold. Understandably, Kelly was disappointed.

According to Dobie, Kelly left the Reagans to seek help in developing his mine, and in the process mysteriously exited from the pages of history. He was, however, replaced by a host of other true believers who invested both time and money but were no more successful than the old horse wrangler. Their "scientific explorations" follow a similar scenario: the ore is found in place, but the finder is either frightened away or dies before he can report the location. One exception to this formula occurred in 1940, actually before Frank Dobie's very eyes, but amazingly enough, without his apparent knowledge. Prospectors, one has to assume, sometime work in strange and mysterious ways. This description fits Guy Skiles to a tee; he claimed to have found the ore in place. Knowing Guy as I did, I am hesitant to doubt his claim. He was indeed a rare breed.

As the following story unfolds, it is important that the reader bear in mind that Skiles was not the typical inheritor of the Coronado tradition. And while he may have exhibited some rough edges, he was unquestionably a man of substance. Michael Collins, Skiles's close friend and research fellow with the University of Texas Archaeological Research Laboratory, described "The Sage of Langtry" as "the absolute consummate naturalist; he had intimate knowledge of his surroundings." He was, in addition, an avid book collector, read the classics, and was well versed in Texana and Western Americana. And to quote Dobie, who was his friend, "he was a man you could ride the river with."[7] In fact, that was what he was doing. Sometime in 1940, Skiles, his brother, and Dobie began a float trip down the Rio Grande. That's when it all happened. Skiles told his story as follows:

> Well, I guess you might say you'd start in down there about at Stillwell Crossing. . . . Actually, there's not anything much below Stillwell Crossing. There's no habitation on either side; there's not anything. . . . Well, there's only [one] thing in history and that's the Lost Nigger Mine. J. Frank Dobie wrote that up in his book, Coronado's Children, but I found the mine![8] I guess it was in 1940, my brother and I and Dobie put in over there at Reagan Canyon, coming down the river fishing and hunting. And I think the first day out we stopped where we could get out

from the river. . . . There was only one place we could get out. The mouth
of the canyon had come [into view] and [there was] a trail coming in.
. . . And I walked out there aways. It was dry; there weren't no deer signs.

When Skiles returned to the river he saw "two or three veins of quartz
there in kind of an upheaval. I got to looking at the little streaks and the
further down, the bigger they got. We got down there to a vein about two
or three inches wide. Why, it was rose looking quartz and I got to thinking, well, that might be the Lost Nigger Mine."

Skiles collected some ore samples, which were later lost downriver in
a boat accident, an event that follows the typical pattern of a *Coronado's
Children* treasure story. He would, however, take another float trip down
the Rio Grande. He continued:

The next spring in February I come there with [Henry B.] duPont [vice
president, E. I. duPont de Nemours and Company], and Dobie, and
another man. And we stopped and stayed all night there and that vein
was still there. . . . I got me out two or three more samples and put them
in a sack . . . to bring them home with me. . . . We come on down and
[another member of the party] was griping about me carrying them
damn rocks around. . . . Course, after we got back he'd heard a lot about
Dobie and he read that book, Coronado's Children, *and he read about*
the Lost Nigger Mine. He come by out here [to Langtry] one time after
that and he said, "Say, what'd you ever do with them rocks you found up
there and brought home?" I said, "Oh, I got 'em out in the barn." He
said, "Well, let me take them to San Antonio and have them assayed.
They might be something." I said, "All right." And I give them to him. I
never did see him or the rocks anymore! He moved off up to Denver or
somewhere.

Well, [this] went on for another year or two and [Henry] duPont
wanted to make another trip down there with his two boys. I thought
well, we'll come down there and I'll stop and get me some more of those
samples. When we got there, there wasn't nothing but a dadgum gravel
pile as big as this house. The only way you could have got down to it was
to dig it with a shovel, and I didn't even have a shovel. I said, "To heck
with it."

Skiles, however, did not give up the search. On a subsequent float trip
with duPont, he planned to collect more ore samples, but that was not to

be. In the interim the Rio Grande had flooded, and "it filled the mouth of that canyon up, and that ledge . . . with gravel. And it's still thataway. I went by there time and time again after that and it was still nothing but a big gravel bar. And that's the reason they never could find that Lost Nigger Mine."

Did Guy Skiles really discover the source of the Bill Kelly legend? And if he did, would it have been the bonanza so many had sought? And was the fact that it was apparently on the Mexican side of the Rio Grande sufficient reason not to develop the prospect? International boundaries offer scant restraint for Coronado's—or Dobie's—children. To them, gold is where you find it, and many have spent small fortunes trying to locate that elusive deposit of ore. They were the true believers.

Bill Kelly, however, had his detractors, the disbelievers. Frank Dobie headed that list. He once told me that he did not believe any of the treasures described in *Coronado's Children* actually existed. He viewed these treasure stories solely as important social documents. To him they revealed the philosophical perspectives of those who told the stories, which, in turn, enabled Dobie and other scholars to gain better insight into the social and cultural fabric of the Southwest. Dobie also told his secretary, Willie Belle Coker, if he had known where any treasure was buried, "'I wouldn't tell anyone about it. I'd go dig it up myself.'"[9]

Then one must raise the question, who was right, Dobie or Skiles? Was "The Lost Nigger Mine" fact or fiction? Hallie Stillwell, that legendary matriarch of the Big Bend country, sided with Skiles. She believed that there are indeed gold deposits in that area, possibly on both sides of the Rio Grande. Hallie explained that "Allan Burnham from San Antonio spent seventeen years down here [on Maravillas Creek] looking for that gold mine and he found enough gold to live on, you know, panning for gold out of the Maravillas [where it enters the Rio Grande]. He lived there for seventeen years and that's how he made his living. He used to come by our place all the time."[10]

Hallie's narrative of Allan Burnham's experience on the Maravillas adds credence to Guy Skiles's description of the area where he claimed to find the gold-bearing quartz, "where this canyon comes into the river." It fell, however, to Hallie's daughter, Dadie Potter, to shift the focus of the lost gold mine from the past to the present. "We have some prospectors that [recently] have found gold down there and are getting ready to core drill," she explained. "They are down on the Maravillas in Black Gap coring near the river," Potter added. "They're just real excited about what they've found."[11] Can it be possible that, after more than a century of searching, a "scientific exploration" is about to confirm what Bill Kelly tried to tell everyone who would listen—there's gold down there in the Big Bend country? *¿Quien sabe?*

El Muerto Springs, a picturesque oasis nestled in the foothills of the Davis Mountains, is located some 150 miles northwest from the confluence of Maravillas Creek and the Rio Grande. This onetime Butterfield stage stop is another mecca for dedicated Big Bend treasure hunters. For almost a century, treasure hunters, many of them Dobie's children, have labored in vain to recover the "Monterrey holdup stuff." According to Dobie, this was "the most magnificent booty, not even excepting Pancho Villa's, to have been buried in modern times."[12] The genesis of this legend is contained in chapter 10 of *Coronado's Children,* "Los Muertos No Hablan" [the dead do not talk]. A brief summation of Dobie's account follows.

In 1879, a quartet of American outlaws—Zwing Hunt, Jim Hughes, Red Curly (also known as Sandy King), and Doctor Neal—formed a partnership with a band of nineteen Mexican bandits who were terrorizing the Big Bend country. The objective was to stage a quick assault on the wealth of Monterrey. According to Dobie's account, "they looted the mint, raided the smelter, and sacked the cathedral."[13] With the loot loaded on twenty-five mules, the bandits embarked on a 390-mile nonstop ride to El Muerto Springs with the Mexican cavalry in pursuit.

Evading their pursuers, the bandits crossed the Rio Grande at the mouth of Reagan Canyon, continued northward, passing near the present site of Alpine, and began a slow trek northwestward to where they planned to bury their treasure. While en route, the four Americans devised a plan to reduce the number of shareholders. As the milelong convoy proceeded up the blind pass leading to the Springs, they ambushed their Mexican compadres, and according to legend, only one escaped to tell the story. During the encounter, however, Zwing Hunt sustained a serious machete wound, rendering him unable to travel. Fearing detection, Hunt's three partners placed him in an adjacent cave, providing him with water and provisions. Next, they cached their loot in a temporary excavation and departed for a hiding place somewhere in the high country to the north.

Two weeks later they returned to the Springs to find Hunt virtually recovered. The quartet, temporarily solvent with withdrawals from the Monterrey treasure, embarked for El Paso and points west. They hoped to enjoy the rewards of their effort while further increasing their capital.

"In the spring of 1881," according to Dobie, "the gang made three separate robberies—apparently not from need of money but for the love of the game. . . . They now had new riches to add to their storage, and they decided to make a thorough job of burying it."[14]

Now follows one of the more implausible aspects of the Dobie story. Traditionally, outlaws are not prone to save for the future; they live for the moment. Yet these decided to stash the Monterrey treasure in a virtually impenetrable depository before departing to seek new fortunes elsewhere. They engaged four Mexican miners working nearby to excavate what appeared to be the final resting place for their joint holdings. They dug a vertical shaft eighty-five feet deep, much through solid rock, and then dug an eighteen-foot offset tunnel. The treasure was then placed in this earthen vault, which they sealed with mortar made of granite dust and the blood of slain antelope. (What was wrong with the water from El Muerto Springs?) As further insurance of total secrecy, they killed the four Mexican miners and buried the bodies in the original treasure excavation. Their work was now complete; they departed the secluded oasis confident that the secret was theirs alone. *Los muertos no hablan.* Yet they apparently never returned to claim their treasure.

There were, however, others who did, all true believers, and all members of Dobie's extended family. There was never a truer believer than Bill Cole of Valentine, Texas. Finding the "Monterrey stuff" was his single mission in life. He worked the El Muerto Springs site for nearly a half century; his confidence never waned. Most important, Cole apparently was Dobie's single source of information, and when the two first met in the mid-1920s, Dobie knew Cole by reputation, but Cole knew nothing about Dobie. He mistakenly thought Dobie was a fellow treasure hunter. Dobie visited Cole in Valentine, listened to the old man's stories, and examined his workings at El Muerto Springs. Cole outlined for Dobie his search for the Monterrey treasure, including his acquisition of a treasure map on which he recognized the El Muerto Springs topography. In addition, Cole had located thirteen reference points called for on the map. He believed implicitly that the real Monterrey loot was still there for the taking.

After Cole began digging, his belief was further substantiated by his findings: cement made of granite gravel mixed in antelope blood, clots of antelope hair, chisel marks on rocks, and fifty feet down a piece from a juniper tree and pieces of surface rock. Cole, however, finally had to face reality. On reaching the eighty-five foot level and ready to tunnel back into the treasure room, he struck water. Realizing he needed help to pro-

Ruins of the Bill Cole residence in Valentine, Texas. Many latter-day treasure hunters, believing Cole stashed some of the recovered "Monterrey stuff" here, pillaged the building searching for the re-buried wealth.
Courtesy Roger Conger

ceed further, he formed a partnership with a Marfa, Texas, well driller to whom he proposed drilling an offset hole to control the water that withheld his long-awaited bonanza.

Lee Bennett, a former award-winning Marfa High School history teacher, picks up the story here. She knew the well digger; his name was Dave Wease. Bennett explained that in 1926, Bill Cole approached Wease with a map and a proposition. Wease liked what he heard and formed a partnership with two other Marfa citizens, Orr Kerr, a garage-service station operator, and Lee Glascock, an insurance agent. The three agreed to join Cole in his pursuit of the Monterrey riches. Glascock was Bennett's father. Since she was about five years old at that time, her knowledge of the episode came primarily from her mother. "They got very excited," Bennett explained, "because he [Cole] said that on certain rocks there would be certain marks. And from the map, if you walked so far you would find a little cave, and from there you would find something else. And when you would walk it out, that's exactly what they found. Anyway, they found every marking called for on the map."[15]

To reinforce further Glascock's confidence in Cole's claims, once they began digging the offset hole, they encountered everything exactly as Cole had predicted. Bennett remembered that "he [Glascock] was sold on the fact that everything that they were supposed to go through, like so many feet of concrete that was made of caliche and antelope blood, they went through it at exactly the footage they were supposed to. They [also] found cement underground that had never been moved. It's hard not to believe after [finding] things like that." After drilling below the eighty-five-foot level, they installed a pump that began lowering the water level. This enabled Cole to resume work on the floor of the shaft. It was at that point, according to Dobie, that Cole jabbed "his crowbar into solid silver. A bit of silver stuck to the bar."[16]

It was that discovery that prompted Glascock to call his wife. Bennett remembered there was excitement in his voice; his message was brief. They were 100 percent sure the stuff was there and were ready to bring it to the surface. She (Mrs. Glascock) was to pack a bag for a long trip and bring along their daughter (Mrs. Bennett). She was to have everything ready and wait for the next telephone call. In order to insure complete secrecy he would only say, "Come." "He told mother," Bennett recalled, "to be prepared to drive straight through to Denver where they planned to deposit the gold and silver in the Denver mint. But the call never came. They never did get to where they were supposed to find the gold because they hit an enormous [underground] river. Like an enormous amount of water. They couldn't pump it down. It was just more than they could handle."[17]

Bennett added that many people in that area "just laugh about Bill Cole. But Bill Cole was not trying to con you. He really believed that they would find something. And the water was the only reason they failed." Pausing for a moment, she added thoughtfully, "I don't know if [the treasure] is not still there."[18]

During the next quarter century, Bill Cole's confidence in the El Muerto Springs site remained firm. He had no doubt that this was where the four outlaws buried the loot. Lack of funding and underground flooding, however, continued to haunt him. During the 1930s and the 1940s, Cole could find no solutions for these problems. The 1950s, however, ushered in a new and more sophisticated age of exploration and a new brand of treasure hunter. Technology was destined to enter the search, along with a cast of characters seldom encountered on the treasure frontier.

Herbert F. Hamilton was a University of Texas at Austin architectural student with a fascination with hot rod cars. Ed Wallace, an avid treasure hunter, operated a hot rod shop adjacent to Herbert Hamilton's fraternity house. Their interest in modified vehicles brought them together, but when the conversation turned to buried treasure they discovered they shared another common bond. "The next thing we knew we became partners," Hamilton explained. "I had three jobs when I was going to college, so I financed Ed to stay in the field and prospect while I worked and went to college. In the summertime we would go out and prospect together. It all made complete sense to us."[19]

The Big Bend country became their theater of operations. Wallace worked first in Reagan Canyon searching for the "Lost Nigger Mine," and when his initial leads played out, he began prospecting other sites. The one that appeared most promising was "Governor Murrah's Loot."[20] According to legend, when Governor J. Pendleton Murrah left Austin he took with him more than just bad memories and a broken heart. Herbert Hamilton believed he "took the entire treasury of the state of Texas out there . . . and buried it and nobody ever found it." In the process of searching for the "governor's loot," Ed Wallace met Bill Cole. This not only marked the beginning of a new association of treasure hunters, it also brought to light unknown facts about the Dobie-Cole relationship. During Dobie's original two-day interview with him, Cole "thought he was talking to a fellow treasure hunter," Hamilton explained, "and he [and Cole] had gotten all liquored up out there," and Dobie collected the data without Cole ever learning either Dobie's true identity or purpose.[21] Cole's mistake is understandable. In the mid-1920s few people outside of the University of Texas or the Texas Folklore Society knew Dobie by reputation—and certainly not an old West Texas treasure hunter. When Cole later learned that his buried treasure secrets were revealed in a best-selling publication, he was livid. What had been his semiprivate treasure site quickly became public domain for other treasure hunters.[22] According to Hamilton, Cole told Wallace that "if he ever saw him [Dobie] again he was going to kill him [for printing the story]. . . . He had promised to kill Mr. Dobie and Mr. Dobie knew it. So Dobie stayed out of his way. He never contacted Cole again after he gleaned the story from him."[23]

After meeting Cole, Valentine became Ed Wallace's base of operations. He believed the Governor Murrah site was near El Muerto Springs, and on some of their early trips he and Hamilton worked both locations. Wallace, however, spent much of his time working with Cole at El Muerto Springs. Water remained their primary obstacle. Still convinced that the treasure was theirs for the taking, Wallace and Hamilton developed an engineering concept that they felt would finally give them access to the offset shaft. That was where they believed the treasure was stored. Hamilton, the architectural student, designed a wooden raft on which they planned to mount a centrifugal pump. This was to be constructed in Austin, trucked to the treasure site, and lowered into the shaft. With this unit in place, they planned to pump the water down to a level that would give them access to the offset shaft. There remained, however, one unknown factor in the equation—the actual diameter of the shaft. The raft had to fit within the shaft in order to be lowered to water level. This necessitated another trip to the treasure site. The year was 1957. Wallace drew the assignment; two surprises awaited him. First, when he arrived in Valentine he learned that Bill Cole had died. Next, when Wallace went to the Springs to make his measurements he discovered the hole was dry. The reason for this remains unclear. The most logical explanation is that the 1950s drought lowered the water table, thereby eliminating the flow into the shaft.[24]

Cole's death offered Wallace and Hamilton an opportunity to explore another facet of the Monterrey treasure story. They believed that Cole had already recovered some of the treasure and had probably reburied it elsewhere, most likely at his home in Valentine. So they temporarily switched the center of operations from the treasure site to Bill Cole's residence, where they searched in, around, and under the house. Robert Coffee, who visited the Cole residence with Hamilton on a later trip, remembered that "when we walked up on the porch of the house, the planks had all been removed and there was a hole about seven or eight feet deep. We walked in the [abandoned] house and the floors were torn up and there was another hole straight down into the floor. So [other] treasure hunters had been in there before us."[25]

With the death of Bill Cole, the ownership of the treasure passed to Wallace, which he shared with Hamilton. They lost little time in moving ahead with the exploration. On their next trip they continued working in the main shaft, and according to Hamilton, "We dug about forty feet or so [by hand] before we got back into the water."[26] This took them to the opening of the offset shaft. And still the water prevented their entrance to where they believed the $800,000 "Monterrey loot" was stored.

With water no longer standing in the main shaft, the two young treasure hunters had to rethink their strategy. They abandoned the idea of a floating raft. But with the offset shaft still flooded, that water would have to be pumped out before the exploration could continue. Wallace thought he had a solution. He and Hamilton acquired a gasoline-powered water pump, which they lowered into the shaft. To this they attached a discharge pipe designed to carry the water to the surface. This plan appeared to be working, except Wallace had overlooked one key consideration—he made no provision to discharge the exhaust fumes. When the shaft filled with carbon monoxide fumes, Wallace became disoriented. Attempting to climb out of the shaft, he collapsed. Falling across the pump, his body shorted the ignition system, which stopped the engine. Hamilton quickly lowered a second man into the shaft to rescue Wallace. He also collapsed and fell across Wallace's body. By then, however, the fumes were no longer lethal, so the surface crew hoisted this man, still unconscious, to the surface where he was revived.

After more than an hour at the bottom of the shaft, Hamilton assumed Wallace was dead, but he was determined to bring him to the surface as soon as possible. He descended into the shaft himself, placed Wallace in a body sling, and began hoisting him to the surface. "He was almost out of the hole," Hamilton recalled, "when he fell [out of the sling]" and dropped some eighty-five feet to the bottom of the shaft. The actual cause of Wallace's death will never be known; either the carbon monoxide or the fall would have been fatal.[27]

With Wallace's death, the torch was passed to Hamilton. "Herbie kinda became the caretaker of the secret," a former associate explained. "He was the only one who knew anything about it or cared anything about it."[28] But time was working against him. News of Wallace's death alerted a new wave of treasure hunters to the possibilities at El Muerto Springs. And while Hamilton had permission from the landowners to work the site, its remoteness favored clandestine intrusion. However, with his close identity with the project, Hamilton had no intention of sharing the anticipated wealth; he immediately began making plans for his next assault on the treasure site. New technology formed the basis of his plan. Accepting water in the offset shaft as an ongoing obstacle, Hamilton believed he had at last devised a scheme to make a thorough search of the treasure chamber: send in a team of divers equipped with aqua lungs. The concept appeared valid; he began assembling a crew to make one last attempt to recover the treasure.

Membership in this unique aggregation comprised the composite skills Hamilton thought necessary to complete the mission. First to join the group was Hamilton's father-in-law, Waco businessman James R. LeBlond. LeBlond, in turn, invited former Waco mayor Roger N. Conger to join the group. Conger was an excellent choice. The future president of the Texas State Historical Association, book collector, author, and student of Texas history, Conger drew the assignment as project historian. He documented the operation in careful detail.

Hamilton chose the remaining crew members from the roster of his fraternity: Robert Coffee, a second-year architectural student; Jim Eller, an engineering student; and Don Wukasch, a premedical student. Eller emerged as the crew leader. He was the only skilled diver in the group, who offered Coffee and Wukasch a crash course in underwater skills. Lake Travis near Austin became their classroom, and according to Coffee, "we all learned to dive in a hurry, but he [Eller] damn near drowned me."[29]

When the crew headed west from Austin on that June morning in 1960, they unknowingly were accompanied in spirit by a former East Texas farm boy who, twenty-six years before, had dreamed of embarking on such an adventure. He would, some thirty-six years later, experience that drama vicariously by helping document this "scientific exploration" and fulfilling a dream from long ago. But when the crew arrived at the treasure site late that afternoon, it fell to his good friend, Roger Conger, to begin a running narrative that remains one of the venture's enduring treasures. Conger wrote:

> The location is about as picturesque as even Hollywood could desire. . . .
> The canyon of Muerto Peak . . . gets its name from its striking resemblance to the profile of a man lying on his back with arms crossed, the customary posture of muerto [death]. At the foot of Muerto Peak, trickling into the granite sand of the valley, is the celebrated watering hole of Muerto Spring. It was the water of Muerto Spring which made the canyon a camping . . . ground for the Mescalero Apaches for centuries. Their "pot holes," pecked into the granite ledges around the spring for grinding corn and mesquite beans, are still there. . . . The celebrated stagecoach line running from San Antonio, Texas, to San Diego [California] erected a station at the mouth of the canyon, and the crumbling adobe walls of the old station, and the rock corrals, still stand within 300 feet of the great hole which Bill Cole dug.[30]

When the crew began surveying the site the following morning, they found the steel framework over the shaft, erected during a previous expedition, still intact. Their first chore was to remove the gasoline engine that had caused Ed Wallace's death. Conger picks up the story here:

A group of young treasure hunters prepare for a descent into the "treasure hole"
at El Muerto Springs. They are, left to right: *Robert Coffee, Jim Eller, James R.*
Le Blond, Herbert Hamilton, and Don Wukasch. Courtesy Roger Conger

One of the trucks . . . equipped with a power winch and some 200 feet of
strong steel cable was backed into position. The cable [was then] fitted to
a "snatch block" suspended from the steel frame, and everything was set
for the first descent. Jim Eller and Bob Coffee were the two skindiver
experts, so they went down first, equipped with portable telephone
equipment through which constant communication could be maintained
with the ground crew. They soon reported that the water level was down
to a depth of approximately four feet but that the offset passage [which
supposedly held the treasure] was still flooded, and rather badly choked
with silt and fallen rock.

During the progress of this clean-out operation, the writer [Conger]
conducted an intensive exploration of the canyon walls and mountains
of the nearby region. At least six ancient Mexican or Spanish mine shafts
were located in the immediate vicinity. On the canyon side just south of
the treasure hole was located the shallow cave where legend records that
Zwing Hunt [one of the outlaws] lay for several days and recuperated
from a bullet wound [machete, according to Dobie's account] he
received at the time he and his American companions shot it out . . .
with their Mexican associates under Juan Estrada.

Among the scattered . . . granite boulders near the canyon mouth,
the writer picked up a bulging hunting coat pocket full of ancient
cartridge shells, some of them Henry or early Winchester rifles, some
Spencers, and others from the old Springfield Needle gun. Almost
without doubt this must have marked the location of the ambush [cited
in the Dobie account].

While Conger surveyed the countryside, the three divers continued working underground, removing the debris from the clogged entrance to the offset shaft. By the afternoon of the fourth day, the passage, still under water, had been sufficiently cleared and enlarged to permit the divers to enter what they referred to as the "treasure room." To the young adventurers the moment of truth was at hand. "When we ran into that [inner room] we really thought we were onto something," Coffee recalled. Poor visibility, however, restricted their search. "We had some very powerful flashlights. But this was so muddy that you could hold those flashlights right up to your mask and you could just barely see a little glow." Despite the poor visibility, they began recovering relics of past explorations: blasting wire, a miner's hard hat, plus much evidence that there had been considerable "fairly sophisticated digging down there." Working underground in a small, mud-clogged chamber differed greatly from the clear blue waters of Lake Travis. "At first it was pretty scary—pretty hair-raising," Coffee admitted, "but after we got used to it, we'd go down there every day."[31]

The chill of the water and the divers' skimpy attire greatly limited the time they could remain submerged, and the lack of visibility further hampered their investigation. "We were just feeling around the walls," Coffee explained. "What we were looking for were antelope skins, that, according to Dobie's story, the treasure was wrapped in antelope skins. And Bill Cole supposedly had gotten to those antelope skins." However, time, fatigue, mud, and equipment failure eventually doomed an effort that was launched with high expectations. Specifically, "we ran out of air [for the aqua lungs]," Hamilton explained. "And we ruined all of our diving regulators. We had three regulators and we ruined them all swimming around in the mud."[32] It, however, remained for Roger Conger to pronounce the weeklong operation's final benediction. He wrote:

[They] *had made it into the treasure room all right. No ricks of silver*
and gold bars, nor sacks of adobe dollars awaited them, however. Instead
the floor was deep—at least arm's length, probably four or five feet—

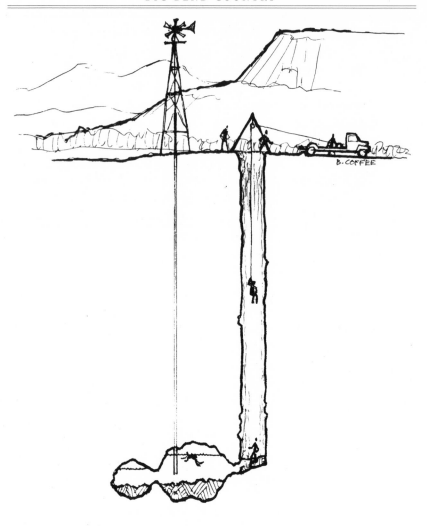

Artist's rendition of the underground workings at El Muerto Springs buried treasure site. One treasure hunter with an aqua lung explores the "treasure room," while two others, including the artist, provide support services. Courtesy Robert Coffee

with silt and caved-in rock and rubble, possibly the work of the original depositors, plus the years of erosion. . . . The condition in the treasure hole itself seemed to indicate definitely that some much heavier, power-operated dredging machinery would be needed. So after extensive deliberation, it was decided to terminate the present expedition, return to civilization, and get the plans in motion for a subsequent and final

*assault. . . . So the camp was struck, the campfire coals extinguished, and
the empty bean and tomato cans buried. As the vehicles zigzagged across
the valley . . . heat waves shimmered above the canyon floor, and the
lonely silence of the mountains seemed to settle once again about grim
Muerto Peak.*

And so Herbert Hamilton and his colleagues, as reportedly did the
four bandits before them, departed El Muerto Springs without the legendary treasure. Some three decades later as I talked with these "young"
treasure hunters, then all middle-aged, they still dream of another assault
on the El Muerto Springs treasure site. They are certain the $800,000 trove
remains exactly where the bandits placed it more than a century previous. My first impulse was to ask why, after almost a century of failed effort,
they believed the treasure was theirs for the taking. Monetary gain would
definitely not be the answer. These were high achievers; all have made
their mark on contemporary society.[33] In scanning the literature on treasure hunting, Bill Mahan, a latter-day urban treasure hunter, may have
provided a partial explanation. "Of course, buried treasure is the main
objective anytime I go out looking," he explained. "But that's only half
the fun—finding relics and uncovering long lost sites of historical interest are the great by-products. Besides, 99 times out of 100 trips you don't
find any buried treasure anyway."[34] What Mahan discovered was the treasure of the imagination, that intangible, yet romantic relationship with
the past.

I, too, had unknowingly discovered that same treasure while fantasizing about that 1937 "scientific exploration" to recover the elusive $37,500
in silver and opals. Once, when the excitement of that imagined treasure
hunt reached fever pitch, I suddenly stopped to ponder an unlikely prospect: "*What if we were to actually find the treasure?*" The idea of actually
removing the silver and opals from that imagined site seemed to negate
whatever value the treasure may have possessed. Actually removing the
treasure from its earthen depository seemed strangely to cheapen the
dream. It was not until years later that I realized the true appeal was not
the treasure itself but the lure of the unknown that had captured my imagination. The unknown can be visualized and imagined, but for a rural
teenager in the Depression years who probably never had more than three
dollars in his life, possessing $37,500 was a matter totally beyond my com-
prehension. A mind, like water, seeks its own level.

Herbert Hamilton, whose dreams of the past have kept the spirit of

El Muerto Springs alive, concurs with both Mahan and me. "A lot of it [treasure hunting] is the touch with history and the fact that this was all handled by men who came from a little different civilization than ours," he explained. "They represented what we like to think was an earlier and better element of ourselves. They had a bit of that old savage in them that we think is essential to preserve man to this point, and too much of that may be gone. Civilization wears it away." While he may find gold, silver, or jewels in some underground cache, the other treasure that Hamilton seeks is essentially antiquity. "It's the touch of history," he added. "And it's something that has almost eluded us. The better parts of it, I feel, would have gotten away from us except for Walter Prescott Webb, Frank Dobie, and some others like yourself who are trying to preserve it. It's that very elusive thing that has the great value that is so hard to grasp."[35]

Hamilton then added another dimension to this ongoing pursuit of the past—the treasure site. "Also, it is that marvelous contact with the earth; it's a very close involvement. These things tend to develop a mystic quality of their own." When asked if given a choice between searching for Jean Lafitte's gold in Barataria and the $800,000 supposedly buried at El Muerto Springs, he answered without a pause: "Monterrey loot by far." Why? "Barataria doesn't have that spiritual quality. That's just a load of loot that fell in the water. The spirits don't live there. But that other country, the Big Bend country, it has that very special quality that you don't find in many parts of the world. I have looked for it in so many places, and *there it is.*"[36]

Within the broad expanse of the Big Bend country, Hamilton had succumbed to the spell of the region's "very special quality," the accumulation of layer upon layer of Spanish, Mexican, and Anglo cultural traditions. From his almost half century vantage point, Dr. Ross A. Maxwell, first superintendent of Big Bend National Park and the definitive scholar of the region, agreed. "Folklore and legend concerning buried treasure, lost mines, Indian raids and battles, cattle rustlers, smuggling activities, and bandit raids abound," he wrote. In addition Maxwell notes that "the Big Bend retains more features of the Old West than perhaps any area of its size in the United States."[37] The ever pervasive romantic mystique of the Big Bend country provides a setting for all who seek that unique relationship with the past, be it physical, philosophical, or aesthetic. Writers, philosophers, photographers, botanists, geologists, archaeologists, anthropologists, and even treasure hunters discover in this still pristine wilderness a haven to fulfill their objectives. They, like Herbert Hamilton, may have looked for it in so many places, but "*there it is.*"

With motivation established, there remain only two unanswered questions: One, brushing legend aside, was there treasure actually buried in the eighty-five-foot shaft at El Muerto Springs? And two, if indeed there was, has it ever been recovered? The answer to the second question, of course, is contingent upon the first. Although Frank Dobie claimed that "history has no more business interfering with legend than legend has interfering with history," scholarly inquiry, however, requires historical projection. Specifically, according to legend, did the four bandits and their accomplices actually raid the mint and smelter at Monterrey and sack the cathedral? Since I am not bilingual, Laura Gutierrez-Witt, head of the Benson Latin American Library at the University of Texas at Austin, offered to aid in this phase of the research. Her report is as follows:

> *I did a quick search of some of the basic sources on the history of Monterrey, including Vito Alessio Robles' work, and I found no indication—no mention—of a raid on the cathedral of Monterrey during 1879 or 1880. I also checked about three sources on the cathedral itself, to see if there was some history of the cathedral that might mention it, [and] there was nothing there. I looked in a couple of histories of currency in Mexico and found no mention of a mint in Monterrey. I also looked in a couple of books on banditry, one written by [John] Hart and the other by [Paul] Vanderwood, to see if there was possible some mention of this incident and I couldn't find it.*[38]

Will the "Monterrey loot" ever be confirmed, denied, or recovered? *¿Quien sabe?* But appropriately it fell to Frank Dobie, courtesy of Robert Coffee, to have the last word in the matter. After returning to school that summer, Coffee thought often about his recent Big Bend adventure and "wanted to go talk to J. Frank Dobie, who I thought could shed a little more light on the tales of Bill Cole and the 'Los Muertos No Hablan' story. But I also thought he would just love to hear about my experiences searching for the 'Monterrey loot.'" So near the end of that semester, Coffee summoned sufficient courage to call the old professor at his home one night and "got him on the phone." Coffee continued, "I introduced myself and told him I had read his story about 'Los Muertos No Hablan' and wanted to come over and talk to him about it. There were a lot of questions I wanted to ask and I wanted to tell him about our trip out there looking for the treasure. At that point he stopped me—there was a long period of silence—and then he said, 'Well, I'll tell you son, I wrote those old treasure hunting stories for people to read. Nobody but fools believe them, and nobody but bigger fools like you would go out and look for them.'" Coffee added parenthetically, "That ended that conversation."[39]

But not the story. Coffee's recollection of his week at El Muerto Springs does indeed live on. Never a true believer, Coffee could, some thirty years later, still view the entire episode with a certain academic detachment. Although they found neither gold nor silver, there were, however, residual benefits. They too discovered the treasure of the imagination and for one brief moment touched the past. Almost audible were the sounds of the bandit's rifle shots echoing off the canyon walls, and as they explored the workings of the eighty-five-foot shaft, they had walked hand-in-hand with the ghosts of Zwing Hunt, Jim Hughes, Red Curly, and Doctor Neal, each young treasure hunter assuming the pseudonym of one of the bandits. In the quiet serenity of El Muerto Springs they had indeed found antiquity. To Coffee, and probably to the other treasure hunters, the expedition was its own reward. "It was an interesting seven days," he recalled. "We still talk about it years later."[40]

CHAPTER

10

W. D. Smithers

BIG BEND RENAISSANCE MAN

My friendship with Bill Smithers began on the morning of June 7, 1966. I was in Alpine, Texas, collecting material on the Terlingua quicksilver mines. Practically everyone I interviewed offered the same suggestion: "See Smithers the photographer. He's been around a long time and knows more about this country than just about anybody." Their instructions were easy to follow: "Go down Holland Avenue till you come to that little house with a yard where a lot of cactus is growing. His name is on the sign on the front porch." The inscription told only part of the story: "W. D. Smithers, Writer-Photographer."[1] I would soon learn that Smithers's skills far exceeded the scope of the inscription.

Smithers greeted me cordially. Being a university graduate student doing Big Bend research, he obviously recognized in me a kindred spirit. He responded to my questions with knowledge and enthusiasm. But as the interview progressed Smithers exhibited an annoying habit. In response to each question he would jump up from his chair, search through stacks of boxes, and return with a handful of photographs to illustrate his answers. Smithers's thoroughness was not fulfilling my needs. I sought verbal data, not visual illustration.

But as I bid Smithers farewell that June morning, I carried with me valuable research data, plus the additional information that his entire photographic collection, totaling some eight thousand prints and negatives, was for sale. I had no way of knowing that this last bit of information was probably the most valuable research data I would ever collect.

Returning to Austin, I shared this information with University of Texas history professor Joe B. Frantz, who launched negotiations with the administrative hierarchy. With minimum discussion and paper exchange—thanks largely to Chancellor Harry Ransom's astute executive assistant, Frances Hudspeth—the deal was made. The university agreed to pay Smithers his asking price: twenty thousand dollars for some eight thousand photographs, each with negatives and extensive captions, plus approximately two thousand handwritten and typed pages of manuscript material. This was in addition to various items of photographic equipment Smithers had used during his some six decades of professional activity. Needless to say, the university got a bargain. Yet both parties were equally pleased with the transaction. To Smithers, the acquisition of his collection by a single academic depository represented the fulfillment of a life's work. And during the remaining fifteen years of his life, he continued to contribute to the collection.

Smithers's work focuses primarily on northern Mexico and the Big Bend region of Texas, documenting military activities (horse cavalry, mechanized cavalry, and military aviation), civilian aviation, Mexican revolutions and border troubles, Mexican religion and folk culture, Big Bend ranching, border trading posts, and desert plant life. Through this collection of data, both visual and verbal, our knowledge of the southwestern borderlands is being greatly expanded.

In order more fully to appreciate the man and comprehend the importance of the data he compiled, it is necessary to peer behind the camera, if you will, and learn something of the man that created this collection. In any creative endeavor the artist and his cultural environment must be viewed as the singular matrix from which his product emerges. Other scholars share this view. The biographers of L. A. Huffman, the pioneer Great Plains photographer, wrote: the "background of understanding begins with the man himself and requires a knowledge of something more than the photographic techniques used in securing the pictures. One needs to know something of the man's activities outside of his profession and, above all, something of those personal peculiarities which set one individual apart from another."[2] Bill Smithers was indeed an "individual apart."

Born in San Luis Potosi, Mexico, in 1895, the son of an American mining company bookkeeper, Smithers attended a Mexican school in San Luis Potosi for three years before the family moved to San Antonio, Texas. He reentered school there, but four years later economics forced his withdrawal. His subsequent literary, scientific, and journalistic achievements, however, belie his meager formal training. During this period Smithers encountered a complex of cultural forces that greatly influenced his later work. "Our years there [in San Luis Potosi] were strongly Mexican in orientation," he wrote later. "Mexican rural enterprise surrounded us, and many of our family habits reflected not American but Mexican tradition."[3] Understandably, Mexican topics—their culture, folk culture, religion, archaeology, and revolutions—comprise approximately one half of the Smithers photographic collection. San Antonio, however, became the second great wellspring of inspiration in Smithers's photojournalism career. Its cultural environment too was strongly Latin, but other local factors, the military especially, helped shape his photographic career.

Because of his stringent upbringing, the work ethic became a dominant factor in Smithers's lifestyle. Gainfully employed at age fourteen, he first prepared layouts for displays in Schuler's Art Shop, worked at Rayburn's [Photographic] Studio, and from 1912 to 1915 served as an unpaid apprentice at Archer's Art Shop. Charles Archer, a leading San Antonio photographer, taught Smithers "to make pictures in exchange for me helping him. . . . He always stood near me to correct me if anything went wrong." Smithers's primary assignment was "to lug his tripod and glass plates for an 8-by-10-inch view camera."[4] Despite the hardships, he learned the basics of his craft. There was, however, one apprentice assignment he fondly remembered. At 9:30 on the morning of March 2, 1910, Smithers was permitted to squeeze the bulb on an 8-by-10-inch view camera that recorded Lt. Benjamin Foulois standing before a primitive-looking airplane on the Fort Sam Houston parade ground. A few minutes later the young lieutenant made history; his takeoff marked the beginning of United States military aviation. "It was on March 2, 1910, when I decided that I wanted to be a photographer and free lance news reporter," Smithers wrote later, "not to work for a newspaper and get stories where they sent me; but to go where I thought [there] was a good story."[5] Smithers fulfilled his career aspirations: he found many good stories.

Shortly after moving to San Antonio, Smithers made the acquaintance of Juan Vargas, a 114-year-old Zapotec Indian, who fascinated the youngster with stories of his century of experiences. Vargas's death in 1910, however, added a new dimension to Smithers's professional agenda. "Thinking of all the things this old man had seen that could never be recaptured," he wrote, "I began to feel that my photography should direct itself to historical and transient subjects—vanishing lifestyles, primitive cultures, old faces, and odd unconventional professions. Before my camera I wanted huts, vendors, natural majesties, clothing, tools, children, old people, [and] the ways of the border. I was to find all of these and more in the Big Bend."[6] It was the military, however, that took Smithers to his photographic promised land.

In the meantime Smithers experienced a growing dislike for the urban lifestyle; he longed for the primitive remoteness of his birthplace, a region like "San Luis' nature's great domain." When later visiting the cavalry barracks at Fort Sam Houston, the soldiers told young Smithers of just such a place—the Big Bend region of Texas. But the nine-year-old realized it would be many years before he could visit there. "I had hopes that the lower Big Bend would remain unsettled until I could go there," he wrote, "as the reports in 1906 described it as the last frontier of the Southwest."[7] In the meantime Smithers bided his time learning his craft while earning a living driving horsedrawn vehicles in San Antonio.

Smithers's skill handling draft animals led to his military affiliation, and ultimately to the Big Bend country. During the pre–World War I era when the army relied mainly on horsepower, four remount stations supplied the animals. Smithers joined the Fort Sam Houston unit in 1915; a few months later he was assigned to a civilian pack train "eagerly headed for the bandit plagued border, never without camera and note pad."[8] This assignment took Smithers throughout southwest Texas, into New Mexico, and eventually to Dublan, Chihuahua, headquarters of the Pershing punitive expedition.

Life with the pack train helped fulfill Smithers's professional objectives. "For me, the . . . pack train offered opportunities for countless fascinating observations," he wrote later, "some of which I found time to photograph. A photographer couldn't ask for better subjects than the packer and cavalry life, or the natural beauties of the Big Bend."[9] The primitive quality of the region he had longed to see fulfilled his fondest expectations. Some of Smithers's rarest photographs were taken during his civilian pack train assignment. He recorded in detail the horse cavalry's role in national defense, as well as the cavalry's early, and frequently unsuccessful experiments in mechanization. Combined, these images document an important facet of early-twentieth-century military history.

The United States' entry into World War I offered the fledgling photographer another view of the military. After enlisting in the army in April, 1917, he subsequently transferred to the United States Army Signal Corps and was assigned to Rockwell Field, located on North Island in San Diego, California. His photographic expertise garnered him this new assignment, and Smithers suddenly found himself pioneering another facet

Smithers's journalistic coverage of Big Bend military activities included the change from horsepower to mechanization. This 1918 photograph shows an Avery tractor pulling a string of nine army wagons up a winding Big Bend road. Courtesy Smithers Collection, Harry Ransom Humanities Research Center, University of Texas at Austin

of military aviation. Assigned to the aerial gunnery school at nearby Otay Mesa he taught fighter pilots aerial gunnery using the recently developed camera gun. Smithers gave the young cadets their first instruction on this new training device. "It looked just like a machine gun," he explained, "[except] right in front of the film was a glass plate with a bull's-eye engraved on it.... They would fire that [camera] gun at the target plane and [snap the shutter which] stopped the picture."[10] The developed film enabled the instructors to evaluate their students' progress.

After achieving proficiency with the camera gun, the young pilots graduated to actual machine guns that fired live ammunition at targets towed by other aircraft. This assignment also fell to Smithers. "I was in the rear cockpit [of a Curtiss JN-4 trainer] holding that cord to that tow target," he recalled. "And my instructions were that if some wild shooting took place and bullets came whizzin' by our plane, to turn the tow target loose. And I turned it loose several times. [Laughter.]" Smithers, however, found another phase of aerial gunnery practice more to his liking. "Sometimes in the late afternoon," he added, "we'd go out over the Pacific and our ship [airplane] would make a shadow on the water and they [the fighter planes] would dive and fire at the shadow."[11]

Smithers remained at Otay Mesa until February, 1919, when the Signal Corps abandoned that facility. He returned briefly to Rockwell Field, from which he transferred to Camp Marfa, where he received his discharge on April 7, 1919. Although Smithers's photographic record of his Signal Corps experience is minimal, it had a profound impact on his later career. Understandably, aviation and the Big Bend country—sometimes together, sometimes separate—form a dual theme of his subsequent work, especially during the 1920s and 1930s. This subject had lain dormant in the mind of the young photographer since that historic moment in 1910 on the Fort Sam Houston parade ground. But for the interim, the Big Bend would be Smithers's theater of operation.

Following his discharge, Smithers rejoined the civilian pack train, again serving in the Big Bend region. In retrospect, this was indeed a fortunate assignment. With the border seething with unrest, changes were in the offing, and with camera in hand he documented a tragic yet fascinating era of that region's history: Mexican bandit raids along the Rio Grande, launching the 1919 Border Air Patrol, ransoming the army flyers lost in Mexico, cavalry maneuvers, and the growth of military aviation along the United States–Mexican border.

Foreseeing the decline in the military's use of horsepower, Smithers decided it was time for a career change. With freelance photojournalism still his ultimate goal, he resigned his packer assignment on September 1, 1921, and the following morning he boarded a train for San Antonio. "The twelve hour train ride [from Marfa] was somewhat melancholy," he wrote later, "and I wondered several times if leaving was the best thing. But the Big Bend was [still] much in my future."[12] Smithers, however, quickly found success in his new San Antonio photographic shop. With money saved from his military service, he invested some one thousand dollars in equipment that included an 8-by-10-inch view camera, and a 4-by-5-inch and a 5-by-7-inch Graflex camera.[13] There was immediate demand for his services; clients included the *San Antonio Light,* the *San Antonio Express,* Underwood and Underwood news service, and Fox News Films.

With San Antonio emerging as an important military aviation center, aviation events dominated his news coverage. On September 4, 1922, he photographed Lt. James H. (Jimmy) Doolittle's arrival following his record-setting cross-country flight, the arrival of the first around-the-world flyers in 1926, while covering the activities of Katherine and Margery Stinson, who had operated a flying school for British pilots near San Antonio during World War I. It was during this period that Smithers pioneered a new facet of his profession—aerial photography. In association with Dick Hair, a former Stinson student and World War I Air Service pilot, Smithers developed a thriving aerial photography business in San Antonio. "Dick Hair flew me in one of those old Curtiss Jennys [Curtiss JN-4 Air Service trainer] to make all of those aerial pictures of San Antonio," Smithers recalled.[14]

Smithers later developed an informal working relationship with several Army Air Corps officers stationed at various San Antonio area bases. Recognizing the uniqueness of his aerial work, they offered to cooperate in his photographic coverage of military-related activities. This included flying him in Air Corps planes. It was through these associations that Smithers documented the first experiments in the use of parachutes at Kelly Field. His friend and pilot in this operation was a young lieutenant named Claire Chennault, who would later organize the legendary "Flying Tigers" and command the 14th Air Force during World War II. Gen. William L. Kennedy, another early Air Corps friend, explained later that the military system was far more casual "back then. You [a civilian] did not necessarily have to get official permission to use military aircraft to make photographs. Hell, Twining [Gen. Nathan G. Twining, later chief of the Air Force and chairman of the Joint Chiefs of Staff] flew Smithers on all sorts of photographic missions in Air Corps planes."[15] This military cooperation aided Smithers greatly in developing the aviation-related news stories he filed regularly with the *San Antonio Light*.

Smithers's early success in aerial photography resulted from a camera he designed and constructed specifically for that purpose. Discovering that the propeller blast against the fabric camera bellows greatly reduced the field of coverage, he constructed a camera with a rigid wooden cone unaffected by the wind. The commander of the photo section at Kelly Field recognized the fine quality of Smithers's work and often borrowed his negatives to print "official" Army Air Corps photographs. He once told Smithers he regretted being unable to pay him for the negatives used by the Air Corps. Smithers explained, "This was not necessary; since Brooks Field is loaning me a plane and a pilot to make them, why shouldn't I loan the photo section the negatives?" The commander, however, devised a clandestine method of compensation. With the receipt of each new allotment of photographic materials, government regulations required that the remaining inventory be destroyed. "'So in place of burning it up at the end of next quarter,'" he told Smithers, "'I'll tell the men to stack it outside the boiler room . . . and you can drive your car over and help yourself.'"[16]

To the young freelance photographer this free and seemingly unlimited supply of photographic materials was indeed a welcomed windfall. When the supply exceeded his needs, Smithers shared the photographic paper with Noah H. Rose, another San Antonio photographer, who used it to copy original prints that would later comprise the historic N. H. Rose Collection. Through Smithers's encouragement Rose expanded his collection of historical photographs to include famous early Texans—military heroes, cattlemen, gun fighters, train robbers, bank robbers, other outlaws, and Indian chiefs. Smithers explained that he would borrow what he considered rare and unique photographs, give them to Rose to copy, and then return the originals to the owners.

Smithers is credited with locating the best known and probably the most reproduced photograph in the Rose Collection—Judge Roy Bean holding court on the porch of his Jersey Lilly saloon in Langtry, Texas. McArthur C. Ragsdale, the pioneer West Texas photographer, recorded the original image. However, after Smithers delivered the print to Rose, and before making his copy, Rose, according to Smithers, typed a new caption bearing his name, which he pasted over Ragsdale's inscription. The Pearl Brewing Company of San Antonio later used that image in developing one of the company's most successful and long-running advertising campaigns.[17]

In addition to news reporting, Smithers developed a thriving commercial photographic business. Motion picture companies scheduling location filming in the San Antonio area engaged the ex-cavalry packer to photo-document set design and produce publicity stills for their films. Assignments included *Rough Riders* in 1926 and *Wings* the following year. The latter, a World War I aviation saga starring Clara Bow, Buddy Rogers, and Gary Cooper, won the first Academy of Motion Picture Arts and Sciences award.

Finding show business to his liking, Smithers also developed several circus accounts by producing publicity photographs for the performers. Ringling Bros. and Barnum & Bailey, Sells Floto, Al G. Barnes, Gentry Brothers, Hagenbeck and Wallace, and Clyde Beatty all used his services. Traveling with the shows throughout Texas in his 1920 Dodge Roadster, Smithers made the action exposures during performances and, lacking darkroom facilities, rushed back to his hotel room to develop the film and print the images before daylight. Even in the mid-1920s economy, he considered this work very profitable. "He sold 8 x 10 [inch] prints for 50¢ each, 5 x 7 for 25¢ and 100 postcards for $3," one writer reported. "Postcards sold wholesale were $1.50 for 100."[18]

Ever vigilant for "historical and transient subjects," Smithers attended many reunions of elderly citizens in the San Antonio area. At one such gathering he met centenarian Amasa Clark, a Mexican War veteran who, in late 1859, joined the United States War Department's military camel experiment. Clark reminisced at great length with Smithers, explaining that he remained with the project fourteen months, helping care for thirty-two dromedaries imported to the United States for the military experiment.[19]

As Smithers's San Antonio photographic business prospered, he fell victim to his own success. "My new photography shop was so successful; I couldn't break away," he recalled. "I found it impossible to get away to the Big Bend as regularly as I wished."[20] By 1922, however, Smithers was scheduling periodic news-gathering forays into that region, primarily to cover military activities. As the decade progressed, however, his news coverage switched from the military to the border patrol. Prohibition had created a new industry along the United States–Mexico border—bootlegging. Mexican smugglers fording the Rio Grande with their contraband liquor provided some of the decade's more exciting news stories. Smithers soon discovered a frustrating dichotomy in his coverage of these border depredations; his friendship with the Texas Rangers and customs officials, necessary to achieve on-the-spot coverage, alienated the Mexican people, whose folkways and native culture were topics Smithers planned to explore in the future. "The popular suspicion," he wrote later, "was that I was an informer for the Texas Rangers or the U.S. Customs, or that I was some sort of prohibition officer."[21] Thus, in the regional vernacular, he was forced to tread a narrow path.

To the Mexicans living along the Rio Grande, Smithers represented a strange phenomenon. He appeared at their homes periodically, never carried a gun, was bilingual, was always alone, and came bearing his ever-present camera. To those avoiding the law, photographs could be damning evidence. However, in order to establish his credibility with the Mexican people, Smithers launched his own personal relations campaign; honesty and openness helped garner the Mexicans' confidence. To prove that he was only a photographer (*el fotógrafo*) and journalist (*escripto*), at each

home he visited he displayed every item he carried in his Dodge Roadster: bedroll, provisions, clothes, newspapers, camera, and film. But it was
through the Mexican children that Smithers finally gained acceptance.
He took them riding in his car, the only car many had ever seen; but most
important, he made their pictures. "I loved the children as photo subjects," he explained, "and they loved to receive pictures of themselves. It
was a real delight to give the parents photographs of their sons and daughters cuddling a favorite pet goat, burro, or puppy."[22]

The creditability Smithers gained through human kindness was subsequently threatened by his professional ingenuity. Frustrated by the two-
day drive back to San Antonio to file his news stories, he proposed to Sam
Woolford, *San Antonio Light* feature editor, using carrier pigeons to deliver his field copy to the newspaper. Woolford agreed, and at 6:45 on Saturday morning, November 28, 1928, Alpine Chamber of Commerce
president Dr. Joel Wright released the first bird. The blue-checked cock
arrived in San Antonio at 5:00 P.M. the same day, bearing a canister containing Smithers's news story. Both Smithers and the bird made the front
page in the Sunday edition of the *San Antonio Light*. "Special by Carrier
Pigeon" became a regular feature; frequently the pigeon's picture—but
not Smithers's—appeared with the article.[23]

Although the news-bearing pigeons proved to be great time savers,
launching them from various Big Bend sites prompted the Mexican people
to again regard Smithers with dark suspicion. Castolon merchant Wayne
Cartledge issued the first warning; his life could be in danger. Cartledge
said the Mexicans were *muy rabioso* (very mad); they thought the messenger pigeons were launched to inform authorities about liquor smuggling along the Rio Grande. He further advised Smithers not to continue
his customary route along the Rio Grande and not to camp out alone in
that area as someone "might take a shot at me." Smithers, however, disagreed, electing instead "to continue my regular route, make all the usual
stops and explain everything." From house to house—to the Domingues,
the Holguins, the Baizas—he displayed copies of the newspaper and read
them his news stories delivered by the carrier pigeons. While most understood, others remained suspicious. He continued on to Glenn Springs
where he encountered his most steadfast defender, a fourteen-year-old
orphan girl, Marie Landrom. Smithers reported:

> As expected, little Marie did the most to help clear me of the false reports
> that everybody in Glenn Springs had been hearing for nearly a month. . .

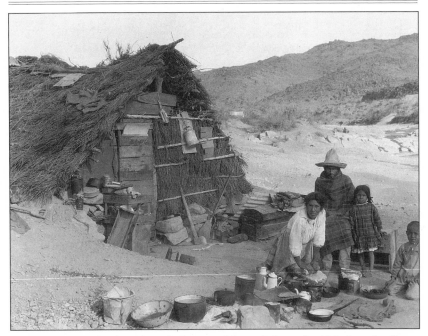

Much of Smithers's Big Bend photographic work focused on Mexican family life. This candelilla wax worker and his family pose in front of their home at Glenn Springs in 1917. The wife is making "masa," a corn batter to make tortillas. One can be seen cooking over the fire. Courtesy Smithers Collection, Harry Ransom Humanities Research Center, University of Texas at Austin

. She spoke English and Spanish, so when she saw all six stories in the papers, she went to each Mexican home and read them in Spanish. . . . They [the Mexicans] again had faith in me and [this] proved that they did not doubt my use of pigeons. They became very interested and curious, [and] asked many questions about [the carrier pigeons]. At first they thought they could go any place I sent them. One [Mexican even] asked [me] to send a message to a relative at Monclova, Mexico.[24]

Smithers's Big Bend news gathering excursions continued throughout most of the 1920s, but a chance meeting with Elmo and Ada Johnson at Castolon in May, 1928, helped alter the course of his professional career. The Johnsons were fascinated with the itinerant photojournalist. Smithers was equally intrigued with the two modern pioneers who had recently established a farm, ranch, and trading post at that remote outpost, located some fifteen miles downriver from Castolon. Accepting the Johnsons' invitation, he accompanied them to their new home. Seeing that riverside setting, he foresaw the fulfillment of a lifelong dream to live permanently in a region "like San Luis' nature's great domain" and conduct an in-depth study into the life and culture of the Mexican people. But considering his San Antonio commitments, Smithers realized those plans would have to be delayed. There were, however, impending factors he could not foresee that would unexpectedly bring that scenario to almost immediate fruition.

Continuing his monthly news-gathering trips to the Big Bend, Smithers arrived at Castolon on the morning of April 12, 1929, unaware that his most sensational story awaited his coverage. He learned from border patrolmen that a band of renegade Mexican soldiers from the Escobar Rebellion had raided Elmo Johnson's trading post the night before. Smithers proceeded immediately to that outpost, interviewed the Johnsons, made some photographs, and rushed back to San Antonio to file his story. En route a devious plan began to take shape in his mind; the trading post raid seemed to forecast a return to an earlier era of border banditry.[25] If he could persuade the Army Air Corps to establish an emergency landing field in the Big Bend to protect the ranches and trading posts, he would also have access to military aircraft to shoot aerial photographs of some of the Southwest's most spectacular scenery.

After filing his story with the *San Antonio Light*, Smithers went directly to Fort Sam Houston where he presented his proposal to an old Air Corps friend, Col. Arthur G. Fisher. Surprisingly, the 8th Corps Area air officer accepted Smithers's plan, acknowledging that the Air Corps was already considering establishing a landing field in that area. When Smithers offered the use of Johnson's ranch (with Johnson's prearranged approval), the deal was made. On April 21, 1929, the first airplane landed at the newly designated Big Bend airfield; Smithers was there to welcome the pilot, Lt. Thad Foster, another old Air Corps friend. Although the facility never fulfilled its strategic mission—there were no subsequent border raids—the site, nevertheless, became a popular destination for United States Army Air Corps pilots for the next fourteen years.[26]

Smithers subsequently closed his San Antonio studio and moved his operation to the Johnson ranch; his first chore was to construct a darkroom. With the aid of Elmo Johnson and a Mexican laborer, he designed and constructed a half-dugout adobe darkroom. In lieu of a controlled light source—as well as running water and refrigeration—Smithers

*U.S. Army Air Corps Lt. Hugh A. ("Lefty") Parker and Elmo Johnson visit
one of Johnson's goat camps near the Rio Grande. Because of his freelance
photographic work with the Air Corps, W. D. Smithers was largely responsible
for the establishment of the emergency landing field on the Johnson Ranch.
Courtesy Smithers Collection, Harry Ransom Humanities Research Center,
University of Texas at Austin*

adapted his photographic technique to the setting. He explained: "At Johnson's I built an adobe building for a darkroom, but by an error I made in
the roof, I had to make the enlarger into a horizontal model. A hole was
made in the north wall, [the] enlarger was set against the hole and adobe
mud was filled in between the enlarger and wall to make it light tight. . . .
The daylight for exposures was perfect, but the horizontal enlarger seemed
clumsy compared to the vertical."[27]

Using this changing light source, Smithers learned through experi-
mentation to vary the exposure time in accordance with the time of day.
The military soon learned of this unique facility and began sharing enlarger time with Smithers. While mapping the United States–Mexican
border, the Army Air Corps photographic teams frequently used Smithers's
riverside darkroom to field test their work, as did the National Guard re-
connaissance units that also landed at the Big Bend airfield. Smithers ex-

plained later that, in appreciation of his cooperation, "they would load up their planes with [government issue] photographic supplies for my darkroom," including "rolls of enlarging paper 36 inches wide and 100 inches long" which he used in compiling a pictorial history of the lower Big Bend area.[28]

Smithers felt he produced some of his best work in this primitive facility. For about two years he enjoyed the best of two worlds, photographically. Working from his riverside studio, Smithers developed a close rapport with the Mexican people still living in the most primitive conditions. He spoke their language, learned their names, and shared their folk secrets as did few people outside their native culture. Smithers claimed that in a year he had been a guest at every home in Mexico within fifty miles of the Johnsons. His pictorial studies of the people, their dwellings, their lifestyle, and their folkways reveal the fulfillment of a professional commitment inspired by his childhood friendship with Juan Vargas. And through the cooperation of the Army Air Corps, Smithers was able to add a new dimension to man's view of one of America's last frontiers.

Smithers's fascination with Mexican primitive culture stemmed from his early childhood in San Luis Potosi, where Pancho, his adolescent role model, introduced him to the mysteries of *curanderos*, folk healers, and *avisadores*, message senders. "My two years with Pancho," Smithers wrote, "are still vivid, and I appreciate them now as having been instrumental in my adult decisions to return, work, and linger in and around Mexico for much of my life. . . . It seems I was the only [member of my family] truly curious about the Mexican people, and mine was an insatiable curiosity."[29] And now living in a remote and predominantly Mexican community where the inhabitants still practiced the folkways of their ancestors, Smithers could at last embark on his study of what would soon be a disappearing lifestyle. With camera and notepad always in hand, he was destined to learn much about the practice of *curanderismo;* his *avisadores* investigation was less productive.

Curanderos, the men, and *curanderas,* the women, were Mexican folk healers who practiced their craft solely for the benefit of their fellow man. Serving as doctor, nurse, and pharmacist, compounding their own medicines from native plants and herbs, "they charged no fee for what they did for the patient," Smithers wrote, "and beside the treatment they often fed them [the patients] for several days while they were in their care."[30] Living in total isolation, the *curanderos* had, over the centuries, discovered that the desert—"nature's pharmacy"—held a rich storehouse of medici-

Smithers moved to the Big Bend to study and photograph the disappearing primitive culture of the Mexican people. He found children, especially their relationship with domestic animals, particularly appealing. He notes the two Holguin children are "the burrito's [small burro] tutor, not for lessons about work, but in kindness and amicability between people and the beast of burden." Courtesy Smithers Collection, Harry Ransom Humanities Research Center, University of Texas at Austin

nal benefits. For example, for heart ailments they prescribed two teaspoons of pulverized deer antlers dissolved in a half cup of blood drawn from a freshly killed deer. A poultice of ground sunflower seeds relieved the swelling of a sprained ankle, while a brew made from San Sipriana (sagebrush), when taken over a prescribed period, cured diabetes. For those suffering from kidney or liver disorders, they prepared a potion made from the popotillo (*Ephreda Trifurca*) or kidney weed, and for women having "female disorders" or wanting an abortion, diamiana (Chrysactinea Mexicana) was the herb of choice. And for patients needing a blood tonic, the *curanderos* recommended they devour a specially baked Chaparral bird. "The list of plants that were used by the *Curanderos* is a long one," Smithers adds, "and they knew exactly what was best for each ailment and [in] what strength to make it up."[31]

During Smithers's tenure at Johnson's ranch, he not only collected much data on the methods of materials of *curanderismo* but also became the beneficiary of their care on three different occasions. A *curandera* ministered to him when he had *Telfo* (typhoid fever), yellow jaundice, and

Smithers informal portraiture recorded not only interesting facial expressions, but wearing apparel and disappearing folk cultures as well. He saw "El Viejo" (old man) as "a typical type of Mexican that was an authentic curandero, avisador *and* chivero*." Courtesy Smithers Collection, Harry Ransom Humanities Research Center, University of Texas at Austin*

sunstroke (*pico el sol*). The latter was probably his most critical illness; he remembered Juana Ramirez, a goat herder's wife, as his angel of mercy.

In June, 1930, learning that a neighbor, a Mrs. Harloe, had been accidentally shot, Smithers grabbed a medical kit and began a brisk walk —sometimes a trot—to their home, located some three miles from the Johnsons. With the temperature around 110°, he quickly felt the discomfort of the midday sun. Arriving at the Harloe residence, Smithers discovered that some key items had been omitted from the medical kit. He immediately began a return trek to the trading post, again walking at an exceptionally fast pace. En route, exhausted from the heat, aridity, and exertion, Smithers became weak, nauseated, and dizzy; he finally collapsed, unconscious. Elmo Johnson found him later, but instead of taking him back to the trading post, he decided this was a case for Juana. In the shade beside her house, the *curandera* first prepared a bed of goat skins and then sent the children to gather leaves from a wild tobacco plant (*Hojo de Igera*). She next prepared a mixture of ground sunflower seed and cotton-seed oil, which she spread on the leaves. These were then placed on Smithers's forehead and temple. "Within a few minutes after she applied the leaves I felt some relief," he remembered. She applied fresh poultices every half hour. Although weak from the stroke and sore from the fall, he realized by late afternoon that the crisis had passed.[32]

Smithers returned the following morning for a second treatment. This consisted of an application of a shampoo-like substance made from boiled sunflower seed, which the *curandera* poured over his head from his neck to his brow. Following a second treatment in about thirty minutes, she then asked her patient to sit erect while she massaged his scalp with the same preparation. That completed the treatment. Although still weak, Smithers realized that he had just survived one of the desert's most frightening and sometimes fatal experiences—sunstroke. In retrospect, he compared Juana's procedures with that followed by the military when cavalrymen experienced similar attacks. "I think it was from three to five days that they were on the 'sick list,'" he explained. "Mine was 24 hours."[33]

This experience had a profound effect on Smithers and his views of the *curanderos*. In his later writings he cites both biblical and historical sources to affirm his belief in the native healers. A prime example is aloe vera, both the scientific and common name for a plant that, according to Smithers, was "known to have been used to treat human ills for more than 3,000 years. From the earliest written history," he continued, "we find references to Aloe Vera. One such in John: 19–39, in the Bible: 'Nicodemus also, who had first come to him at night, came bringing a mixture of myrrh and aloe about a hundred pounds weight.'"[34] Had Smithers lived another two decades he would have relished academia's endorsement of "nature's pharmacy." In the mid-1990s, Texas anthropologists and herbalists launched a joint effort, petitioning the United States Food and Drug Administration to give recognition to native medicines.[35]

In his research on the *avisadores* (message senders), Smithers experienced the same frustration as the proverbial husband who knew his wife is having an affair with a neighbor, but since neither would admit their involvement, proof was never forthcoming. Because he was a friend and *compadre* of the Mexican people, they frequently accommodated him by dispatching personal *avisos,* yet his attempts to penetrate the secrecy of the "Mexican grapevine" yielded little. He had absolute proof that it existed, yet he could learn nothing of its mechanism. This he understood. Even Pancho, his childhood friend, shared many ethnic secrets, but "it was not intended that I learn all the facts of either craft [*curanderismo* and *avisos*]," Smithers explained. "This is an example of how the Mexicans prevented anyone but one of their kin or clan to gain knowledge of some of their parental teachings."[36] Life along the border did, however, evolve as an ongoing learning experience for *el fotógrafo.* And while he never learned the basics of this primitive method of communication, he did indeed become its beneficiary, thereby confirming its existence.

An *aviso* dispatched by Alejandro Garcia in the spring of 1932, for example, enabled Smithers to complete a difficult wildlife photographic assignment in record time. His commission required that he photograph a specific number of birds' nests in their original location, each representing a species unique to the Big Bend area. Garcia's *aviso,* enlisting the aid of boys ten to fourteen years old, explained that the nests were not to be disturbed, and must be located within three to four miles of the Rio Grande. The *aviso* stated further that Smithers would reward each finder with a Boy Scout knife, and if the nests were extremely rare, an additional monetary bonus awaited them. When the response exceeded Smithers's expectations, Garcia dispatched a supplementary *aviso,* canceling the original request. Viewing that experience in retrospect, Smithers concluded: "It was clear to me that much could be said in *aviso* communication—its two way signaling a simulation of spoken dialogue, with messages that could be corrected or amended. Even reprimands could be given."[37]

Other than basic methodology—sunlight reflected with a mirror or shiny object—and confirming beyond a doubt that the system worked, Smithers learned little of the *avisador's* craft. On one occasion he reported seeing a flashing light on a distant hilltop as a contingent of border patrolmen approached a well-known smuggler's river crossing. He assumed the *avisadore* was dispatching a warning message to those living in that immediate area. Smithers also learned that Juana Ramirez, his elderly *curandera,* was also a skilled *avisadora.* And while he never discussed the matter with her, there always appeared a bulging object in her dress pocket that he assumed was a mirror. "She was the only woman I knew who carried a mirror," Smithers wrote, "a fact supporting my conclusion that most *aviso* senders were men, who were never without their pocket mirrors."[38]

While still living at the Johnson trading post, Smithers began corresponding with an official at the Smithsonian Institute about a projected photographic expedition to northern Mexico to record images of pre–Columbian archeological ruins. When negotiations reached the conference stage, he traveled to Washington to finalize plans for the expedition. Disappointment, however, awaited his arrival; federal appropriations had been cut and the project canceled. Smithers returned to Texas via a Depression-enforced yearlong stopover in St. Louis, where he survived by taking odd jobs, including a few freelance assignments with the *St. Louis Post-Dispatch*. He returned to the Johnsons in 1933, remained there a few months, but was soon offered a new photographic challenge.

When the General Electric Company failed to get a satisfactory operational photograph of the huge McDonald Observatory telescope, the responsibility of completing the project fell to University of Texas director of public relations Arthur L. Brandon. On someone's recommendation, Brandon offered the assignment to Smithers, who embarked immediately for the Mount Locke construction site to survey the installation. He concluded that the desired perspective could be achieved only by lying on his back on the floor of the observatory and shooting upward with his hand-held, homemade camera. (Others had attempted the assignment with a tripod-mounted camera.) Once he achieved the desired exposures, Smithers faced another challenge: developing the negatives and printing the images without a darkroom. Again he was forced to improvise. With the help of construction workers, he converted a gravel pit into what he referred to as his "hole-in-the-ground" darkroom; for chemical trays, the carpenters built wooden frames that Smithers covered with oilcloth. Also lacking electricity as a light source for his enlarger, he repeated the technique he used in his dugout darkroom at Johnson's trading post—controlled sunlight. "The [observatory] darkroom, which Smithers considered the best he ever used, had the capacity for making enlargements up to 30 x 40 inches," one writer reported. As a tribute to his skill and ingenuity, the General Electric Company used a Smithers McDonald Observatory photograph on the company's 1942 calendar.[39]

After completing the observatory assignment in late 1934, Smithers moved his base of operations to El Paso, where he began producing and marketing postcards and lantern slides. This proved to be only temporary.

The following year the United States Immigration and Naturalization Service offered him another difficult assignment. The service commissioned Smithers to photograph and develop maps of various landmarks along the United States–Mexican border between the Gulf of Mexico and the Pacific Ocean. Subjects included towns, bridges, roads, canyons, streams, mountains, geological formations, and all of the 258 boundary markers. The remoteness of many markers forced him to walk much of the 1,900 miles, carrying the equipment necessary to complete the assignment. En route, he encountered vast climatic extremes. In the mountains west of El Centro, California, "I had to wear skis and dig this monument, Number 247, [out of snow] to make a picture of it," he recalled. "An hour later I was on the hot desert [floor] again, traveling west on the boundary line to Monument 258, right on the coast." The almost four-month assignment yielded nearly two thousand photographs, which he delivered to the United States Immigration and Naturalization Service.[40]

The lure of the Big Bend country, however, remained with Smithers. In 1935, he moved to the Grandview Courts in Alpine, and a year later opened a shop at 207 East Holland Drive, where he resumed production of postcards and lantern slides. Dr. W. H. Morelock, then president of Sul Ross State College in Alpine, who used Smithers's lantern slides in his classes, encouraged him to expand production. He explained that since other colleges and universities were beginning to employ projected visuals in both the humanities and the physical sciences, a ready market awaited this product. Smithers liked the idea and launched a well-organized, if unusual, production and distribution program of educational lantern slides. After transferring images from his black-and-white negatives to 3¼-by-4-inch glass plates, he painstakingly hand-colored each slide in accordance with educational requirements. Smithers explained the marketing process as follows:

> I'd make up a set of 100 slides and make a wooden box [for shipping] and [then] decide on some professor or dean around the country [to send them to]. I'd get the names from the president of the old School of Mines [The University of Texas at El Paso] . . . and [would] then ship them to him by express and then I'd write him a letter and ask him to run the slides through a projector . . . "and if you can use them for the university you can buy them for $50. If you can't use them send them back to me by express collect." I never got one set back, not a one.[41]

Smithers's lantern slides quickly gained him international recognition. German professor Dr. Heinrich Frick, an authority on religious history at the University of Marburg, learned of Smithers's work through the National Geographic Society, and began a brisk correspondence with the Alpine-based photographer. Dr. Frick was deeply interested in obtaining images of Mexican religious shrines and proposed that they begin planning a photographic research mission to sites in northern Mexico. Smithers relished the idea. This was essentially an extension of the earlier program of work he had pursued with Mexican folk culture along the Rio Grande. He could, however, foresee certain technical and cultural obstacles. First, from his recent experiences, he knew the Mexican people were *tenian miedo* (very afraid) of cameras and having their photographs taken; and second, since much of the projected work would be interior low-light exposures in churches and cathedrals, the use of flash powder and flash bulbs would likely be forbidden. Again *el fotógrafo* was forced to improvise, or at least adapt his equipment to the assignment that lay ahead. The result: a new Smithers-designed camera "that would take indoor pictures without the use of [artificial] light," wrote historian Dudley R. Dobie. "The only manufactured items in this homemade camera are the lenses and shutters; all other parts were made by W. D. in machine shops and with his own woodworking tools."[42]

In December, 1935, Smithers and his German colleague embarked for Mexico via Juarez, Chihuahua City, Guanajuato, and eventually Mexico City. Although the unsettled political climate in Europe forced Dr. Frick to abandon the expedition after eight days, Smithers remained in Mexico and completed the mission. Even in the depressed economy of the mid-1930s, Smithers's compensation for this assignment appears minimal: $750 for 1,500 lantern slides, 25 cents each for an undetermined number of 8-by-10-inch enlargements, his railroad fare, plus $300 for expenses. The project, nonetheless, yielded some 3,000 photographs in the following categories: Mexican archaeology (1,015), Spanish missions (219), Mexican religion (1,629), and rural religion (110). When considering that some of the religious structures no longer exist and that photographs are no longer permitted in many shrines, the cultural and historical value of this work is multiplied manifold.[43]

The development of commercial color film in the late 1930s forced Smithers to terminate lantern slide production. By that time, however, he had already adapted the materials and the process to another commercial product that proved to be even more profitable—photographic lamp shades. Smithers fabricated the prototypes by gluing four glass plates together, which were then mounted on a wire frame. This formed a transparent lamp shade through which four separate scenes could be viewed. Since these were heavy, fragile, and time-consuming to construct, Smithers began searching for alternative materials. He first sent the glass panels to the Eastman Kodak Company, suggesting that they develop a transparent photographic material, similar to X-ray film, but yielding a positive image that could be hand-colored. The company responded that the concept was indeed valid, but since they felt the product would have a limited market, they rejected Smithers's proposal. He turned next to the Defender Corporation, and that company, unlike Kodak, saw the commercial potential of his proposal and soon began producing Adalux, a transparent material upon which photographic enlargements could be projected. At last he had the product to launch a new enterprise. In early 1937, he opened the Photo Color Lamp Shade Shop, "Home of the Photo Color Lamp Shade," at a new location at 116 North Fifth Street in Alpine. "The Photo shades were a tremendous success after a few days," Smithers recalled, "as the shades advertised themselves."[44]

Smithers's production line began at two o'clock each morning in his kitchen-darkroom. During the early morning darkness he began printing photographic panels sufficient to produce one hundred lamp shades. When his two college-student employees arrived at eight o'clock the panels were ready to color and assemble. (The four panels were laced on a wire shade frame.) As orders for the unique product grew, so did the size of Smithers's production staff. With fourteen employees, Smithers became the largest private employer in Alpine. His staff received $1.25 an hour when the minimum wage was 75 cents. The company produced shades in six sizes, from 5¾ inches to 10½ inches in height; prices ranged from $2.50 to $5.50. Customers could choose from 120 models, each containing four separate scenes on a single theme.[45]

Smithers's client base eventually included both national and international accounts, and when orders exceeded his shop's production capacity he encouraged others to establish businesses of their own. He felt husband-and-wife teams were ideal; men were more adept at developing and printing the photographic panels, while women were usually more efficient at coloring and assembling the shades. Smithers, however, never applied for a patent, and eventually one of his protégés was sued by a competing Arizona firm marketing a similar patented product. When the plaintiff filed the suit in federal court in Phoenix, Arizona, Smithers appeared as a surprise witness for the defense. The plaintiff's attorney was unprepared for Smithers's testimony. When asked to define his position in the proceeding, Smithers startled the attorney by explaining "how long I had been making [the lamp shades]. One of the first ones I made [was] for President Roosevelt. I had a [dated] letter from Mrs. Roosevelt. . . . I had a lot of letters from people around the country. I didn't want no patent myself. I studied up on the patent laws when I first made the things and I found out you had to apply for a patent before you put the product on the market." Smithers testimony sealed the outcome: the plaintiff lost.[46]

Smithers produced the Photo Color Lamp Shades for some twenty-five years. "In 1960, I made the last Photo Color Lamp Shade," he explained, "but today, twelve years later, many letters are received from all parts of the United States requesting a shade."[47] Escalating material costs had gradually eliminated the margin of profit. In retrospect, closing the shop appears as a watershed event in Smithers's life; with no fixed income save his small military pension, this decision seemed to portend a vague and uncertain future.

In his late sixties, Smithers faced the sobering reality that he, at last, was living on the down side of life. His eyesight was failing and he was no longer able to drive an automobile; younger journalists began receiving Big Bend freelance news assignments he once fulfilled. Other than an occasional story for the *El Paso Herald-Post* and infrequent articles in the *Cavalry Journal* and the *Western Horseman,* Smithers did little writing. His interest in aviation and aerial photography did, however, endure. On March 17, 1966, the *Alpine Avalanche* reported: "Bill Smithers has accomplished something that no other person in the world can equal. Bill is completing his 53rd year of aerial photography! He first started shooting pictures from airplanes over San Antonio in April, 1913, and he took his latest aerial picture Monday morning of this week. And, believe it or not, he took his first color pictures on that same flight. . . . Bill says in all his 53 years of photography he just never got around to shooting color before."[48]

Smithers's historic flight occurred some three months before our first meeting on June 7, 1966. I had no way of knowing that one day that meeting might also be considered somewhat historic, especially in view of the ensuing chain of events. When the University of Texas acquired the entire Smithers collection the following year, that transaction released into the channels of knowledge the greatest single source of historical documentation on the Big Bend country of Texas. But for Bill Smithers, it was something more, much more; specifically, a new lease on life. When I

Smithers, a pioneer aerial photographer, displays the camera he designed and constructed especially for aerial work. The rigid bellows were unaffected by the airplane's propeller blast.

handed him his first partial payment check in December, 1967, I asked him: "Bill, this is probably the most money you have ever had at one time in your life. Are you going to retire?" He responded emphatically: "Heck no! I'm going to buy me a new camera."

And he did indeed purchase a new twin lens reflex camera, but that was merely a gesture of delayed self-indulgence. To Smithers that transaction was both a symbol of accomplishment and a source of unprecedented personal pride. The product of a life's work was going into the archives of one of the nation's major universities, and it would forever bear the creator's name—the Smithers Collection.

Smithers felt there was still much left to be done. For the next three years he worked almost constantly preparing the various sections of the collection for transfer to Austin. The agreement with the university provided that a negative accompany each 8-by-10-inch print, and since some images were still on glass plates, this meant transferring these to permanent film stock. He also rewrote many photo captions and made what he considered substantive additions to the some two thousand pages of original manuscript. "His days began before sunrise in his kitchen darkroom," Mary Cook wrote. "Later in the day he spent writing out captions. A woman in Alpine typed the captions which were then attached to both negatives and prints by a high school student who worked on Saturdays." He paid for these services with money from his monthly pension.[49] Smithers also felt the Mexican religion and archaeology collections required additional scenes. On September 9, 1968, he wrote that he planned "to make a trip to Mexico to make the last of the needed pictures, also to have a short vacation I need. I have worked seven days each week for almost a year without a day off."[50] He also visited the El Paso Public and University of Texas at El Paso libraries to gather supplementary data on Big Bend military activities, specifically, testimony given before the [Senator Albert B.] Fall Committee.

When the last shipment of the collection reached the University in October, 1969, Joe Coltharp, curator of photography, had already begun the arduous task of filing and cataloging the material. Once the Humanities Research Center administrative staff (now the Harry Ransom Research Center) realized the enormity of the collection, they began making plans for a public exhibition of the photographic material. That event coincided with the Fifth Annual Meeting of the Collectors' Institute, a private organization of collectors of library materials. Held in the University of Texas Undergraduate Library auditorium on November 18, 1972, the meeting honored Smithers with a showing of his work. Four Big Bend scholars, Dr. Ross Maxwell, Hallie Stillwell, Virginia Madison, and I, addressed the meeting, with additional comments by Sam Woolford, Smithers's former feature editor at the *San Antonio Light,* and Joe Coltharp, curator of the collection.[51] Smithers narrated a presentation of some fifty photographic slides of his work. The event also marked Smithers's first visit to the university campus and the Humanities Research Center that housed his collection. Although typically reserved in his response, he was noticeably moved by the day's events, a public acknowledgement of his life achievement.

The November 18, 1972, meeting represented unquestionably the apogee of Smithers's entire career. He was seventy-seven years old when accorded that honor, an event that also marked the beginning a period of renewed literary activity. He was already working on a manuscript published by Madrona Press in 1976 as *Chronicles of the Big Bend: A Photographic Memoir of Life on the Border.* Smithers invited me to write the foreword. This was also the year Texas A&M University Press published my doctoral dissertation, *Quicksilver: Terlingua and the Chisos Mining Company*, the research project that first brought us together. "Glad that your book on the Chisos Mine will be published," he wrote on June 22, 1975. "You worked hard and long on it."[52]

Later that year I visited Smithers at his new residence in El Paso to discuss a projected history of military aviation activities along the United States–Mexican border. With the airfield at Johnson's ranch as the center-piece of the study, I solicited his cooperation. He was pleased to learn of the project, but before we talked he insisted on dinner, his favorite—Mexican food. Eighty years old and appearing in robust health, he joined me on a vigorous three-mile walk across town to his choice purveyor of *comida sabrosa*. Finding it closed, another two-mile-trek took us to an alternate facility. Breathless and twenty years his junior, I discovered mine was no match for his apparent boundless energy. After dinner and another long walk to the Del Norte Hotel, we talked long into the night about his unofficial Air Corps affiliation at Johnson's ranch. His help proved in-valuable. Some two hours later, the interview complete, he refused my offer to call a cab; said he "thought he needed the walk."

With the combined incomes from the sale of his collection, his social security, and military pension, Smithers was free to devote his time to research and writing. "Sure have been working hard on the big [uni-dentified] manuscript," he wrote. "Now have 177 typed pages, and about 40 to go."[53] Failing eyesight, however, seemed more of an annoyance than an impediment. Still he forged ahead. On July 18, 1977, he explained that he was "working on another story that should have been done long ago. It is about the Texas Rangers, the U.S. Mounted Custom[s] Patrol, and the U.S. Immigration. . . . I now have 17 p[ages] written and I have started making a map of the northwest corner of the Big Bend showing where Custom[s] Officer Joe Sitters and Ranger Eugene Hulen were killed in 1915." This letter ended optimistically: "My new glasses are much better than what I had and I can write more hours with them."[54]

As work progressed on my aviation manuscript our correspondence became more frequent. During 1978, I received nine lengthy letters from Smithers, all containing valuable data on Big Bend aviation activity. This obviously was a book that he would have wanted to write had he had access to the sources, but working with me gave him a great sense of plea-sure; he was reliving vicariously some of his most pleasant years along the border. "I am glad you are getting a lot of information about the field," he wrote on February 27, 1978. "It [the research] should have been done earlier but you seem to be finding the facts. . . . I am sure glad that you have contacted as many of those old flyers that you have and got a lot of first hand information." He concluded: "When you write Gen. Kennedy, or any of my old Air Corps friends, tell them howdy for me."[55]

Later that year Smithers sent me two books, one, *Border Patrol,* which contained many of his photographs, and his latest work, *Early Trail Drivers,* published in the Texas Western Press Monograph series. Although he attempted to maintain a strict writing schedule, time and age began to take their toll. In December, 1978, he fell on an ice-covered sidewalk, injuring his left arm and hand. A passing university student helped him to his feet as he continued his walk downtown. But pain and weakness forced him to take a bus back to his apartment. And there were increasing financial problems. His *Chronicles* royalties led to the temporary cancellation of his pension at a time when medical bills continued to mount.[56]

When Joe Coltharp, curator of the Smithers Collection, visited Smithers shortly after his fall, he confided to Coltharp his difficult financial position. He had no telephone, and even postage stamps had become an almost luxury expenditure. Coltharp later suggested that, in the future, I send Smithers a supply of stamped envelopes in order for us to maintain our correspondence. Our exchange of letters continued but with less frequency; failing eyesight continued to plague him. From March to May 1979, he had to stop writing completely. New glasses, however, enabled him to continue but on a much restricted schedule. Smithers wrote in June that "between 3 PM and 5 PM when there is good daylight from a window at my desk [and] with a strong electric [light, I am] trying to finish the last manuscript I'll write."[57] His vision, however, continued to deteriorate, and by September he was able to write only "two hours a day in two periods. I am still on the big story [unidentified]. Now have 326 pages, only two or three more pages [to go]."[58]

There were other stories to be told, and seemingly aware that his time was running out, Smithers engaged a student research assistant to help him fulfill his literary agenda. His contribution was obviously limited; between February 29 and May 2, 1980, Smithers paid him only $54.00.[59] Now using his limited faculties to complete his manuscripts, he had less and less time for correspondence. During the next few months his letters arrived sporadically, and finally none at all.

Returning from California in February, 1981, I arranged to visit Bill in

El Paso, specifically to get his help in identifying photographs to be used in *Wings Over the Mexican Border*. Although he greeted me warmly, it was obvious he was in failing health. He had lost considerable weight; his clothes, noticeably soiled, hung loosely on his frail body. He was, however, excited about seeing photographs of his former Air Corps friends. He first examined them under a lighted magnifying glass and, failing to identify the images, carried them outside in the sunlight where he studied them closely for a long time. Finally, returning to the apartment, obviously dejected, he admitted he could no longer see well enough to identify the subjects. After talking a while about old friends and our individual research and writing projects, I bade him farewell. As we drove away from the apartment, my wife, who accompanied me, commented: "That man is almost blind, ill, and undernourished. I don't believe he will live very long." Her words were indeed prophetic; that was the last time I saw Bill Smithers.

Virtually blind and still attempting to write, hoping to remain mobile while faced with immobility, Smithers's final six months were a struggle to survive. There were doctors' appointments, hospital visits, discomfort from a hernia, all the while purchasing new glasses in the vain hope of improving his eyesight. Between November 29 and Christmas Day, Smithers notes six doctor appointments, primarily with his optometrist, to whom he paid $123.45. Also faced with dwindling finances, he closed his savings account on December 9, 1980, transferring the balance to checking. Day Book entries between March 4 and May 30, 1981, document the endeavors of a lonely old man, a body weakened by age, yet still possessing a determination to persevere. There were many stories yet to be told.

> *May 16. "To V.A. [Veterans Administration Hospital] for hernia. Will*
>   *go to Med. Center in New Mexico in three or four weeks."*
> *March 25. "Lawyer's Office."*
> *March 26. "Lawyer, $50."*
> *April 7. "To V.A.—lost bill fold."*
> *April 17. "Appointment to V.A. Med Center—Medicare Card came.*[60]

Frail, ill, and legally blind, Smithers refused to give in; he appeared self-driven to complete "the big manuscript." On May 23, 1981, he sent a request to Mary Ellen MacNamara, staff assistant at the Harry Ransom Research Center, for four pages of captions with numbers of corresponding photographs with which he planned to illustrate his autobiography. "On Wednesday May 27, 1981," he concluded, "I am leaving to go to the V.A. Medical Center in Albuquerque, New Mexico, to have an old rupture corrected . . . . After that I plan to request my cataracts removed, so I expect to be there at least a month."[61] According to his day book, Smithers's departure was delayed approximately one week because of interim health-care appointments. His day book entries continued:

> *May 20. "Eye doctor, $17.50"*
> *May 28. "To Hospital"*
> *May 29. "Returned from hospital" [Writing almost illegible]*
> *May 30. "Hospital paid $51.20"*
> *June 7. "Operation Day"*[62]

This was Smithers's final entry. "I remember the day he left for the [Veteran's] hospital," recalled Mrs. Jimmie Grim, who managed the apartment complex where Smithers lived. "He came in and I straightened up his clothes and he had blood on his face [from shaving] and I wiped it off. And got him sent off to the Veteran's Hospital. He rode the bus to Albuquerque."[63]

For a man who documented some seven decades of his life, both visually and verbally, nothing is known of Smithers's final days. He arrived at the hospital, apparently surgery was performed, and it is assumed he died of cardiac arrest. As there were no next-of-kin, confidentiality prevented the Veteran's Administration from releasing any details of Smithers's passing. "They called me," Mrs. Grim recalled. "He had evidently put me down as his only survivor. They called me and asked if I wanted his body shipped back here. Of course, he was nothing to me except a good friend. I said I had no way of taking care of that."[64] Smithers was buried at the Santa Fe National Cemetery with only the mortuary chaplain and the internment staff present. He had no survivors. He did, however, leave a will. Mrs. Grim explained: "He had a girl friend. A very young Mexican girl. She didn't speak any English at all. I finally got in touch with her because he left her everything he had. It was very little." Then after a short pause, she added approvingly, "She took very good care of the old gentleman."[65]

Although Smithers had no family survivors, he was, nevertheless, remembered fondly by those who knew him and admired his work. Air Force general William L. Kennedy, who knew Smithers both at Kelly Field and at Johnson's ranch, considered him "a most unusual human being, possessing the mind of a scientist and the perception of an artist. Always pleasant, yet he seldom spoke unless he had something worthwhile to say. He had no time for a phony. A true scientist doesn't either."[66] Elmo Johnson, Smithers's friend and Big Bend host, agreed that he was well liked by the other area residents but could never be considered one of them. "He was a loner," Johnson explained, "but he had lots of friends. Everybody liked him. He was congenial and honest. He had no bad habits. . . . But he just lived alone. . . . He said he never learned anything by talking. He'd talk when spoken to. But he never brought up a subject. . . . He enjoyed living."[67] Dudley R. Dobie, librarian and history teacher at Sul Ross State College, viewed Smithers within an academic context. Although Smithers had only the equivalent of a seventh-grade education, Dobie saw him as "a most remarkable person," as well as a "brilliant historian . . . with his toes dug deep in Border Country soil, and one whose heart and soul are consumed with a burning desire to record every detail of history."[68] Historian Virginia Madison inscribed a copy of *The Big Bend Country of Texas* as follows: "For W. D. Smithers, who has told the story of the Big Bend Country and her people through the eye of the camera and with his fine writing about the events which present day writers can know only from 'hear say.'"[69]

Yet it was this man, unquestionably "a most remarkable person," whose self-proclaimed mission in life was preserving a photographic image— no matter the subject—of that one brief moment in time. For Smithers, the image, that bit of action or impression frozen in time by the camera's shutter, was the sole objective of his some seven decades of professional activity. His reaction to the death of Juan Vargas in 1910 had deemed it so. Photojournalism was his profession; art and commerce seldom entered into his calculations.

In any broad-based assessment of Smithers's work, his visual legacy must be examined within the complete context of early-twentieth-century photography. One critic writes that unlike E. O. Goldbeck, another San Antonio photographer and Smithers's contemporary, "Smithers was not a commercial photographer; his sense of worth was bound up in providing a historical record rather than a business service. As the country moved [forward] . . . Smithers simply could not resist looking back. . . . His intention at all times was to preserve a story rather than create one."[70] In preserving the story, Smithers did indeed assume a backward perspective in his view of life, but at the same time he was looking forward. Within his frame of reference is the impoverished goat herder juxtaposed with mechanized cavalry vehicles and the Air Corps' latest fighting equipment. Singularly dedicated to neither, he, nevertheless, continued to explore both as overlapping layers of change within the ongoing phenomenon of human progress.

This element of change is ever apparent when examining the Smithers Collection. Smithers was fascinated not only by the photographic process but by the subjects he chose, as well; his interest, not commerce, made the determination. He loved airplanes, the cavalry, border life, all aspects of nature, and above all the Mexican people and their culture. This personal philosophy is most evident in his studies of the Mexican goat herders along the Rio Grande. For example, where photographer Dorothea Lange would have seen abject poverty and hopelessness in their primitive dwellings, Smithers recognized cleanliness and order. Where Russell Lee would have photographed the Mexican child with her pet goat as an act of social protest, Smithers was celebrating the beauty and innocence of childhood. Thus, in every topic he examined he saw only its enduring worth, importance, and uniqueness.

When considering the technical aspects of Smithers's photographic images, his skill often fell short of his ambition. Many images are not clearly focused; others lack sufficient contrast to be aesthetically appealing; few negatives show any evidence of cropping. Yet when viewing the collection in its entirety, and considering the adverse conditions under which Smithers worked, these shortcomings appear relatively unimportant. One scholar who made a careful study of the collection writes: "His equipment . . . [was] largely homemade and makeshift. He rarely had anything resembling a permanent darkroom. Even in the last years of his photographic career, he did his laboratory work before daylight in his kitchen. The film, paper and chemicals he used would be considered almost unworkably slow by today's standards; and they were always at the mercy of the tortuous Big Bend heat."[71]

Yet despite these technical and, for most practical purposes, unimportant flaws, Smithers compiled a remarkable body of data. And in a final assessment one salient fact must not be overlooked: his work stands alone as a visual and verbal document of the southwest borderlands. There is nothing else like it. All who knew Smithers, and all whose lives will be enriched by his legacy, will no doubt agree with Dudley R. Dobie's assessment: Wilfred Dudley Smithers was indeed "a most remarkable person."

Adios, el fotógrafo.

11

When Hollywood Came to Marfa

During the years of my Big Bend travel I frequently visited the area in a dual role: doing independent historical research while serving as education director of the Texas State Historical Association. It was in the latter role that I first visited Marfa, Texas, and met Lee Bennett. A popular history teacher at Marfa High School, Lee had achieved national recognition as sponsor of the Marfa Junior Historians, the association's education affiliate. It was on my first visit with Lee in 1967 that I became aware of the enduring *Giant* mystique. I learned from her that I, like every other visitor who had seen the movie, wanted to see the "Reata" set, the magnificent Victorian mansion occupied in the film by Rock Hudson and Elizabeth Taylor. Lee explained it had long since succumbed to the elements.

But as I became more acquainted with the community, it was readily apparent that while the physical evidence of the filming had long since vanished, the *Giant* legacy lived on. Lee, like many others I met, had served as an extra in the film and casually referred to the stars on a first-name basis: Rock and Elizabeth. I began asking questions; the answers intrigued me. *Giant* was indeed a monumental event and had touched the lives of many living in that region; it appeared that 1955 was a watershed year in local history. I wanted to know why.

In the ranching country a man's stature is frequently judged by the attendance at his funeral. But to apply this criterion to the passing of Henry T. Fletcher would be unfair. As this prominent Big Bend rancher was being laid to rest at 4:00 P.M. on June 4, 1955, only family members and five friends gathered at his graveside. His other friends and mourners, and just about everyone else in the Big Bend country, including Marfa mayor Henry Coffield, were headed for the Marfa airport to greet the incoming cast of the movie *Giant*.[1]

With no disrespect intended, the excitement of seeing Elizabeth Taylor and Rock Hudson in person took precedence over an old rancher's funeral. Henry Fletcher represented the past; they were looking to the future. This West Coast invasion was destined to jolt the social, cultural, and economic foundations of the Big Bend community. The impact would be felt far and wide. Producer-director George Stevens's selection of Marfa for the location filming of *Giant* was the most exciting news to hit the Big Bend country since the era of border bandit raids along the Rio Grande. And since it occurred in the midst of a record-breaking drought, the prospects of an infusion of new money into the depressed ranching economy had wide appeal. So for the next six weeks, Marfa, Texas, became Hollywood East. The Big Bend country would long remember the summer of fifty-five.

Edna Ferber had started it all some three years before with the publication of *Giant*, her mythical Texas saga of ostentatious exaggeration. As a Book-of-the-Month Club selection, *Giant* commanded wide attention, especially in Texas. "Instead of making her ranchers rich," Bill Brammer complained in the *Texas Observer*, "she made them incredibly rich—and unbelievably stupid instead of merely provincial."[2] The national press tended to agree. *New York Times* reviewer John Barkham explained that "Miss Ferber makes it very clear that she doesn't like the Texas she writes about, and it's a cinch that when Texans read what she has written about them they won't like Miss Ferber either."[3]

It fell to erudite Lon Tinkle, literary critic with the *Dallas Morning News*, to defend his home turf in the ongoing debate over Ferber's view of Texas. He accused the author of possessing a misguided "passion for hilarious exaggeration, the irresistible impulse to turn everything into a 'tall tale.'... Her book on ranch and oil empires of South Texas reads like a parody of that grand old melodrama, 'A Texas Steer.'... But Miss Ferber is a bum steer.... Her vexation with Texas leads her berserk."[4]

The book's success and the ensuing debate did not escape the ever-watchful eye of movie producer-director George Stevens. Highly regarded in the film industry for his demand for artistic perfection and visual authenticity, Stevens recognized the novel's potential as a major film property. While still in production with *Shane*, he began negotiations with fellow producer Henry Ginsberg, and on March 5, 1953, the two consummated a partnership agreement with Edna Ferber.[5] To produce a film of this anticipated magnitude, the trio turned first to the problems of securing funding, studio facilities, and production personnel. The Warner Brothers studio offered all three, including a $2.5 million loan, plus $100,000 for marketing.[6]

Stevens, aided by Ivan Moffat and Fred Guiol, began work on the screen adaptation in early 1954.[7] With the first draft of the screenplay still in revision, Stevens began scouting for an appropriate site for location filming. Logic indicated Texas, the setting of the novel and the state where Ferber had already incited the wrath of many of its more literate citizens. And so began the trek east. It remains unclear when and exactly how the Marfa site was chosen, but according to Emma Mallan, owner of Marfa's Paisano Hotel, it was "an accident of history." She recalled that five studio representatives spent the night at the hotel en route to California; they had unsuccessfully scouted various location sites in Texas, including the King Ranch. When Mallan mentioned Marfa as a possible site for the filming, they questioned the community's ability to provide extended accommodations for the film company. As the owner of the town's largest hotel, she thought otherwise, as did the Marfa Chamber of Commerce. Mallan remembered the visitors made some notes, returned to the West Coast, and finally concluded that "the Marfa area had everything needed to shoot the film."[8] By early February, 1955, the word was out: Hollywood was coming to Marfa to film *Giant*. From that time forward, the pace of preparations quickened.

On February 5, Joseph Barry and Mel Deller of Warner's location department began checking various locations for the filming. After rejecting sites in the Presidio area, they met with Worth Evans, a Marfa rancher, and chose his ranch for the major location filming. With herds depleted, pastures burned dry by the drought, and little ranch work to do, Evans viewed *Giant* as a windfall. The company designated that site for the Benedict Mansion "Reata" set and the famous barbecue scene. While there is no studio record of the contract with Evans, his son, J. W. Evans, recalled his father received about $25,000 for the film rights to his father's 35,000-acre ranch and the use of "about one thousand head of cattle—cows and calves—for the roundup scene." He remembered the camera crew was at the ranch some five or six weeks. Evans and some of the other cowboys received additional compensation for working the cattle during the filming. And while he could not remember his salary, he thought "it was good wages for that time. The economy at that particular time—we were in a bad drought—was pretty bad. It [the filming] really helped the community and the surrounding area. It brought a lot of money into the community."[9]

Some of that "new money" found its way into the bank accounts of other Big Bend ranchers, especially Cole A. Means and Ben Avant. The company chose the Means ranch for the "Reata" railroad station set and also agreed to use approximately fifty head of Brahman cattle for seven days prior to filming. He received $50 per day while the company prepared the set and $250 per day during filming. In addition, the company supplied the feed for the cattle and paid Means's cowboys for managing the herd.[10] Giant Productions also chose a site on the Ben Avant ranch for Jett Rink's shack and oil well. Avant agreed to release the site for one month—three weeks for construction and one week for filming. For this he received $1,000—$500 upon execution of the contract and $500 payable when the company released the property. Avant also received an additional $15 a day from the company for guarding his own ranch. The local economy had already taken on a brighter hue.[11]

A photographic-interview-social research team led the next wave of movie folk. They left the studio on Tuesday, February 22, 1955, for a two-week tour of the state. The objective: capturing local color. The team, headed by Stevens, also spent five days in Marfa in late February, conducting final inspections for the filming locations.[12] Stevens liked what he saw. In his pursuit of visual authenticity, especially in his action dramas—*Gunga Din* (1939) and *Shane* (1953)—Stevens chose settings that he believed would both reflect and enhance the story line, as well as the stature of the film's primary characters. By choosing Wyoming's Jackson Hole country as the exterior setting for *Shane*, the towering Teton Mountains seemed to enlarge the already larger-than-life image of the itinerant gunfighter. And when Stevens viewed the vast sweeping plains of the Big Bend country interrupted only by the backdrop of the Davis Mountains, he knew he had found the perfect stage upon which Ferber's epic *Giant* could reach fruition.[13]

After establishing the location sites, the largest task still lay ahead. Moving the 250 members of the cast, crew, and construction staff some 1,000 miles for a five-week location filming in semirural isolation required the ultimate in preplanning. Stevens seemed to recognize early on that he would have to come to terms with an unfamiliar environment, and in the process acknowledge that Marfa was not Hollywood. The company compromised; Marfa gave its very best. Arranging food and lodging were the next priorities. For a village of 3,600, the sudden influx of some 250 temporary citizens placed an unprecedented strain on facilities. The company, however, moved with dispatch, taking over the two hotels and one motel. At the Paisano Hotel, Marfa's largest, Giant Productions guaranteed Mallan a minimum of 2,832 man-days at $16.50 per day. This included breakfast at $2, lunch at $3, and dinner at $4.50. This agreement provided accommodations for 118 people for twenty-four consecutive days, with an extended option at the same rate. Paisano residents included feature players, members of the technical staff, and some company executives. Since the Paisano lacked both staff and equipment to serve that many permanent guests, the company gave Mallan an additional $6,625 to engage a professional caterer, the Gillespie Catering Service of El Paso, which transferred a temporary staff to the Paisano for the duration of the filming.[14] The film company also took over the smaller Crews Hotel and the Toltec Motel.[15] Stevens and coproducer Henry Ginsberg approved these arrangements on May 5, 1955. For the stars, the publicity staff, some company executives, and visiting journalists, the company rented five private residences in Marfa.[16]

Location filming of this magnitude required a plethora of skills and services normally provided by an established studio staff. But with Marfa situated some 1,000 miles from the film capital, it fell to the Big Bend community to fill the gap, both before and behind the cameras. The economic benefits were extensive. The company engaged Lois Baygent of Marfa to contract local people as film extras. By mid-April she had 135 individuals listed on the extra call sheet. They were to receive $10 per day, $100 if given speaking lines. Other beneficiaries included the local Future Farmers of America chapter, who received the location snack bar concession; the Marfa High School band, with majorettes who performed to play-back recordings; and Edna Adams, who agreed to conduct a Mexican boys' choir for the military burial scene. Each choir member received $10 a day; Adams commanded $500 for a three-day minimum, plus $100 for each day she was required to be on the set.[17]

Because of the widely dispersed filming sites, transportation emerged as a priority item for the location department. Lee Williams of Fort Davis provided three trucks with a 150-mile-a-day allowance at prices ranging from $25 to $75 per day, without drivers. The company engaged drivers and paid for the gas and oil. To transport cast and crew to the location sites, Giant Productions acquired six twenty-nine-passenger coaches, two five-passenger cars, and two station wagons. The company insured all leased vehicles. Other local vendors included the Big Bend Feed Company, which delivered fifty tons of alfalfa hay to the Worth Evans ranch site, and arrangements were made with the Highland Cleaners and Bennett Cleaners "to work at night for any rush cleaning."[18]

Acquiring operational space was another priority item for the production department, much of which, surprisingly, local citizens offered free. Mallan donated a makeup room, a prop storage room, and an additional office that served as a radio room to contact various units in the field. The Paisano Hotel beauty parlor agreed to share shampoo facilities morning and evening, before and after closing hours. Also, the owner of a closed motion picture theater offered that facility free for the company to view the "dailies." In appreciation, Giant Productions paid the owner $100.[19]

But the skills the company needed most—carpenters and laborers—were in short supply in the predominantly ranching country. The studio's areawide canvas for those skills apparently succeeded. On the morning of April 14, a twenty-nine-passenger bus, a pickup truck, and a five-passenger car loaded with workmen departed from the Paisano Hotel for the Worth Evans ranch; on-site preparations for the first camera day were at last under way. They first had to unload the sixty prefabricated sections of the "Reata" house set that had been shipped from Warner studio on five railroad flat cars. After erecting the two-sided flat, the construction crew moved to the Ben Avant ranch to begin work on the Jett Rink's oil derrick set. Welcome Hollywood dollars were finding their way into the pockets of many unemployed Big Bend ranch hands.

The initial contact between members of the film company and the local Big Bend citizens was harmonious. On May 4, in appreciation for the economic windfall, the Marfa Chamber of Commerce staged an "old fashioned western barbecue and dance . . . honoring Marfa's Hollywood guests." Entertainment was provided by "some talent from as far away as El Paso." Admission was $1, thirty technicians attended, and studio representative Carl Benoit commented on the "delicious vittles."[20] There was, however, other news emanating from Marfa in which studio executives expressed far greater interest. By May 21, with set construction almost complete, construction costs were well below original estimates. The "Reata" house set, for example, estimated at $98,450, cost only $85,071.21, or $13,388.79 below estimate. The same was true of the Mexican village set, Jett Rink's shack set, and the oil derrick set, which combined were

$10,330.29 below estimate. Although still almost three weeks away from filming, Stevens seemed assured that choosing the Marfa location was a sound business decision.[21]

Throughout the four months of site selection and set construction, George Stevens pondered two other facets of filmmaking that, more than any other, held the keys to success: cast selection and script revision. Both required the ultimate in patience, persistence, and diplomacy, personal skills in which Stevens excelled.

Casting the major roles, especially Bick Benedict, the male lead, presented both advantages and disadvantages. With the national publicity accorded the best-selling novel, and news that Warner's was financing the big-budget production, many of filmdom's brightest stars literally begged for the opportunity to work with the legendary director. The choice role, Bick Benedict, eventually went to Rock Hudson, but not without much deliberation. Every male star in Hollywood wanted the part; the names of Clark Gable, Alan Ladd, Errol Flynn, and William Holden top the original casting list. In the final selection, Stevens had to choose between Holden and Hudson. Youth won out; the makeup artists could make Hudson look old, but they could not make Holden look young. Hudson's youthful versatility—he was twenty-nine—was worth $10,000 a week for a ten-week minimum.

Stevens originally offered the leading female role, Leslie Benedict, to Grace Kelly, but she declined. Elizabeth Taylor was next on the preliminary casting list. Three years before, she and Stevens had worked together in *A Place in the Sun*, the film that won Stevens his first Academy Award as best director. Although he approved Taylor's selection, her acquisition also created a temporary budget crunch for the company. "We had to pay MGM a bundle of cash in addition to loaning James Dean for one picture," Stevens explained later.[22] Taylor also felt the crunch, but for a different reason. While in Marfa she confided to fellow actress Carroll Baker that " 'those bastards at MGM make me do five pictures a year for my hundred thousand, and on this *Giant* loan-out they are collecting two hundred and fifty thousand from Warner Brothers.' "[23]

Robert Nichols, whom Stevens chose for the role of Pinky, strove for regional authenticity on his first reading. "I went out and met Mr. Stevens and I talked with him for about ten minutes in what I thought was a Texas accent," Nichols recalled. "And he said, 'Well, you're our Pinky, but you had better learn how to talk Texas.' " To teach the entire cast "to talk

Texas," Stevens engaged native Texan and former rodeo performer Bob Hinkle as voice coach. Nichols added that they worked with Hinkle for about five weeks "before we started to get the right sound."[24]

While Stevens grappled with the details of casting the film and coordinating set construction at Marfa, other unexpected preproduction problems continued to plague the producer-director. First, there was the steady stream of correspondence from Edna Ferber, challenging the literary quality of the screen adaptation. Citing one scene on page 78 of the script, she wrote on April 23, 1955, "I can't bear to read it, much less hear it. . . . I want to say this: I know nothing about making motion pictures. I know about writing. I know dialogue, characterization, situation. I know how forceful words are to convey the meaning of the situation. . . . As a writer I find some of these 'Giant' speeches wooden, unvital and uncharacteristic. A writer of proven talent and experience could not have written them. . . . This picture is a huge business venture. We cannot afford to use dialogue which is inept."[25] While there is no record of Stevens's response, it can be assumed that, with the film's ultimate success, Ferber's admonition received careful consideration.

In addition to their preoccupation with production details, Stevens and his staff were also concerned with creating a compatible working environment in an unfamiliar area. Hence the social interaction between members of the film colony and the star-studded cast, as well as citizens of that remote ranching community, also received high priority. One month before filming began, production manager Ralph E. Black challenged each member of the company to exhibit their best behavior: "Because of the length of stay at this location and the restriction of recreation, it is very important that all members of the company make every effort to conduct themselves in such a way as to prevent criticism from the local people. They will make us welcome in their town, and will show us every possible cooperation. We must, in turn, cooperate with them."[26]

By the time May gave way to June, all appeared in organized readiness. The million-dollar-plus inventory of production equipment stood in place: cameras, camera dollies, fifteen short-wave radios, sound trucks, generators, props, wind machines, refrigerator trucks for preserving the motion picture film, and portable dressing rooms. All that was needed to begin filming was the cast, and at a few minutes past four o'clock on Saturday afternoon, June 4, they began arriving. Some thirty-six hours later the cast and crew heard the director's familiar command, "Picture up!

And we are rolling." The filming of *Giant* was at last under way. During the ensuing five weeks Marfa and the Big Bend country became the entertainment news capital of the world. Representatives of the state, national, and international news media converged there to file their copy as George Stevens's long-planned epic film slowly became reality. And all the while local citizens experienced the things of which dreams are made. And those dreams would linger on.

Like most days in Marfa, Texas, Monday, June 6, 1955, dawned bright and clear. But for some *Giant* cast members, their day began long before sunrise. Rock Hudson reported at the Paisano Hotel makeup room at 4:30 A.M., and left in a limousine at 7:15 bound for the Worth Evans ranch. Elizabeth Taylor followed the same schedule. Dennis Hopper and Earl Holliman began makeup at 5 A.M. and left the hotel at 7:15. James Dean, requiring less makeover, arrived at 7:00 A.M. and by eight o'clock was en route to the "Reata" set.[27] Seldom had Marfa witnessed that much early-morning activity.

June 6 marked the first day of shooting;[28] first item on the call board was the "Barbecue Scene." In the *Giant* scenario this event documents the return of tall Texan, Bick Benedict, from Virginia with his new bride, Leslie. To celebrate the occasion, Benedict's neighbors stage a Texas-style barbecue. This scene, and the following christening scene, required the services of more than one hundred local residents who worked as extras at $10 per day. They considered the money important; the experience, a pleasant break from ranch work. For most, this was their formal introduction to Hollywood, and, in turn, Hollywood's initial on-the-job contact with Marfa. This was essentially the meeting of social and cultural foreigners who spoke the same language with different accents but who had come together for a common purpose. Initially, both groups reacted with guarded amazement, amazement that grew eventually into fondness and respect.

The extras, like the stars and feature players, also greeted the dawn early. They met at the old USO Building for makeup and costuming. The objective: turn back the visual clock some three decades to the mid-1920s. Makeup artists armed with powders, paints, brushes, and apparel began performing their miracles; the women loved the Hollywood touch. Wigs, hairpieces, and buns added length to the short hairstyles of the mid-1950s, while a combination of big hats, long sleeves, long waists, and cotton hoses created the prescribed image of rural femininity. The men, already rugged and sunburned, were largely ignored in makeup; cowboy images seldom change. By the time most extras normally would be beginning their daily ranching chores, they boarded chartered buses en route to the Worth Evans ranch to make a movie.

Eighteen miles later the extras saw the "Reata" set for the first time. On the crest of a small rise in a sea of dry tabosa grass stood the facade of the three-story, sixty-foot-high Victorian mansion. All gingerbread and rococo, and utterly inelegant, the surreal vision was, to them, at last, the vision of reality. That confirmed it; Hollywood had indeed come to Marfa. For many of the costumed extras, that set would be their home away from home for the next several days. It was there, in the shadow of that empty prefabricated shell, that they would discover the magic of filmmaking—the myth, the romance, as well as the reality.

Disembarking, they, like any layperson visiting a movie set, began looking for the obvious—movie stars. They were there, stars of national and international fame: Rock Hudson, Elizabeth Taylor, James Dean, Mercedes McCambridge, Carroll Baker, Dennis Hopper, Chill Wills, and, of course, the real star of the film, producer-director George Stevens. But on that June morning there was one essential difference. These people were no longer projected images on a movie screen, *they were real live people—colleagues, fellow thespians!* During the filming of the barbecue scene that marked the fictional homecoming of Leslie Benedict (Elizabeth Taylor), the extras, in their roles of neighboring ranchers, "greeted" Hollywood's most glamorous and most beautiful star of stars with hugs and handshakes and a verbal—but unrecorded—welcome home.

There were takes and retakes, and three days work in the hot desert sun yielded possibly five minutes of screen time. By the time the extras viewed *Giant* on a theater screen, their image would emerge as little more than a fleeting blur. But they were there, part of an epic film in the making, part of the drama—both dramas—the one captured on film and the one being played out behind the cameras. It was the latter that the extras remember best.

Their first contact with the film industry was through the assistant directors, those responsible for crowd management while filming the barbecue scene. Their directions, terse and usually shouted with a sense of urgency, were preceded with a well-calculated "please." Totally missing was the fictional ranting of the harried movie director. "I noticed so much the patience and seemingly easy way the directors and other workmen handled people—never ruffled, never relaxing, and always on their toes and always seeming to enjoy it," wrote *Giant* extra Evelyn Davis. "It all makes me think those men in charge are very fine people."[29]

Filming *Giant* was essentially a dawn-to-dusk affair, with few breaks. But the one break all looked forward to was lunch. The company erected a large tent behind the "Reata" set where the Gillespie Catering Service served both cast and crew in that common area. Actress Carroll Baker remembered the repast with great enthusiasm: "We ate the catered noon-day meal at long picnic tables, and that made every lunchtime a party. The buffet was sumptuous: caldrons of stews and curries; serving planks with roasts and fish and chicken, mashed, baked, boiled, and fried pota-toes; a wide variety of vegetables and salads, assorted cheese, freshly baked rolls and bread; and dozens of yummy desserts. I had never seen such a quantity of delicious foods!"[30]

It was in that common area that Marfa got to know Hollywood, and vice versa. Most agreed, movie people were "very fine people." Actor Rob-ert Nichols, who played Pinky, emerged as one of the local favorites. "With the first sequence being the barbecue, which was so much fun, and we all got to know each other at that point," he recalled. "And it was like a big party; it went on for a week. . . . It sort of opened things up."[31] The "big party" continued during breaks. Cast members not involved in a particu-lar scene headed for the big tent where snacks and cool refreshments were always available. This was indeed a common area; stars and extras met and conversed on a casual basis. Rock Hudson and Jane Withers are re-membered with special fondness. To extra Lee Bennett, Hudson was "just great. He was so casual, so charming. Just hung out with us and loved to talk." Jane Withers was a "great yakker, laughing and talking all the time." And Mercedes McCambridge was "a lovely lady, sweet and charming. They all seemed to enjoy our company as much as we enjoyed theirs."[32]

The one person who did not mix well with the locals was Elizabeth Taylor. Unlike other cast members, she is remembered as "spoiled," "de-manding," "arrogant beyond belief," and "an exhibitionist." According to one extra, she seemed to relish flaunting her sexuality. On one occasion the evocative star emerged from her air-conditioned trailer dressed in short shorts and, in lieu of a blouse and brassiere, had wrapped a loose fitting bandanna around her more-than-ample breasts. To some of the women extras, it was an example of poor taste; to the men it was a memo-rable day on the range.[33]

The extras were equally intrigued by the more mundane aspects of filmmaking. The difference between myth and reality, so nebulous when viewed on the motion-picture screen, disappeared completely as the cameras began to roll. They saw imitation rocks made of sponge rubber, dead grass sprayed green to look alive, thick molasses used in lieu of crude oil, and cutouts of life-size cattle attached to sharp sticks that, when driven in the ground, added dimension to Worth Evans's already substantial herd. Between takes assistant director Dick Moder would shout: "Move the Texas [live] cattle over here—move the Hollywood cattle over there."

During the filming of the barbecue scene, however, the extras did indeed witness one genuine touch of reality. Following an old Texas custom, the fictional ranchers prepared a cooked calf's head, from which they served the steaming brains, considered a rare delicacy in the ranching country. In the film when Leslie (Elizabeth Taylor) sees the brains being served from the decapitated animal's head, she faints in Bick's arms. According to one extra, her reaction was not too far removed from reality. "The calf's brains had been fresh to begin with, and every night they would refrigerate it and bring it out the next day," Lee Bennett explained. "By the end of the third day, it was really gross, both in look and smell. Although Elizabeth was acting, the rest of us felt like joining her."[34]

As the filming proceeded day after day in the searing summer heat, the dawn-to-dusk routine eventually took its toll on individual patience. As a result, the extras were accorded a rare view of Hollywood's seamier underside—the stubborn, temperamental, demanding, and explosive "movie star." James Dean, a recent newcomer to films, became the first to incite director Stevens's wrath. Trained at the Actors Studio in New York and steeped in "the Method" tradition, Dean's perception of how a scene should be played did not always coincide with Stevens's. In one scene Stevens placed a mark on the set where he wanted Dean to stand. When Dean stated that he did not use marks, Stevens responded emphatically that the cameraman did. "I wanted to nail him quick," the director explained later. "There's always a testing period in the beginning of a picture when an actor wants to find out who's the boss. Jimmy was predisposed to do a scene as he saw it, and I had my way of doing it."[35]

Elizabeth Taylor, like Dean, also ignited some on-the-set fireworks, much to the amazement of the extras, especially Lee Bennett, who wrote:

> I do not remember what caused her to throw a temper tantrum on the porch [of the "Reata" set] as the birthday scene was being filmed. It was terribly embarrassing to everyone. We didn't know what to expect next.

Marfa and Hollywood meet at Giant barbecue. "This was the first sequence we shot in Marfa," actor Robert Nichols explained, "and a great introduction to the people of that town." Nichols and Jane Withers, facing camera, converse with Rock Hudson and Elizabeth Taylor; Mercedes McCambridge stands in background. Mansion in background was actually a "flat" supported by utility poles. Courtesy Academy of Motion Picture Arts and Sciences

Everything got awfully quiet. Then George Stevens stepped toward Elizabeth and positioned himself right in front of her. I have read of "steely" eyes and an "ominous" voice and he used both as he said in a quiet voice, but one that carried to every ear: "Elizabeth, your conduct does not become you." He waited until she obviously wilted a little and turned away. That was enough.[36]

The spectacle of on-set temper tantrums and emotional eruptions was not limited to cast and crew. Uncounted thousands whom the company invited to view the filming in designated visitor areas also saw the show-within-a-show. Stevens had designated *Giant* an "open set." Press observers visiting Marfa reported that never before had the public been accorded such a free and intimate view of a film in production. For a layperson to be invited on set was rare, but the opportunity to visit a star-studded location like *Giant* had unprecedented appeal. "People are coming here from all over—distance makes no difference," stated Ben Avant, on whose ranch some scenes were filmed. "We have people here from everywhere. Monday a special drama class from Lubbock came down. Distance doesn't make any difference. They load up a car full of kids and they're off."[37] Stevens stated his purpose was to build up public interest in the film before it was completed. His decision, no doubt, stemmed from his awareness of the negative reception the novel had initially received in Texas. "The freedom of the press and public on location," he explained, "is good for pre-selling an audience."[38]

Emma Mallan, whose Paisano Hotel provided the food for the *Giant* location, recalled that the visitors were frequently invited to join the cast and crew for lunch. "This was a tremendous thrill for people who had never seen a motion picture in production," she explained, "and certainly not one of this magnitude involving performers of this stature."[39]

The daily rush of spectators to view the filming resulted from the studio's carefully orchestrated media coverage. With local accommodations provided by the company, a steady rotation of state, national, and international journalists converged on that small West Texas hamlet, from which they filed their daily copy. Not since the days of Pancho Villa and the border bandit depredations had the region received such national publicity. Actor Earl Holliman reported he had never seen "press coverage like that in my life. They flew in press from Paris, London, New York, and the West Coast. Every flight that came in had a certain amount of press people on board."[40]

Producer-Director George Stevens declared Giant *an "open set" and
invited visitors to observe a motion picture in-the-making. A group of students,
in a designated area, watch a camera "set up" for filming the next scene.
Cameras are protected from elements with plastic covers.*
Courtesy Marfa Public Library

The Warner Brothers publicity department carefully staggered the
arrival and departure times of media personnel to insure ongoing coverage. The publicity blitz also included representatives of the state press.
John Rosenfeld of the *Dallas Morning News,* arrived on Saturday, June 11,
and remained through the following Monday; John Bustin, representing
the *Austin American-Statesman,* conducted his interviews on June 22–23.
His assignment complete, the company accorded Bustin a special courtesy; actress Mercedes McCambridge drove him to the Marfa airport in a
studio car.[41]

While in Marfa, the journalists visited the set, interviewed the stars in
their homes or at the Paisano Hotel, dined with them, and joined them in
the old Texas Theater to view the daily "rushes." But wherever the journalists appeared with their notepads, they found a story waiting; after a
day's work on the set, the stars were ever visible in downtown Marfa. For
both press and public, the favorite spot for stargazing was the Paisano
Hotel dining room; each evening the cast assembled there for dinner.
Unlike some of the more exclusive Hollywood celebrity hideaways, the
Paisano advertised movie stars on exhibit. The *Big Bend Sentinel* reported,

"Mrs. E. F. Mallan, owner of the Paisano Hotel, extends a cordial invitation to all the public to partake of his [Caterer Leon Gillespie's] delicious meals and at the same time have an opportunity to hob-nob with Hollywood royalties."[42] Ralph Lowenstein, staff writer for the *El Paso Times*, visited Marfa during the filming and reported:

> And they are making this West Texas town of 3,600 people a mecca for movie fans in the Southwest. Little noses press against the windows of the Paisano Hotel at all hours of the day, their owners hoping to catch a glimpse of a movie hero. Bands of teenagers wait outside the Paisano dining room to pounce on Rock Hudson with a shrill scream when he hoves into view. And their parents head out to the sets to watch movieland in action, or arrange to eat dinner in the Paisano dining room about 9 P.M., the time when most film stars come in for supper.[43]

Actor Robert Nichols experienced this public scrutiny on his first day in Marfa. He had just met Rock Hudson in the hotel lobby, and Hudson had invited Nichols to join him and Elizabeth Taylor for dinner. When they first entered the dining room it was virtually empty, but that soon changed; within five minutes it was full. "Every eye was watching us," Nichols recalled. "And out on the street there must have been 200 people collected, all resting their noses against the window. I said, 'Look, it's nothing personal, but I have really lost my appetite. I'm going back to my room.'"[44]

And while much of the stargazing and autograph hunting was limited to juvenile transients, there also developed genuine social interchange between members of the film company and the local citizens. Earl Holliman, who lived in the Paisano Hotel and shared a room with Dennis Hopper, remembered "people were very nice to us. People really got involved with the movie and movie people." He said that as he was checking into the Paisano Hotel, he met Robert Nichols, who was leaving to attend a bridge party at a rancher's residence. This local involvement also included watching the daily rushes in the Texas Theater, which was open to the public. "Everyone sat there and watched the 'dailies' together. It all had a wonderful friendly feel to it," Holliman added. "I remember one rancher taking me out to his spread and showing me his cattle. We had met him down in Ojinaga drinking those straight tequila shots. They welcomed us with open arms."[45]

Big Bend ranch life particularly appealed to some actors. Lee and

Murphy Bennett, local ranchers who also worked as *Giant* extras, became friends with Alexander Scourby, who played "Old Polo" in the film. Lee remembered on one visit to the ranch, they discovered Scourby seated on the living room couch reading a Davy Crockett Golden Book to their two small sons in his most dramatic voice.[46] Robert Nichols, who met extras Bill and Jane Shurley on the *Giant* set, enjoyed a weeklong visit to their ranch. "We went sheepherding and jack-rabbit hunting, and I had a wonderful time with them," he recalled. "We met a lot of the local people."[47]

As the filming continued, the avid stargazers at the Paisano dining room began observing some noticeable pairings. One that received the most attention was the recently engaged Rock Hudson and the soon-to-be-divorced Elizabeth Taylor. Their consistency led to the erroneous assumption that they were "going steady." And Carroll Baker's ever-changing companions also drew much attention. First, it was James Dean. "Our main diversion was making fun of Rock and Elizabeth," Baker wrote. But when Dean sought other companionship, Dennis Hopper and Earl Holliman competed for her company. Holliman, the consistent winner, would later escort Baker to the theater to watch the "rushes." "Jimmy would be there already, in the balcony," Baker noticed, "where he would sit there all by himself to view the rushes."[48]

Dining at the Paisano also had its lighter moments. Owner Emma Mallan remembered the evening the ceiling collapsed. Director George Stevens and members of his staff were having dinner with several cast members when, without warning, the Sheetrock ceiling above their table fell in, showering them with debris and gallons of what turned out to be someone's bathwater. "Instead of being upset or even disturbed," Mallan explained, "Mr. Stevens acted as though it was written in the script. He simply stood up, backed away from the table, dried himself off, and wondered what had occurred." Mallan soon learned what occurred, but refused to identify the culprit, an actor who had fallen asleep in the bathtub, allowing the water to run over and drenching the unsuspected victims below.

Stevens exhibited the same emotional stability and good humor when he experienced another unexpected interruption in food service. This occurred on the Worth Evans ranch when a sudden windstorm struck the set, collapsing the food tent on the cast and crew while they were dining. As they scrambled from beneath the huge canvass, Stevens, well known for his many retakes, shouted above the crowd, "'Let's get ready for a retake on this.'"[49]

Stevens was less philosophical about other unexpected delays in production. One such interruption occurred on June 19, when a violent thunderstorm dumped more than an inch of rain on the Marfa area, including the "Reata" set. "Hail followed the rain," the *Sentinel* reported, "which began early in the afternoon and continued to well past dark."[50] Stevens was despondent, the drought-stricken ranchers elated, and the cast members delighted with the unexpected break. Elizabeth Taylor and Rock Hudson celebrated the downpour by collecting hailstones to cool their Bloody Marys.

Filming continued throughout June, and on Friday night, July 8, the final wedding scene was shot in Marfa's St. Mary's Church. That was an event that no one, neither cast, crew, nor local citizens, looked forward to. Carroll Baker apparently spoke the sentiments for all when she wrote: "It was a sad day when the Marfa filming was completed. Everyone felt a terrible let-down when 'That's a wrap' was called. . . . We had a private train which was supposed to pull out at 9:00 P.M. to take us back to L.A., but it didn't leave until well past midnight because of the 'farewell' cocktail party. The local people didn't want to see us leave and we were all reluctant to go. . . . a very special time passing away."[51]

Earl Holliman also remembered that last day in Marfa: "When the train was pulling out, I remember it seemed like the whole town turned out to say good-bye. . . . It was a lovely time. . . . a marvelous experience that I am proud to have been a part of."[52] It fell to journalist Sue Flannagan to write the final "wrap" to the location filming: "Saturday the Warner Bros. company folded its tent, wind-blowing machine, and No. 1 cameras and departed for Hollywood. . . . The stardust here today has lost its prefix and settled back down to just good old, plain, Texas dust."[53]

The departing cast left behind more than fond memories. Assistant director Fred Guiol and the second unit remained in Marfa another week for retakes on the Worth Evans ranch and at Valentine. These scenes also involved James Dean and Dennis Hopper. The perfectionist Stevens wanted additional footage.[54] And there were other delays. First, in a bucking horse scene the only available horse refused to buck, and still it rained, further delaying completion of the location assignment. Despite the handicaps, Guiol's efforts pleased Stevens, who again telegraphed his assistant director in Marfa: "Ran all the unseen film last night—39 reels. . . . All of it was great. . . . Your long shots of the Reata House from the high view points are magnificent. Fine pictorial quality. . . . These are as fine photography as anything in the picture to date."[55] Despite Guiol's achievements, there was still work to be done. By July 19, at least one full day of shooting remained for the second unit, plus an additional day to gather footage for television coverage.

Betty Coryell, George Stevens's secretary, also remained behind to terminate the company's business and supervise the postlocation cleanup. On July 12 she approved a $2,974 bid to repaint several structures on the Evans ranch used in the filming and on Monday, July 24, closed the company's Paisano Hotel headquarters. She was the last to leave. Her departure on the westbound train appeared symbolic; it marked the end of a rare and exciting episode that occurred in that remote ranching community. In that one brief moment in time, Hollywood came to Marfa to make a motion picture and the nation turned its attention to the Big Bend country. And like an unbelievable dream, suddenly it was over. But the friendships endured. On September 14, Mallan wrote Betty Coryell: "We think of you all so often and wonder if you are still working on the 'Giant.' This truly was a wonderful experience for the whole community—one we shall never forget. And one that has many pleasant memories. When you have a few free moments please write and let me know some news as I still feel you are all part of my family."[56] Coryell responded the following week. "My stay at the Paisano will not soon be forgotten. . . . Texas was fun. We are still hard at work on 'Giant,'" she continued, "and the one working hardest and putting in the most hours is, as usual, Mr. Stevens. We are scheduled to finish the actual filming sometime next week."[57]

By the time Coryell wrote Mallan, the company's first unit had been working on a Warner Brothers sound stage for some two months, filming the remaining interior scenes. With a final "wrap" only days away, Stevens was, nevertheless, still being plagued by two ongoing problems that had their origins in Texas.

First, there was the Eppenauer matter. While still on location, Marfa attorney Hunter O. Metcalfe, representing rancher A. R. Eppenauer, filed suit in the United States District Court in El Paso on June 21, citing Warner Brothers for breach of contract. Eppenauer claimed the company breached an earlier agreement to use his cattle in the film. For the time and expense of removing the herd from the range and placing them on special feed for exhibition, Metcalfe pleaded for a $25,000 judgment against Warner Brothers.[58] After filing a general denial on July 18, 1955, the company engaged the El Paso law firm, Edwards, Belk, Hunter, and Kerr, to represent its interest in Texas. Negotiations ensued, and by September, Metcalfe indicated that the matter might be settled for $12,500. The studio, however, remained suspect. Company attorney R. J. Orbringer recommended an $8,500 counteroffer to avoid the possibility of going to court. "And with the Texas jury sitting in on a claim for damages of a Texan," he wrote on September 9, 1955, "I do not feel we Californians will have much of a chance."[59]

Although Metcalfe realized he had the advantage, he remained flexible in his demand. On September 21, he settled the case for $8,500, plus costs. Viewing the case in retrospect, Metcalfe acknowledged that Eppenauer's prize bull played a key role in the settlement. "What won the case for me was those Hollywood folks knew nothing about ranching," he recalled. "I asked their lawyer, 'How can an overweight two-thousand-pound bull service a seven-hundred-pound heifer?' When he couldn't answer me, that did it! That little 1955 Chevy Mama [Mrs. Metcalfe] is driving around town was paid for out of that settlement."[60]

James Dean was the other proverbial thorn in Stevens's side. After returning to California, Dean's social life, especially his late-night dates with actress Ursula Andress, prompted his late arrival on the set, a matter that infuriated Stevens. On August 23, he waited all day for the young actor, who never appeared at the studio. "The next day when Jimmy arrived Stevens berated him in front of the entire cast and crew," biographer Joe Hyams wrote, "using Mercedes [McCambridge, who had sustained a broken arm] as an example of professionalism, finally working himself into a caustic rage while Jimmy stood silently and took it." Later that week while viewing the rushes with New York Times correspondent Tom Pryor, Stevens remarked, "Just once, I'd like to fire the bastard."[61] Realizing that the completion of the film would terminate their association, Stevens contained his anger.

The hotel dinner sequence in which Bick Benedict and Jett Rink exchange blows in the wine cellar were some of the final scenes shot in the studio. Benedict's closing line, spoken by Rock Hudson, were: "You know, Jett, you're all through." Neither realized the prophetic overtones of those lines. That scene, subsequently referred to as "the last supper," was completed on September 22, and on the evening of the twenty-seventh Stevens called Dean back to the studio to view the rushes. Arriving characteristically late, Dean sat in the rear of the viewing room occupied by other members of the cast, studio executives, and their guests. In a tribute to the rising young star, Stevens introduced the sequence "as one of the most difficult ever undertaken by a screen actor." After viewing the scenes, all agreed with Stevens's assessment. Dean, however, appeared unmoved by the applause. He quickly left the viewing room, pausing briefly in the hall to say good-bye to Stevens. "Now it's all over, we don't have to bug each other any more," he said. "And I can go back to my motor racing." That screening was held on Tuesday. During Friday night's "rushes" the telephone rang; Stevens took the call. A studio executive reported that James Dean had been killed in an automobile accident.[62]

The news threw the cast into shock; Elizabeth Taylor broke down completely. Stevens, nevertheless, insisted that she return to the studio the following day for retakes. "She sobbed throughout the scene," journalist Joe Oppenheimer reported, "which Stevens was forced to film from behind her head."[63] Hudson also shared her grief; his line in his final scene with Dean—"You know, Jett, you're all through"—continued to haunt him.[64]

Stevens directed the final scene on October 12, 1955, and over the ensuing months he edited and reedited, spliced and respliced, and eventually released the final cut. After some four years in preparation—*Shane* required five—*Giant* was at last "in the can." When filming began in Charlottesville, Virginia, on May 19, 1955, probably no one, not even Stevens, could fully comprehend the magnitude of the project. From the initial $2.5 million budget, expenses multiplied more that twofold; the final cost exceeded $5.5 million. In that period of declining film revenues, growing television competition, and the phasing out of the studio system, launching a project of that enormity was a courageous undertaking. And while Edna Ferber had written a financially successful novel, successful novels do not always translate into financially successful films.

On October 17, 1956, the producing partners were ready to submit their creation to a panel of the toughest critics in the world—the Hollywood film community. Warner Brothers scheduled the West Coast premiere in Graumann's Chinese Theater in Hollywood where filmdom's elite sat in judgment. When the lights came up at the end of the three-hour-and-seventeen-minute film, Stevens, Ferber, and coproducer Henry Ginsberg received the wholehearted confirmation of success; the applause seemed interminable. And when Warner Brothers released the film nationwide, that applause continued from those who would lead the masses to the box office: the film critics. The *Time* review seemed to reflect best their composite appraisal: "In the hand of a master moviemaker," the magazine reported, "*Giant* has been transferred from a flashy bestseller into a monumental piece of social realism. In mood, in movement, *Giant* is something the film colony often claims but seldom achieves: an epic."[65]

Good reviews quickly translated into box-office gold. *Variety* reported one week's business in its unique showbiz vernacular: "October 31, 1956. 'Giant' Terrif. . . . With new pix ranging from big to terrific, the Loop [in Chicago] in current stanza is loaded by great figures. . . . 'Giant' shapes spectacular $72,000 or near for first frame at the Chicago [Theater]. . . . Chinese Theater [in Los Angeles] in second week $42,000, last week above estimate at $48,100."[66]

Throughout the remainder of the year, exhibitors nationwide continued to report record-breaking attendance. The project Stevens, Ferber, and Ginsberg launched some four years previous proved to be a box-office bonanza; by 1958 studio income reached $12 million. A later rerelease pushed that figure to $14 million, ranking *Giant* ninth in all-time box-office receipts.[67]

And so George Stevens came to the Big Bend country, produced an epic movie, and in the process helped the community through a period of hard times. But the story does not end there. Stevens was dealing with a socially, culturally, and ethnically volatile property; the *Giant* theme ran counter to views held supreme by many Texans. It was Edna Ferber who had originally set the stage for controversy. She made it infinitely clear in the novel that she was offended by Texas's bigness, especially the wealthy Texans who controlled the land, the cattle, and the oil—and the political power that control drew into the hands of the fortunate few. To some, Ferber was, in essence, attacking the success symbols that many Texans held as role models. And it is especially ironic that Stevens chose a site for the location filming that had become symbolic with bigness and vastness—the Big Bend country of Texas. Although Stevens chose that site for its visual characteristics, it appears more than coincidental that it was within that setting that he chose to articulate his message of humanitarian concern.

In *Giant* race develops as the most divisive factor in the Benedict household. That tension is resolved in the film's closing scene, where Stevens makes his strongest appeal for tolerance. Returning home from a trip, the Benedicts, accompanied by son Jordy, his Mexican wife Juana, and their infant son, stop at a roadside restaurant for lunch. When the burly, red-faced owner, Sarge (played by Mickey Simpson), approaches the booth to take their order, Bick asks his grandson, obviously Mexican, what he would like to have. When Bick answers for him, "ice cream," Sarge replies insultingly, "Ice cream. I thought that kid would want a tamale." Bick exhibits mild anger but restrains himself. However, when Sarge attempts to evict an elderly Mexican couple solely because they are Mexi-

Memories of Giant. A local citizen holds an original publicity still before the decaying ruins of the Benedict mansion set. Courtesy Jim Lincoln

can, Bick intercedes and a fight ensues. At this point in the film, Bick, for the first time, is motivated not by self-interest or social convention but by his concern for the feelings of the defenseless Mexican couple being violated by one who is stronger than they. The fight between Bick and Sarge, a Stevens film additive, constitutes the dramatic high point of the film, and while Bick loses, he has at last come to terms with his own bigotry.

As a result of this confrontation, Leslie discovers a new identity with her husband. In the next and final scene, played with almost casual gentleness, Leslie, referring to the fight at Sarge's restaurant, tells Bick, "You were at last my hero. That's what you always wanted to be. . . . You wound up on the floor on your back, and I said to myself, 'After a hundred years the Benedict family is a big success.' "[68]

Although Edna Ferber invested the 447 pages of her novel in attempting to deflate Texas egos, she, and most especially George Stevens, ends the story on a positive note. With the inner tension of racial prejudice resolved, the more perceptive individual could view *Giant* from a different perspective. The upbeat ending did not go unnoticed by some non-Texans; on the basis of Stevens's fan mail, responses to the racial issue in *Giant* did, however, follow regional divisions. The most astute appraisal came from Dr. Richard E. Renneker, associate director of the Psychiatric and Psychosomatic Research Institute at Mt. Sinai Hospital in Los Angeles. Dr. Renneker wrote Stevens:

> *I like your bold handling of the color prejudice theme. You succeeded in making [Bick Benedict] swing over toward a partially changed color attitude dynamically authentic and thus psychologically believable. A basic fault in most novels, and all previous films dealing with this theme, has been their inability to logically account for character shifts toward a position of lesser prejudice. . . . For the first time there is true identification with the downtrodden. It is an emotional event stamped by the physical pain of the fight [in Sarge's restaurant] which he loses—as all Mexicans had lost in their fight with white supremacy. He, Bick, thus feels even more deeply—the role of the defeated.[69]*

Stevens's son, film producer George Stevens, Jr., confirmed to me that, in addition to the film's entertainment value, his father "believed he found the 'Giant' story to be one in which he could express certain feelings and commitments that had developed through[out] his life. . . . He understood and had feeling for . . . the racial aspects of the story, the attitude towards women which, for its time, was very far ahead of the curve. . . . My father was very much a humanist and I think he was able to work his feelings on various subjects into the film without ever becoming a preacher."[70]

And so in the mythical story of Texas, George Stevens conveyed his vision of tolerance to the world. As the final scene faded to darkness, the message that lingered was that both Stevens and Ferber were leading the viewers into a more tolerant and unprejudiced future. And while the citizens of Marfa and the Big Bend country as a whole may or may not have shared George Stevens's social philosophy, they did indeed reap the economic benefits of his brief tenancy. They still remember *Giant* and the summer of 1955 with great fondness. Hollywood literally extended its helping hand at a time when it was needed most. Emma Mallan, the voluble owner of the Paisano Hotel, rated the filming as "the greatest thing that ever happened to Marfa in such a short time."[71] The *Big Bend Sentinel* agreed editorially:

> *The filming of Edna Ferber's "Giant" in this locale, has brought in valuable prosperity to Marfa, in addition to putting many thousand dollars in circulation. . . . Throughout the entire six weeks period all hotels and tourist courts have been filled to capacity. . . . Tourist travel reached an all-time high with people from throughout the state and neighboring states timing their vacations so that they might come here and watch the stars at work. George Stevens' welcoming and urging visitors on the set was responsible for that, for which Marfa can be grateful.*[72]

George Stevens is still regarded by many Big Bend citizens as Marfa's savior and most revered patron saint, and rightly so. Drought is ranching's greatest menace, and in 1955, the entire Southwest was caught in the throes of a decade-long dry cycle that literally paralyzed the ranching industry. Also the previous closure of local military installations—Fort D. A. Russell and the Marfa Army Airfield—further stagnated the local economy. For all the communities bordering the Big Bend country—Pecos, Fort Stockton, Marfa, Alpine, and Valentine—economic growth had long since ceased. And then in 1955, from a most unlikely and most unexpected source—Hollywood—came a sudden injection of wealth, and with it renewed hope for a brighter and more prosperous future. According to

Emma Mallan, Warner Brothers was spending about $60,000 a day in Marfa during the actual filming. In addition, "they left about $750,000 in Marfa from the time their crew first came in February until they left in July. Why, it [*Giant*] saved my hotel."[73]

This new wealth touched all segments of the community, both rural and urban. By early March, 1955, local stores reported sales increases from 10 to 50 percent, and the previously unemployed found work with Warner Brothers. Rancher Charlie Hancock, idled by the drought, gladly accepted a $200-a-week position as studio chauffeur. "'My business went up 33 percent,' added Walter Polksy, who runs a local shoe store. Comments from other shop owners ran pretty much along the same line—30 to 50 percent rise in business."[74] Bennett Cleaners was another local firm that benefited from the *Giant* economic bonanza. "We stayed open every single night," co-owner Lee Bennett reported. "I know we did Rock's and Elizabeth's costumes because they had two outfits. They would get so soiled that one had to be cleaned every night. Every evening they [the studio] would bring in something that had to be ready to go out the next morning."[75]

As president of the Marfa National Bank, W. E. DeVolin occupied a unique position to observe the fluctuations on the local economic barometer. "It [*Giant*] had a tremendous impact," he explained. "It put practically everybody in the community to work that wasn't working. And during the drought that was important. It sure helped 'em to pay bills and buy groceries."[76] Russ Thornburg, president of the Marfa Chamber of Commerce and owner of the City Drug Store, felt an even greater debt of gratitude to the film company. "I don't want to say 'Giant' saved this town," he explained, "but it darn near did."[77]

Many Marfa residents reminiscing about the *Giant* experience some four decades later acknowledge its economic benefits but also accord great value to the psychological rewards of being in a movie and living in the same town with a roster of international celebrities. One movie extra, a young married ranch wife at that time, expressed her enduring feelings: "There was nothing to do on the ranch, so instead we made a movie, had fun, and got paid for it. I'll never forget the summer of fifty-five."[78]

Epilogue

And so we come to the end of my historical tour through the Big Bend country. I hope each of you share my appreciation for the people—all the people—we met along the way, as well as acknowledge their contribution to the history and culture of this remote corner of civilization. While all may not have been the most admirable of individuals, each nevertheless represents a thread from which is woven the region's social fabric. It was their voices, in both Spanish and English, that articulated a composite image of earlier life along the Great River. From their recollections I attempted to recapture the spirit of the times through the eyes and words of the participants.

This book encompasses almost half a century of Big Bend social, cultural, and economic change, extending from the era of covered wagon travel in 1900 to the production of an epic film in 1955. Within that time frame the quicksilver mines closed, a national park was established, isolation gave way to urbanism, vacation ranchettes sprang up where range cattle once roamed, and tourists, filmmakers, ranchers, and the border patrol flying Cessnas, Pipers, and Bonanzas frequented the airstrip at Lajitas. Then there is the unchanging face of the Big Bend. Against the backdrop of spectacular mountains, breathtaking gorges, and hauntingly beautiful sunsets, the summers remain hot and dry, ranchers face fluctuating seasons, and even if one chooses to fly, the distances still seem interminable. And while violence still erupts periodically along the Rio Grande, the Big Bend country today is an infinitely safer place to live. Shootouts at Study Butte no longer occur; they are part of Big Bend history.

My literary departure from the region does not mean there are no other important Big Bend stories to be told. With each sunrise a new chapter of history awaits to be recorded; within every region of the state, either urban or rural, wooded or barren, humid or arid, there are occurring daily events that are the wellsprings of tomorrow's history. The Big Bend country, redolent in drama, romance, and ongoing change, is no exception. Other scholars are encouraged to investigate other topics rich in regional lore and significant in historical comprehension. For example, the settlement pattern of the Big Bend country is a prime topic awaiting the serious scholar. More work needs to be done on ranchers and ranch histories. The following names come to mind: Henry T. Fletcher, E. L. and A. S. Gage, W. B. Hancock, Meyer Halff, Lawrence Haley, the Kokernots, the Nevills, the Rooneys, and the Wilsons. For these topics, the Archives of the Big Bend is a good point of departure.

Big Bend business and economic history is another prime topic. Specific examples are Forchheimer's store in Alpine (we may have waited too long), Spencer Brothers, Inc., in Presidio (Carlos Spencer, president, is articulate and knowledgeable, and company records may still be available), Casner Motor Company, plus the history of banking—formal and informal—in the region. More work needs to be done on the economic importance of the candelilla wax industry. Also Big Bend military history needs further study, especially Camp Marfa/Fort D. A. Russell and the Marfa Army Air Field. Law enforcement is another virgin topic for research, as is the developing pattern of education. (Dr. Albert Tucker of Sul Ross State University is working on this topic.) The increasing importance of tourism and the work of artists and writers being lured to the region are topics frequently overlooked by scholars.

My interest in the region focused primarily on the "historical period," years that encompass the first half of the twentieth century. And while history, by its very nature, projects a retrospective view of the past, many of the episodes I investigated appear to sustain the old adage—"the more things change the more they stay the same." The problems faced by many of those early Big Bend citizens—and the solutions they sought—bear striking resemblance to the problems faced by society in the late twentieth century. For example, the factors that precipitated the Baiza-Acosta feud—poverty, absence of positive role models, and lack of formal education—are also cited as prime factors in contemporary urban violence and social decay. Likewise, the humanitarian impulses and racial sensitivities exhibited by Mary Daniels, Lucia Madrid, and Kathryn Casner could also serve as sociological guidelines for modern-day urban planners.

Frustrated business executives facing cyclical market trends could also benefit from rancher Hallie Stillwell's decision to diversify in order to survive the fluctuating Big Bend cattle market. And America's youth, who feel the age of opportunity has passed them by, should find inspiration in the career of W. D. Smithers. Lacking a proper camera, enlarger, and darkroom facilities to fulfill an assignment, he improvised with material at hand and produced an incomparable collection of historical photographs. Contemporary social philosophers struggling to reverse the decline of public education could also seek counsel with Lucia Madrid. Working virtually alone without funds, computers, or modern facilities, she successfully planted the seeds of knowledge and academic success among the underprivileged in one of the remotest sections of the nation. Madrid proved beyond a doubt that determination, not race, is the best prognosticator of success. Therefore, as these Big Bend residents—Lucia Madrid, Kathryn Casner, Hallie Stillwell, W. D. Smithers, and others—found solutions to their diverse problems, they exhibited traits of character, wisdom, and determination that, when viewed in the context of the late twentieth century, challenge contemporary society to take a more circumspect view of itself. When viewed as a social unit, these people proved that, no matter the obstacles, a measure of success awaits all who seek it.

And it is with a bit of nostalgia that I look back some seven decades to when I first visited the area in my cousin's Hudson Super-Six touring sedan. And it is with that same feeling that I bring this literary excursion to a close. The high adventure of collecting history bears with it the memories of those I met along the way: enjoying good conversation and tasty enchiladas with Bill Smithers (in innumerable Mexican restaurants), coffee and cake with Hattie Grace Elliott, a delightful drive along the Rio Grande with Stanley Casner, a fascinating conversation with Mary Daniels, a meeting with Lucia Madrid while Enrique taught my son how to make tortillas, Sunday dinner with O. C. Dowe, a Saturday afternoon helping Lee Bennett bathe her dogs (that's friendship!), breakfast at the Balia Motel coffee shop in Presidio with Carlos Spencer, a trip to the El Muerto Springs treasure site with ranch owner Mike Orton, a drive with Bill Fleming in a four-wheel-drive vehicle to the remote Johnson's Ranch site in Big Bend National Park, and a visit with Hallie Stillwell, sitting on the steps of her store watching swallows alight on a utility line in the hushed silence of a Big Bend twilight.

And it is with such pleasant memories that I say a final *adios amigos.*

Notes

Prelude. They Came in Covered Wagons:
The Diary of Irene Rogers

1. Alice Jack (Mrs. O. L.) Shipman, *Taming the Big Bend* (Austin: Von Boeckmann-Jones, 1926), 51. See also Robert M. Utley, "The Range Cattle Industry in the Big Bend of Texas," *Southwestern Historical Quarterly* 69 (Apr. 1966): 429.

2. *Texas Almanac and Industrial Guide, 1949–1950* (Dallas: A. H. Belo Corporation, 1949), 101–104.

3. *Alpine Times,* June 29, 1904; Aug. 2, 1905; and Aug. 29, 1906.

4. Oscar O. Winther, *The Transportation Frontier: Trans-Mississippi West, 1865–1890* (New York: Holt, Rinehart and Winston, 1964), 149. See also Martha Mitten Allen, "Traveling West: Nineteenth Century Women on the Overland Routes," Southwestern Studies Series No. 80 (El Paso: Texas Western Press, 1987).

5. "The First Fifty Years," *Texas Highways,* Fiftieth Anniversary Edition, 1917–1967, vol. 14, no. 9 (Austin: Texas Highway Department, 1967), p. 9. In 1899, the eccentric railroad tycoon, Colonel E. H. R. Green, who owned one of the first, if not *the* first, automobiles in Texas, drove his machine from Terrell to Dallas, a distance of thirty miles, in five hours and ten minutes. The colonel noted: "It was amusing to notice the sensation our appearance caused along the road. Cotton pickers dropped their sacks and ran wildly to the fence to see the strange sight" (9–10).

6. Irene Rogers's diary is quoted verbatim; some words have been inserted in place of abbreviations, with minimum punctuation added to aid the reader. Hattie Grace Elliott, Rogers's daughter, holds the original diary; a photocopy is in the author's files.

    The ten members of the Pearsall graduating class were Artie Morrow, Leona Fabian, Clemmie Loggins, Cora Lowe, Hixie DeVilbiss, Mary DeVilbiss, Irene Rogers, Ray Rogers, Edwin Fabian, and Lora Harris.

    Eleven members of the Rogers family traveled in two covered wagons; some of the young men probably rode horses. The party consisted of Thomas H.

Rogers, his second wife, Hattie, and their seven children. These were Irene, the oldest; Ray; two sets of twins, Hallie and Allie, and Ida and Arthur; and May, the youngest child. Also included in the party were Ed and George Rogers, Thomas Rogers's sons from a former marriage.

7. Frio Town was located sixteen miles west of Pearsall on the Frio River and was a major crossing point on the Old San Antonio Road. When the International-Great Northern Railroad bypassed Frio Town in the early 1880s, a new town, Pearsall, became the county seat, and most residents moved there.

8. When the pull was too great for one team of horses, a second was added, hence the term *double teams.*

9. Although some of the dates appear incorrect, the entries are in proper sequence.

10. Irene Rogers is referring to a poem in which Cooke describes the least desirable aspects of the Lone Star State.

11. "Map Showing Proposed System of State Highways," adopted June, 1917, State Highway Department, Office of State Highway Engineer, Austin, Tex. State-funded road improvements came late in Southwest Texas. The portion between Pearsall and Uvalde was completed in six- to ten-mile segments between 1948 and 1951. That portion between Uvalde and Sonora was improved in various stages between 1925 and 1937. Texas Department of Highways and Public Transportation, Transportation Division, Road Life Studies, Austin.

12. *Rand-McNally, 1918–1923,* "Principal Highways of Texas," Center for American History, University of Texas at Austin.

13. *1906 Post Route Map of Texas,* Post Office Department, published by order of Postmaster General George B. Cortelyou.

14. For more information on early wagon roads and stage travel in the Southwest, see Roy L. Swift and Leavitt Corning, Jr., *Three Roads to Chihuahua* (Austin: Eakin Press, 1988); J. W. Williams, *Old Texas Trails* (Burnet, Tex.: Eakin Press, 1979); and Robert H. Thonhoff, "San Antonio Stage Lines," Southwestern Studies Series No. 2 (El Paso: Texas Western Press, 1971). Intermittent points on the "Southern Route" between San Antonio and El Paso included Fort Clark, Camp Hudson, Howard's Well, Fort Lancaster, Lancaster Crossing on the Pecos, and thence to Fort Stockton (Comanche Springs).

15. *1906 Post Route Map of Texas.*

16. J. Evetts Haley, *Fort Concho and the Texas Frontier* (Boston: Houghton Mifflin, 1936), 26.

17. Wayne R. Austerman, "Giddings Station, A Forgotten Landmark on the Pecos," *Permian Basin Historical Annual* 21 (1981): 3. For more information on Pecos River crossings, see Clayton W. Williams, "The Pontoon Bridge on the Pecos, 1869–1886," *Permian Basin Historical Annual* 18 (1978): 3–18; J. W. Williams, *Old Texas Trails,* 354–55; and Lauderdale and Doak, *Life on the Range and on the Trail* (San Antonio: The Naylor Company, 1936), 42–43. Guy Skiles, longtime Langtry, Tex., resident and an authority on the lower Pecos River country, explains: "Before they built the railroad [Southern Pacific] they couldn't get to this country here . . . only [on] horse-back. . . . You couldn't cross the Pecos 'til way up the river a good ways. And most of the time it was always up, especially

during the summer when the snow on the mountains up there's melting . . . up in New Mexico." Undated interview with Jack Skiles, Sr., Langtry, Tex., University of Texas Natural Areas Survey.

18. State-funded road development along the original wagon routes in the trans-Fort Stockton region began in 1924 and was not completed until 1947. For example, Pecos County began construction on one 15.930-mile section of what became State Highway 67 southwest of Fort Stockton in 1936, which the state later rebuilt in 1947. Five years were required to complete the highway between Alpine and Marfa. The segment from the Brewster County line to Marfa was built in 1932–33, while the 9.218 miles from the Presidio County line to Alpine was not completed until 1937. Highway 385 south of Fort Stockton, the Chihuahua Trail "cut-off road," was not completed until the mid-1950s; however, the 47-mile section from Marathon to present Panther Junction, was begun by Brewster County in 1924 and rebuilt by the state in 1947. Texas Department of Highways and Public Transportation, Transportation Department, Road Life Studies.

19. Frances (Mrs. Aaron) Green to Kenneth B. Ragsdale, undated letter in author's files.

20. Unidentified newspaper clipping dated Mar. 5, 1909. Fort Worth University was chartered as Texas Wesleyan College on June 6, 1881; eight years later the trustees amended the charter under the name of Fort Worth University. The school of medicine was organized in July, 1894. In 1911, the institution was consolidated with the Methodist University of Oklahoma City.

21. Interview with Hattie Grace Elliott, Alpine, Tex., Aug. 29, 1975. While a member of the Texas House of Representatives, Everett Ewing Townsend coauthored the first bill to make portions of the lower Big Bend area a state park. He subsequently became known as the "father of the Big Bend National Park."

22. Ibid.

Scene I.
"I've Been Seeing Other Women"

1. Elton Miles, *More Tales of the Big Bend* (College Station: Texas A&M University Press, 1988), 242–43. For a comprehensive biographical sketch of Maggie Smith, see chapter 12, "Maggie Smith: Madrina of the Big Bend," in that source.

Through a fairly simple boiling process, the outer waxen layer of the *candelilla* plant is recovered and marketed for a variety of industrial uses in the United States. The raw wax is smuggled into the United States from Mexico to avoid the Mexican export tax.

2. Ibid., 244–45.

3. After a brief marriage, her first husband, Robert Hay, died of brucellosis. In 1922, she married ranch worker and cattle trader H. Baylor Smith, who died of suffocation in an Alpine hotel fire in 1944.

4. For a survey of early settlement in the lower Big Bend region, see J. O. Langford, *Big Bend, A Homesteader's Story* (Austin: University of Texas Press, 1976).

5. Ross Maxwell, *Big Bend Country: A History of Big Bend National Park* (Big Bend National Park, Tex.: Big Bend Natural History Association, 1985), 25.

6. Miles, *More Tales,* 247.

7. Undated interview with Mr. and Mrs. Frank Wedin, Tape 10, p. 9, Lower Canyons Project Files, Office of the State Archeologist, Texas Historical Commission, Austin.

8. Clifford B. Casey, *Mirages, Mysteries and Reality: Brewster Country, Texas* (Hereford, Tex.: Pioneer Book Publishers, 1972), 123.

9. Undated interview with D. D. Thomas, Lower Canyons Project Files, Transcripts Nos. 1 and 2, pp. 46–47.

10. Interview with Ross Maxwell, Austin, Sept. 6, 1989.

11. Probably not included on Maggie Smith's books was her interest in a herd of Mexican cattle given her by Mexican people whom she had befriended.

Chapter 1. Kathryn Casner:
She Practiced Medicine Without a License

1. Sandra L. Myres, *Westerning Women and the Frontier Experience, 1800–1915* (Albuquerque: University of New Mexico Press, 1982), 2.

2. The Casner family owned Ford distributorships in Marfa, Alpine, Pecos, and Fort Stockton. These were later sold, and the family acquired a General Motors franchise with agencies in El Paso, Marfa, and Alpine.

3. Interview with Kathryn Casner, Austin, Tex., Mar. 30, 1978.

4. Ibid. The climate at Chinati Ranch differed greatly from that at Marfa. The river valley region enjoys a near year-round moderate climate.

5. Ibid.

6. Kathryn Casner had attended Sul Ross State College, West Texas State College, and Howard Payne College, and held a teacher's certificate.

7. Mrs. Herbert G. (Ann) Tavenner to Kenneth B. Ragsdale, May 18, 1978. Letter in author's files.

8. Ibid.

9. Casner interview, Mar. 30, 1978.

10. Ibid.

11. Tavenner to KBR, Mar. 18, 1978.

12. Casner interview, Mar. 30, 1978.

13. Ibid.

14. Ibid.

15. Ibid. Kathryn cited the cooperating physicians as Dr. Francis E. Gibbons and a Dr. Thomas in Presidio, and Dr. Joseph Daracott in Marfa.

16. Kathryn tied a strip of cotton around the razor blade, marking the exact depth she wanted the incision.

17. Casner interview, Mar. 30, 1978.

18. Ibid., Jan. 16, 1978.

19. Ibid.

20. Tavenner to KBR, May 18, 1978.

21.ᐧ Casner interview, Jan. 16, 1978.

22. Undated interview with Stanley W. Casner, Austin, Tex., 1968.

23. Kathryn Casner interview, Jan. 16, 1978.

24. Ibid., Mar. 30, 1978.

25. Ibid; *Austin American-Statesman,* May 2, 1995.

26. Casner interview, Jan. 16, 1978. Stanley Casner, like his wife, was also a humanitarian. Once when a Mexican child sustained a broken arm in an automobile accident and the family was unable to pay the medical bills, he anonymously gave Edmundo Nieto, a Presidio civic leader, one hundred dollars to pay the bill. Interview with Edmundo Nieto, Presidio, Tex., Sept. 16, 1989. Manuel Franco, a former neighbor of the Casners at Chinati, wrote: "All the people on both sides of the border looked upon him [Stanley Casner] as one of their best friends. The Casners always helped people in distress. One time, I do not know how many tons, but he sent corn to be distributed among the poor and needy, and several other ways helped the people." Manuel Franco to Kenneth B. Ragsdale, July 30, 1978. Letter in author's files.

27. Tavenner to KBR, May 18, 1992.

28. Ibid. The Chinati experience apparently launched the Casner children toward useful and productive lives. Stanley, Jr., became a physician, while Ann majored in Spanish, took a Ph.D. at Texas Tech University, served as a Methodist missionary in South America for fifteen years, and later became a college professor.

29. Casner interview, Mar. 30, 1978.

Chapter 2. Mary Coe Daniels:
She Lived Muy A Gusto, A Gusto

1. Interview with Stanley Casner, Presidio, Tex., Dec. 10, 1996.

2. Susan Godbold, "Mary Coe Daniels, Woman of the West," *Junior Historian* (Dec. 1969): 21.

3. Ibid., 22.

4. Interview with Mary Daniels, Presidio, Tex., Dec. 10, 1967.

5. Godbold, "Daniels," 22.

6. Undated interview with Mr. and Mrs. Frank Wedin, Tape 10, page 10, Lower Canyons Project Files, Office of the State Archeologist, Texas Historical Commission, Austin.

7. Godbold, "Daniels," 22.

8. Interview with Carlos Spencer, Presidio, Tex., Sept. 16, 1989.

9. Daniels interview.

10. Laguna Meadow is located on a high plateau south of Mount Emory, the highest point in the Chisos Mountains.

11. Daniels interview.

12. Godbold, "Daniels," 24.

13. Susan Godbold interview with Mary Daniels, Presidio, Tex., Aug. 29, 1968, quoted from Godbold's original manuscript. Junior Historian archives, Marfa Museum, Marfa, Tex.

14. Daniels interview.

15. For more information on the Brite Ranch Raid, see W. D. Smithers, "Bandit Raids in the Big Bend Country," *Sul Ross State College Bulletin* (Sept. 1963); Noel L. Keith, *The Brites of Capote* (Fort Worth: Texas Christian University Press, 1950); and Walter Prescott Webb, *The Texas Rangers* (Austin: University of Texas Press, 1965).

16. Porvenir, a community some fifty miles upriver from Presidio, no longer appears on the highway maps of Texas.

17. Daniels interview.

18. Ibid.

19. Godbold, "Daniels," 31.

20. For more information in the Pilares raids, see Smithers, "Bandit Raids"; Smithers, *Chronicles of the Big Bend* (Austin: Madrona Press, 1976); and Webb, *Texas Rangers*. In *History of Marfa and Presidio County, Texas, 1935–1946* (Austin: Nortex Press, 1985), author Cecilia Thompson states: "On March 25, 1917, some fifty Mexicans crossed the Rio Grande and attacked the E. W. Nevill ranch and killed his son Glenn. . . . Pursued by the United States Cavalry and a company of Texas Rangers led by Captain Jim Fox, the bandits crossed the Rio Grande near Pilares, a well-known bandit stronghold. Allegedly they killed some thirty bandits as well as several inhabitants of the village. For his role in this event, Governor Hobby dismissed Captain Fox from the Ranger service" (152–54). According to this account, one Tom Snyder, a civilian and Mary Daniels's neighbor, accompanied Captain Fox on this mission.

21. Daniels interview. On Feb. 10, 1913, John S. H. Howard was killed in ambush near Pilares. Howard's party had captured Chico Cano and, while escorting him to headquarters, was ambushed by members of his gang. Cano escaped during the attack; Inspector Joe T. Sitters was also killed, and posse member J. A. Havrick was seriously wounded. Letter from Harry P. Hornby to Mrs. Mary M. Howard, Feb. 24, 1938. Copy in author's possession.

22. Daniels interview. Thomas W. Snyder was one of four local citizens who accompanied Captain James Fox and the Texas Rangers on the Pilares raid. See Cecilia Thompson, *History of Marfa and Presidio County, Texas, 1935–1946*, vol. 2 (Austin: Nortex Press, 1985).

23. Daniels interview. Harry (Hawkeye) Townsend operated a cotton gin in Porvenir. As a lieutenant in the United States Cavalry, Samuel L. Myers recalled meeting Townsend at Porvenir in 1929, where he purchased feed for his mounts (Kenneth B. Ragsdale, *Wings Over the Mexican Border* [Austin: University of Texas Press, 1984], 21). Historian Cecilia Thompson, in her history of Presidio County, notes that a Porvenir man, Harry Townsend, was slain on Sept. 16, 1938, by an unknown assailant.

24. Daniels interview.

25. Ibid.

26. Ibid.

27. Ibid.

28. The Conchos River rises in the mountains of Chihuahua, enters the Rio Grande a few miles above Presidio, and from that point usually provides a steady flow of water downriver.

29. Clifford B. Casey, *Mirages, Mysteries and Reality: Brewster County, Texas* (Hereford, Tex.: Pioneer Book Publishers, 1972), 118.

30. Mary Daniels claimed she introduced cotton farming in the Boquillas area of the Big Bend country. However, some forty miles upriver at Castolon, Wayne Cartledge harvested his first cotton crop in 1923. See Arthur R. Gomez, *A Most Singular Country* (Salt Lake City: Brigham Young University, 1990), 163.

31. Daniels interview. Around 1910, C. L. Hannold established a homestead on Tornillo Creek where he raised corn, maize, alfalfa, peanuts, and garden vegetables.

32. Wedin interviews, Tape 10, page 11, Lower Canyons Project Files.

33. Daniels interview.

34. Leon Hale, "No Skirt is Spotless, Says Ma," *Houston Post,* Apr. 9, 1965.

35. Copy of letter in author's files.

36. Interview with Bill Ivey, Lajitas, Tex., Sept. 16, 1989.

37. On June 1, 1942, the state of Texas paid Mary Coe Daniels $14,049.50, for 749 acres in section 4, block G-19, Brewster County, Texas. As the state was limited to $2 per acre for raw land, the Danielses' property apparently contained considerable improvements. *Excerpts from Minutes of the Meeting of the Texas State Parks Board,* Nov. 7, 1942, p. 3. Records of Land Acquisitions, Big Bend National Park, Texas Parks and Wildlife Department, Records Center, Austin.

38. Undated and unidentified newspaper clipping in Mary Daniels file, Junior Historian archives, Marfa Museum, Marfa, Tex.

39. Godbold, "Daniels," 25.

40. Interview with Carlos Spencer, Presidio, Tex., Sept. 16, 1989.

41. Interview with Edmundo Nieto, Presidio, Tex., Sept. 16, 1989.

42. Spencer interview.

43. Ibid.

44. Ibid.

45. Godbold, "Daniels," 31.

46. Letter from Travis Roberts to Kenneth B. Ragsdale, Nov. 6, 1989, in author's possession.

47. Spencer interview.

48. Daniels interview.

49. Content of letter recorded on tape in Dec., 1969, in author's files.

50. Daniels interview.

51. Spencer interview.

52. Ibid.

53. Ibid.

54. Daniels interview.
55. Vol. 2, p. 22.
56. Spencer interview.

Chapter 3. Lucia Madrid:
Planting the Seeds of Knowledge

1. Redford, Texas, was formerly known as El Polvo.

    Secundino Lujan, a married man and "resident-citizen" of Presidio County, received a 160-acre preemption land grant from the state of Texas, on May 3, 1876. The land, surveyed on January 13, 1873, and patented on May 3, 1876, was received under the provision of the act of August 12, 1870. The certificate of occupancy indicates that Lujan had lived on the land for three consecutive years, "beginning on the fifteenth day of January 1871." Mateo Carrasco and Lonjino Aguilar witnessed the transaction; Joseph Wilkin Tays of San Elizario, Texas, made the original survey. Texas Pre-Emption File 388, Texas General Land Office, Austin.

    The settlement process was not achieved without personal conflict. On Oct. 14, 1876, Louis Cardis [or Cardiz] wrote Secundino Lujan and Juan Jose Acosta from Fort Davis, Texas, as follows: "I heard that you still have not resolved the difference that exists between you and Mr. Mateo Carrasco; and seeing that the matter is taking a bad turn and threatens to disturb the tranquility of all of you, I take the liberty of offering this advice: Settle with Mr. Mateo Carrasco and give him his portion of land and pay him for the work he did; because if you do not settle amicably in this way and take the disputes to the courts all of you will end up ruined, both winners as well as the losers." Letter, translated by Enrique Madrid, Jr., in Madrid family collection, Redford, Tex.

    That portion of Southwest Texas was originally part of the Chihuahuan Acquisition, land acquired from Mexico between the end of the Mexican War and the Compromise of 1850. See J. J. Bowden, *Spanish and Mexican Land Grants in the Chihuahuan Acquisition* (El Paso: Texas Western Press, 1971).

2. *Fort Worth Star-Telegram*, Feb. 2, 1987.

3. Unidentified journal article, Nov., 1985; interview with Lucia Rede Madrid, Redford, Tex., Oct. 1, 1991.

4. Letter from Lucia Rede Madrid to Kenneth B. Ragsdale, Oct. 1, 1992. In author's possession.

5. Lucia Madrid interview, Oct. 22, 1991. Lucia was the sixth of eight children, seven of whom became teachers. Members of various generations of the Rede family reportedly have logged more than 120 years teaching school.

6. Telephone interview with Lucia Madrid, Oct. 12, 1992.

7. Andreas Madrid, Enrique Madrid's grandfather, who came from Ojinaga, Mexico, established one of the largest cattle ranches in the Redford area; Enrique's father, Ceferino Madrid, established the Madrid store in Redford in 1910. Later, Enrique became one of the area's leading citizens. He served as a Presidio County commissioner for more than twenty years, served as justice of

NOTES TO PAGES 59–62

the peace, and was instrumental in establishing El Camino Del Rio (the River Road between Lajitas and Presidio) and the international bridge at Presidio. At that time the bridge connecting Presidio, Texas, and Ojinaga, Mexico, was the only privately owned toll bridge on the United States-Mexican border. According to Enrique Madrid, Jr., "My father's assistance to the community went far beyond his friends and neighbors." Interview with Enrique Madrid, Jr., Redford, Tex., Sept. 16, 1989. Cited hereafter as Enrique Madrid interview.

8. Lucia Madrid interview, Oct. 22, 1991. Jaime Madrid attended Texas Tech University, studied for the priesthood at Conception Seminary in Missouri, which led to four years of theological study at Gregorian University in Rome. Following several priesthood assignments, he accepted a professorship (philosophy and theology) at a Catholic seminary in Indiana. Enrique Madrid, Jr., attended St. Mary's University in San Antonio before transferring to the University of Texas at Austin to study philosophy. He later moved to Redford to manage the family properties and continue a program of self-study on the history and archeology of the Southwest, while translating scholarly books on borderland history. Lydia Madrid received her bachelor of arts degree from the University of Texas at El Paso, before transferring to the Pratt Institute in New York City. After teaching printmaking at the Atlanta College of Arts, she studied for her master's degree at Indiana University, before accepting a teaching position in the University of New Mexico art department.

9. *International* (Presidio, Tex.), English Section, Oct. 22, 1991.

10. Lucia Madrid interview, Oct. 22, 1991.

11. The Head Start program evolved from the Economic Opportunity Act of 1964. In early 1965, a committee appointed by Sargent Shriver, director of the Office of Economic Opportunity, recommended a program for disadvantaged preschool children. On May 18, 1965, President Lyndon B. Johnson announced that 1,676 Head Start projects had been approved, establishing 9,508 centers to serve 375,842 children.

12. Lucia Madrid interview, Oct. 22, 1991.

13. Ibid.

14. Ibid.

15. Ibid. Dr. Maria Montessori, an innovative Italian educator, rejected traditional teaching methods and materials, choosing instead such things as beads arranged in graduated-number units for premathematics instruction, small slabs of wood designed to train the eye in left-to-right reading movements, map puzzles, and sandpaper letters that children traced with their fingers. Social manners were taught in serving meals and waiting tables. Dr. Montessori's students learned to read, write, count, and express themselves artistically.

16. Lucia Madrid telephone interview, Oct. 19, 1992.

17. Ibid. Enrique Madrid never told Lucia about the election matter and the trustee's threat. She learned this from his brother, Edmundo Madrid.

18. *Westward Magazine*, July 15, 1984.

19. Letter to the author, Oct. 1, 1992.

20. Telegram from Allen A. Raymond, president and publisher, *Grade Teacher*

Magazine, to H. G. Adams, superintendent of schools, Marfa Independent School District, Dec. 2, 1968; letter from Penelope Karageorge, public relations, *Grade School Magazine,* to H. G. Adams, Dec. 4, 1968, in Madrid personal collection, Redford, Tex. Lucia Madrid cited Superintendent Adams as supportive of her innovative teaching methods.

21. *Fort Worth Star-Telegram,* Feb. 2, 1987.
22. Enrique Madrid interview.
23. Current public library volume holdings in Texas towns with a population of 2,000 or less (Redford reported 110 inhabitants in 1947; later statistics are unavailable) are as follows: Troup, 5,489; McGregor, 9,413; Quitaque, 7,236; Quemado, 7,230; and Rhome, 8,567. Source: *Texas Public Library Statistics,* 1993.
24. Enrique Madrid interview.
25. *Fort Worth Star-Telegram,* Feb. 2, 1989.
26. Enrique Madrid interview.
27. Unidentified journal article, dated Nov., 1985, in Madrid personal collection, Redford, Tex.
28. Enrique Madrid interview.
29. Lucia Madrid interview, Sept. 16, 1989.
30. Interview with Nancy Sosa, Oct. 27, 1992, Austin, Tex.
31. *National Geographic,* Feb., 1984, p. 225.
32. *International* (Presidio), Apr. 20, 1990.
33. Enrique Madrid interview.
34. *Austin American-Statesman,* Mar. 28, 1990.
35. *International* (Presidio), Apr. 26, 1990.
36. Letters to Lucia Rede Madrid from United States senator Lloyd Benson, Dec. 19, 1989; and R. Vic Morgan, president, Sul Ross State University, Mar. 27, 1990.
37. Letter from Mayra Garcia to Lucia Rede Madrid, Jan. 15, 1990, Madrid personal collection, Redford, Tex.
38. *International* (Presidio), Apr. 26, 1990.
39. Ibid.
40. Text from videocassette of television special, in Madrid collection, Redford, Tex.
41. *International* (Presidio), Apr. 26, 1990.
42. Jane Addams (1860–1935), social reformer and pacifist, cowinner (with Nicholas Murray Butler) of the Nobel Prize for Peace in 1931, is probably best known as the founder of Hull House in Chicago, one of the first social settlements in North America. Edna Gladney was superintendent of the Edna Gladney Home in Fort Worth, a maternity home and child-placement agency. Her career inspired the motion picture, *Blossoms in the Dust* (1941), starring actress Greer Garson.
43. Undated interview with Mrs. H. E. Gatlin, Tapes 5 and 6, Page 9, Lower Canyons Project Files, Office of the State Archeologist, Texas Historical Commission, Austin.
44. Interview with Rex Ivey, Alpine, Tex., Sept. 16, 1989.
45. Ibid.

Scene II.
"A Few Men Are Going to Die"

1. Ron Tyler, *The Big Bend: A History of the Last Texas Frontier* (Washington: National Parks Services, 1975), 7.

2. Ibid., 10.

3. Mike Cox, *Red Rooster Country* (Hereford, Tex.: Pioneer Book Publishers, 1970), 62.

4. Interview with Brian Montague, Del Rio, Tex., June 4, 1966.

Chapter 4.
"Somebody Has Got to Be Killed"

1. Kenneth B. Ragsdale, *Quicksilver: Terlingua and the Chisos Mining Company* (College Station: Texas A&M University Press), 1976.

2. Interview with Dr. Ross Maxwell, Austin, Tex., Sept. 9, 1978.

3. For a comprehensive study of the Big Bend cattle industry, see Robert M. Utley, "The Range Cattle Industry in the Big Bend of Texas," *Southwestern Historical Quarterly* 69 (Apr. 1966): 419–41.

4. Brian Montague, Del Rio attorney, stated that "Gillespie, who was in fact a dangerous man, and Mr. E. E. Townsend [Brewster County Sheriff] were enemies. . . . I was told that Gillespie and Townsend met one another on the road—I believe, between Alpine and Marathon—and engaged in a fist fight. Because of Gillespie's dangerous character . . . Mrs. Townsend stood by and held a pistol on Gillespie, while the fight was going on to be sure that he did not, in some manner, get the drop on Mr. Townsend and kill him." Letter from Brian Montague to Kenneth B. Ragsdale, Mar. 15, 1968, in author's possession.

5. For one version of the Jim Gillespie smuggling episode, see C. A. Hawley, "Life Along the Border," *Sul Ross State College Bulletin* 44 (Sept., 1964): 7–88.

6. Hawley incorrectly cites the date as 1911.

7. Hawley, "Life," 81. Hawley apparently erred again; $25,000 seems like a high price to pay for a herd that was later evaluated at $12,500.

8. *Cause No. 375, The United States vs. 603 Head of Cattle,* Fort Worth Federal Records Center, FRC 379,499.

9. Hawley, "Life," 81.

10. Although Gibb's complicity in the cattle smuggling affair was never proven, he was, nevertheless, dismissed from the customs service.

11. O. C. Dowe to Kenneth B. Ragsdale, Apr. 8, 1966, in author's possession. Rozell Pulliam held a deputy's commission from Brewster County sheriff Allen Walton. Hawley gives Pulliam's first name as Roselle; the family spelling is Rozell.

12. A higher duty of up to four cents a pound was imposed on the heavier cattle.

13. Court documents cite the location as Haymond, Texas.

14. *Cause No. 375.*

15. Interview with O. C. Dowe, El Paso, Tex., Dec., 1967.

16. *Cause No. 375.*

17. Dowe interview.

18. Hawley, "Life," 83.

19. Dowe interview.

20. Interview with G. B. Crawford, Alpine, Tex., June 7, 1966.

21. Interview with Mrs. Robert Pulliam, Alpine, Tex., June 7, 1966.

22. Hawley cites the location as "Old Man Peck's" restaurant ("Life," 85).

23. Interview with Wayne Cartledge, Marfa, Tex., June 5, 1966.

24. Ibid.

25. *Alpine Avalanche,* Sept. 19, 1912.

26. Ibid., author's italics.

27. Subsequent to the murder, C. A. Hawley, who aided Gillespie in the financial transactions of the cattle purchase, resigned suddenly from the Chisos Mining Company. Mine employees maintained Hawley was not involved in the smuggling operation. Pressure to resign, they believed, came from mine owner Howard E. Perry.

28. *Cause No. 375.*

29. Ibid.

30. *Alpine Avalanche,* Feb. 6, 1913.

31. A. Rene Barrientos, deputy clerk, Maverick County, Tex., to Kenneth B. Ragsdale, Mar. 25, 1968, in author's possession.

32. Mrs. Pauline Orts, district clerk, Wilson County, to Kenneth B. Ragsdale, Mar. 18, 1968, in author's possession.

33. Dowe interview.

34. Ibid.

35. *Pacific Reporter* (1st), vol. 212, *State vs. Luttrell* (No. 2766), pp. 739–41.

36. Joint interview with Mrs. Robert Pulliam and Mrs. Pearl Pulliam, June 7, 1966, Alpine, Tex. A search of prison archives in New Mexico and Texas yielded no record of Paschal Luttrell's incarceration. According to Mrs. Pearl Pulliam, Luttrell moved to Corpus Christi and "became rather successful."

37. *Alpine Avalanche,* Oct. 8, 1987.

38. Terrence E. Poppa, *Drug Lord: The Life and Death of a Mexican Kingpin* (New York: Pharos Books, 1990), 2.

Chapter 5.
Shootout at Study Butte

1. For a comprehensive study of the Terlingua Quicksilver District, see Kenneth B. Ragsdale, *Quicksilver: Terlingua and the Chisos Mining Company* (College Station: Texas A&M University Press, 1976).

2. Records of the Texas Almaden Mining Company, Sanger Brothers Papers, presently held by the Arter, Hadden, Johnson, and Bromberg law firm in Dallas, Tex. Study Butte, pronounced Stoo-de Butte, was named for Will Study, an early resident in that area.

3. Interview with Robert L. Cartledge, Austin, Tex., Oct. 3, 1965.

4. Interview with H. C. Hernandez, Alpine, Tex., Oct. 23, 1972.

5. Sotol, an inexpensive liquor made from the stalk of the sotol plant, is popular in northern Mexico.

6. Cartledge interview.

7. Ibid.

8. Letter from W. O. Coffman to Robert L. Cartledge, Jan. 22, 1923. Copy in author's files.

9. Trial records, *Cause No. 1078, The State of Texas vs. George Billalba*, County-District Clerk, Brewster County, Alpine, Tex.

10. Ibid., letter from Dan Coffman to his sons, Mar. 5, 1923.

11. Ibid. Billalba is sometimes spelled Villalba; in Spanish B is sometimes pronounced as V. It appears the Coffmans were attempting to settle accounts that local ranchers had established with the mining company store. In this context, "old" is a familiar term and not necessarily intended as derogatory.

12. Ibid., undated correspondence.

13. Ibid., undated correspondence. The "old woman" is not identified; Simmons is probably Robert H. Simmons, former manager of the Texas Almaden Mining Company at Study Butte.

14. Interview with Bill Burcham, Alpine, Tex., June 6, 1966.

15. Cartledge interview.

16. Interview with Brian Montague, Del Rio, Tex., June 4, 1966.

17. Montague interview. Death certificates state Winslow Odell Coffman and Aubrey Douglas Coffman died on May 25, 1923. Cause of death, gunshot wound; homicide. Volume 2, pages 66 and 67, Death Records, Brewster County, Tex.

18. Cartledge interview.

19. *Alpine Avalanche,* May 31, 1923.

20. Ibid.

21. Interview with Hattie Grace Elliott, Alpine, Tex., Mar. 21, 1994.

22. Interview with Hallie Stillwell, Alpine, Tex., June 7, 1966.

23. *Alpine Avalanche Supplement,* May 31, 1923.

24. Ibid. Local opinions differed on Jake Billalba's whereabouts at the time of the shooting. Robert Cartledge and W. D. Smithers placed him at the George Billalba residence asleep. Brian Montague believed he was out driving in a herd of horses when he heard the gunfire. The charges against Jake Billalba were subsequently dropped.

25. Interview with Hunter Metcalfe, Marfa, Tex., June 6, 1966.

26. Montague interview. *Cause No. 1078.*

27. Metcalfe interview.

28. Trial Records, *Cause No. 1077. Cause No. 1077* charged George Billalba with the murder of Jack Coffman. Billalba was tried only for the murder of Winslow Coffman as *Cause No. 1078.*

29. Montague interview.

30. Ibid.

31. Letter from Dan Coffman to Robert L. Cartledge, May 26, 1924. Copy in author's files.

Chapter 6. The Anatomy of a Family Feud:
Part 1, A Sunday Afternoon at Espino's Tavern

1. Kenneth B. Ragsdale, *Quicksilver: Terlingua and the Chisos Mining Company* (College Station: Texas A&M University Press, 1976).

2. Interview with Edith Hopson, Alpine, Tex., June 7, 1966. The family name on local documents is spelled *Baisa,* the family spelling is *Baiza.*

3. *Fort Stockton Pioneer,* July 12, 1979.

4. Ross Maxwell, *Big Bend Country* (Big Bend National Park, Tex.: Big Bend Natural History Association, 1985).

5. Interview with William Warren Dodson, Marfa, Tex., Aug. 19, 1993. Dodson interview, Aug. 19, 1993.

6. Ibid.

7. Dodson interview, Sept. 18, 1993. Curtis Lloyd Hannold taught school at Dugout Wells from 1911 to 1919. This is the earliest record of a school at that site. Other early schools in the Big Bend area include Hot Springs (Boquillas), 1898, H. E. Middleton, teacher; Study Butte (Big Bend), 1892, C. C. Dugat, teacher; and San Vicente, 1900, Nellie Eberling, teacher. Source: Dr. Albert B. Tucker, "Ghost Schools of the Big Bend: Brewster County, Texas," manuscript, Sul Ross State University, Alpine, Tex.

8. Interview with Ramon Franco, Fort Stockton, Tex., Oct. 10, 1991.

9. Interview with W. D. Smithers, El Paso, Tex., Aug. 27, 1975.

10. Santa Elena [Santa Helena], Mexico, is a small village located across the Rio Grande adjacent to Castolon, Tex.

11. Dodson interview, Aug. 19, 1993.

12. Hopson interview.

13. Smithers interview.

14. Letter from Travis Roberts, Marathon, Tex., Nov. 6, 1989, in author's possession.

15. John Hollis's account of the double murder, as told to Robert Cartledge, Cartledge interview, Austin, Tex., Oct. 3, 1965.

16. *Alpine Avalanche,* Feb. 7, 1930. Italics mine.

17. Legal Transfer of Rights from Pablo Baiza to Wayne Cartledge, Mar. 26, 1930, Wayne Cartledge Collection, Archives of the Big Bend, Sul Ross State University, Alpine, Tex.

18. Letter from Edith Hopson to Kenneth B. Ragsdale, Nov. 8, 1965.

19. *Alpine Avalanche,* Sept. 5, 1930. On Feb. 23, 1931, by motion of the district attorney, the remaining case against Adolpho Baiza, *Cause No. 1191,* was dismissed, and "the two cases pending against Pablo Baesa [*sic*], in cause number 1191 and 1195 were [also] dismissed." District Attorney's order dismissing *Cause No. 1191* and *1195,* Feb. 23, 1931, Cartledge Collection.

20. Interview with Valentin Baiza, Fort Stockton, Tex., Oct. 22, 1972. Interview interpreted by Fort Stockton attorney Alex Gonzalez.

21. *Fort Stockton Pioneer,* Oct. 9, 1958.

22. Valentin Baiza interview.

23. Interview with Claudio Baiza, McCamey, Tex., Aug. 25, 1974.

24. Interview with Manuel Franco, Fort Stockton, Tex., Sept. 11, 1989. Ramon Franco, interviewed at Fort Stockton, Tex., on Oct. 19, 1991, also claimed that Cornelio Acosta killed Adolpho Baiza.

25. Carlos Baiza interview.

26. *Fort Stockton Pioneer*, Oct. 9, 1958.

27. Ibid.

28. Ibid.

29. Pablo Acosta, a witness for the state and son of Cornelio Acosta, later became "drug lord" of the Ojinaga-Presidio drug corridor, through which passed an estimated one-third of all illegal drugs consumed in the United States. Pablo Acosta was eventually killed in a Mexican government military-like assault on his hideout at Santa Elena, Mexico. See Terrence E. Poppa, *Drug Lord* (New York: Pharos Books, 1990).

30. Interview with Pecos County sheriff C. S. (Pete) Ten Eyck, Fort Stockton, Tex., Dec. 9, 1967.

31. Letter from Judge Hart Johnson to Kenneth B. Ragsdale, Sept. 14, 1967. Letter in author's file.

32. Ramon Franco interview, Oct. 10, 1991.

33. Interview with Joe Primera, Fort Stockton, Tex., Oct. 22, 1991.

34. *Cause No. 577, State of Texas vs. Pablo Baiza,* Office of the County Clerk, Pecos County, Tex., document dated Jan. 9, 1959. Texas is one of seven states that allows juries to assess punishment.

Chapter 7. The Anatomy of a Family Feud: Part 2, Another Beer Joint Killing

1. Interview with Valentin Baiza (translation by Alex R. Gonzalez), Fort Stockton, Tex., Oct. 22, 1972. Terlingua Abajo (Terlingua below, or lower Terlingua), an abandoned primitive Mexican village located on Terlingua Creek just north of the east entrance of Santa Elena Canyon, is now part of Big Bend National Park.

2. Ibid.

3. Interview with Shelby Blades, Fort Stockton, Tex., Dec. 12, 1957.

4. Ibid.

5. Interview with Roy Baiza, Fort Stockton, Tex., Sept. 12, 1989.

6. Evidence gathered by Fort Stockton attorney Shelby Blades from Augustin Baiza for the defense of Valentin Baiza. Blades interview.

7. Roy Baiza interview.

8. Blades interview.

9. Ibid.

10. *Fort Stockton Pioneer*, Feb. 20, 1966. After Valentin left the bar, Manuel Ramirez, Eulalio Acosta's friend, discovered that he had been wounded in the shooting. One of the bullets that passed through Eulalio's body struck Ramirez in the stomach. He walked to the south end of the bar and pulled up his shirt. "On seeing the flesh wound," Blades explained, "he shook his stomach and the bullet

dropped out on the floor. He handed the missile to the barmaid and left the tavern." The wound required no medication; no charges were filled in the matter. Blades interview.

11. Blades interview.

12. *Criminal Docket, Cause No. 1014, The State of Texas vs. Valentin Baiza,* 83rd District Court, Pecos County, Tex.

13. Interview with William H. Earney, Marfa, Tex., Sept. 13, 1989.

14. Blades interview.

15. *Fort Stockton Pioneer,* Apr. 27, 1967. "The Law of Communicated Threat" provides that if a person is threatened by another, the threatened individual has the right in certain circumstances to arm himself for protection.

16. Records, *Cause No. 1014.*

17. Earney interview.

18. Records, *Cause No. 1014.*

19. Earney interview.

20. Interview with Mrs. Francisca Acosta (translated by Joe Primera), Fort Stockton, Tex., Oct. 21, 1991.

21. Blades interview. Two years later (Valentin's was a five-year sentence) Blades returned to the 83rd District Court and requested a new trial. Judge Patterson granted the trial, and Blades petitioned the court for a dismissal. The judge concurred, and on April 30, 1969, he entered a final notation on the criminal docket: "Order entered terminating probation and dismissing indictment and discharging defendant." Valentin Baiza was again a free man. "Actually," Blades explained, "according to the record, he hadn't been convicted of anything." Blades interview.

22. Letter from Alex R. Gonzalez, Fort Stockton, Tex., Dec. 27, 1972.

23. Roy Baiza interview.

24. Interview with Nona Baiza, Fort Stockton, Tex., Dec. 9, 1967.

25. Roy Baiza interview.

26. Offense Report, Fort Stockton Police Department, Case No. 1A–12, Dec. 26, 1976.

27. Interview with Alex R. Gonzalez, Fort Stockton, Tex., Jan. 31, 1990.

28. Interview with Ramon Franco, Fort Stockton, Tex., Oct. 4, 1993.

29. Roy Baiza interview.

30. Virgil Carrington Jones, *The Hatfields and the McCoys* (Chapel Hill: University of North Carolina Press, 1948), 6.

31. Altina L. Waller. *Feud: Hatfields, McCoys, and Social Change in Appalachia, 1860–1900* (Chapel Hill: University of North Carolina Press, 1988), 11.

32. Jones, *Hatfields,* 5. For a broad interpretation of Texas feuds see C. L. Sonnichsen, *I'll Die Before I'll Run* (New York: Harper and Brothers, 1951).

33. Valentin Baiza interview.

34. Interview with Dr. Ricardo Romo, Austin, Tex., Jan. 17, 1994.

35. Interview with Adan Acosta, Fort Stockton, Tex., Oct. 22, 1991.

36. Romo interview.

37. Nona Baiza interview.

38. Alex R. Gonzalez interview.

39. Interview with Pete Terrazas, Fort Stockton, Tex., Sept. 12, 1989.

40. Interviews with Roy Baiza, Fort Stockton, Tex., Sept. 12, 1989; and Adan Acosta, Fort Stockton, Tex., Sept. 22, 1991.

Chapter 8.
"Hallie Stillwell Is What This Country Is All About"

1. Interview with Hallie Stillwell, Alpine, Tex., Sept. 13, 1989. Unless otherwise cited, all subsequent quotations by Hallie Stillwell are from this interview. For Hallie Stillwell's personal account of this period of her life, see *I'll Gather My Geese* (College Station: Texas A&M University Press, 1991).

2. The original one-room structure was later incorporated in the Stillwell ranch house, a comfortable six-room, two-bath structure.

3. For more on women's roles on the western frontier, see Ann Patton Malone, *Women on the Western Frontier,* Southwestern Studies Monograph, No. 70 (El Paso: Texas Western Press, 1983); Glenda Riley, *The Female Frontier* (Lawrence: University Press of Kansas, 1988); and Sandra L. Myers, *Westering Women and the Frontier Experience, 1800–1915* (Albuquerque: University of New Mexico Press, 1982). The following books, all out of print, also provide good insight into women's roles in the West: Nannie T. Alderson and Helen Huntington Smith, *A Bride Goes West* (New York: Toronto, Farrar and Rinehart, 1942); Mary Hudson Brothers, *A Pecos Pioneer* (Albuquerque: University of New Mexico Press, 1943); and Mary D. Rhodes, *The Hired Man on Horseback* (Boston: Houghton Mifflin, 1938). See also Sally Reynolds Matthews, *Interwoven: A Pioneer Chronicle* (1936; reprint, College Station: Texas A&M University Press, 1997).

4. Roy Walker (Son) Stillwell, was born Sept. 21, 1919; Marie Elizabeth (Dadie) Stillwell, June 18, 1921; and Guy Crawford Stillwell, Sept. 7, 1922.

5. From 1924 to 1929, cattle prices increased from $4.15 to $8.00 per hundred pounds; calf prices ranged from $5.30 to $9.60 per hundred pounds. *1867–1985 Texas Historic Livestock Statistics,* Texas Department of Agriculture and U.S. Department of Agriculture, p. 10. Cited hereafter as *Livestock Statistics.*

6. Between 1928 and 1929, livestock prices stabilized at $8.00 per hundred pounds; in 1930, prices dropped $1.90 per hundred; the following year they decreased another $3.50 per hundred; and bottomed out in 1933 at $3.10 per hundred pounds, or a 61 percent decline. *Livestock Statistics.*

7. Average annual precipitation for that region is 14.74 inches. The decade began with only 12.54 inches in 1930, and the region received 13.55 inches the following year; 1932 was considered a wet year with 21.48 inches, while the region reached an all-time low in 1934 with only 7.72 inches. *Climatological Data, Texas,* Annual Summaries, Weather Bureau of the U.S. Department of Commerce. Cited hereafter as *Climatological Data, Texas.* The rainfall statistics quoted for the Big Bend area are misleading. Alpine, Tex., located some 115 miles north of the Stillwell ranch, is the nearest point where weather data is reported in that area.

Since that area normally receives some 20 to 25 percent more precipitation than the Big Bend area, that differential must be considered in the significance of this data.

8. Hallie Stillwell, Personal Financial Records, Stillwell Store and Trailer Park, Alpine, Tex.

9. *Livestock Statistics.*

10. *Climatological Data, Texas.*

11. *El Paso Times,* Jan. 5, 1975.

12. Preliminary Inheritance Tax Report, filed in Alpine, Tex., June 1, 1948. Copy, Hallie Stillwell Personal Files, Alpine, Tex.

13. *Climatological Data, Texas.* Annual Summaries, Weather Bureau of the U.S. Department of Commerce.

14. Ibid.

15. Letter from Hallie Stillwell to Frank O. Ray, July 20, 1949. Stillwell Family Papers, Alpine, Tex.

16. For more information on the *candelilla* wax recovery process, see Michael Barlow, "From the Wilderness," *Texas Historian* 35 (Jan., 1975); "Wax From Weeds," *Literary Digest* 84 (Feb., 1925); T. A. Wastler, F. M. Daugherty, and H. H. Sineath, "Industrial Raw Materials of Plant Origin," *Bulletin* (Georgia Institute of Technology) 15; and John R. Whitaker, "Wax From the Wilderness," *Nature Magazine* 34 (Nov., 1941).

17. Undated interview with Hallie Stillwell, transcript nos. 1 and 2, pp. 51–53, Lower Canyon Projects Files, Office of the State Archeologist, Texas Historical Commission, Austin. (Apparently page 53 is incorrectly numbered and should be page 52.) Cited hereafter as Lower Canyon Projects Files.

18. Tesa Bunsen, "Silk and Rawhide," *Texas Historian* 39 (May, 1979): 5–6.

19. *Livestock Statistics.*

20. Undated interview with Hallie Stillwell, Lower Canyon Projects Files, p. 44, Office of the State Archeologist, Texas Historical Commission, Austin.

21. *Alpine Avalanche,* Oct. 28, 1955.

22. *Alpine Avalanche,* appropriate dates previously cited.

23. Gerald G. Raun, editor/publisher, *Alpine Avalanche,* to KBR, undated [1990].

24. Interview with Inda Benson, Alpine, Tex., Sept. 13, 1989.

25. The Big Bend National Park Historical Association acquired the unbound remainders of *How Come It's Called That?* from October House, which they had bound for sale in Big Bend National Park. That edition also sold out.

26. Letter from Senator Dorsey B. Hardeman to Hallie Stillwell, Mar. 24, 1964. Copy in author's files.

27. Undated interview with Judge Sam Thomas, Alpine, Tex., conducted by Jim Cullen. Hallie gave high priority to training and preparation for her judicial responsibilities, attending annual seminars conducted by Lamar University and Texas A&M University. These sessions further instilled in her the belief that strict interpretation of the law meant equality to all, including both friends and other public officials.

28. *Alpine Avalanche,* Apr. 30, 1970.

29. Hallie Stillwell, 824; Lewis B. Gordon, 774. Unopposed in the general election, Hallie Stillwell received 1,131 votes; Gordon, 6 write-in votes. Brewster County Election Returns, Democratic Primary, 1970, County Clerk's Office, Alpine, Brewster County, Tex.

30. Founded in Corpus Christi, Tex., in 1929, the League of United Latin American Citizens (LULAC) has addressed such issues as civil rights, education, and living conditions in *colonias* on the United States-Mexican border. It remains unclear why LULAC chose a black man as Hallie's opponent.

31. Hallie Stillwell, 737 votes; Johnny Sotello, 663 votes. Unopposed in the general election, Hallie Stillwell received 638 votes, Sotello, 26 write-in votes. Brewster County Election Returns, 1974.

32. Texas Senate Resolution No. 171, 66th Legislature, Regular Session, February 28, 1979. Copy in author's possession.

33. *Climatological Data, Texas.*

34. *Fort Worth Star-Telegram,* June 25, 1987.

35. "Hallie's Hall of Fame" museum, located adjacent to the Stillwell Store and Trailer Park on FM 2677, documents the life achievements of Hallie Stillwell with photographs, artifacts, apparel, and family memorabilia.

36. *Texas Monthly,* Apr., 1990, 168. In the Apr., 1990, issue, *Texas Monthly* honored ten Texas women by designating them *Grande Dames.*

37. *Stephenville Empire-Times,* Aug. 8, 1990.

38. *Texas Monthly,* Apr., 1990, 168. Various positions held by Hallie Stillwell are as follows: president and board member, Marathon Independent School District; member, Marathon Parent Teachers Association; president, Marathon Study Club; member, Davis Mountain Federated Womens Club; trustee, Brewster County Park at Fort Pena Colorado; president, Alpine Pilot Club; president, American Legion Auxiliary; director, U.S. 67 Highway Association; secretary, Big Bend National Park Development Committee; chairman, Brewster County Historical Survey Committee; president, West Texas Historical and Scientific Society; and member, Texas and Southwestern Cattle Raisers Association.

39. Virginia Madison, *The Big Bend Country of Texas* (New York: October House, 1968), 177.

40. *Fort Worth Star-Telegram,* June 25, 1987.

41. *Alpine Avalanche,* Dec. 21, 1978.

Chapter 9. Dobie's Children:
Discovering the Treasure of the Imagination

1. In 1540, Spanish Viceroy Antonio de Mendoza appointed Francisco Vasquez de Coronado to lead an expedition to locate the reportedly treasure-laden seven cities of Cibola. Although Coronado found no gold (and the seven cities proved to be Zuni villages in western New Mexico), the search for buried wealth continues. Hence the term, "Coronado's children."

2. This device consisted of two highly polished wooden cylinders about four inches long, one inch in diameter, and contained some secret substance. These

cylinders were attached by an eighteen-inch chain. Included with this remarkable device were two small slivers of metal, one supposedly silver, the other gold. The instructions were as follows: if you are seeking gold (as most treasure hunters were), you place the gold sliver over the lifeline of your left hand and then lightly grasp one of the cylinders against the gold sliver, allowing the other cylinder to swing free. That was the key to a successful treasure hunt; as you neared the treasure site, the free swinging cylinder would literally overpower you, leading you directly to the treasure.

3. In the half century since its first publication, *Coronado's Children* has appeared in at least ten discernibly different editions, ranging from the Bantam Books paperback edition in 1953 to the lavish 1983 Neiman-Marcus edition, printed by Andrew Hoyem of San Francisco.

4. *Daily Texan,* Feb. 15, 1931.

5. Ibid.

6. The Presidio Mine at Shafter, from 1880 until it closed in 1942, produced some 30,293,606 ounces of silver along with small amounts of gold and lead. And the Chisos Mining Company at Terlingua, located in the very heart of the Big Bend, was one of the major producers of quicksilver before it closed at the end of World War II. For more information on Big Bend mineral deposits, see *The Handbook of Texas,* vol. 2 (Austin: Texas State Historical Association, 1952–76), p. 611. See also E. H. Sellards and C. L. Baker, *Structural and Economic Geology: The Geology of Texas,* vol. 2, University of Texas Bulletin No. 3401 (Jan. 1, 1934); and Kenneth B. Ragsdale, *Quicksilver.*

7. Interview with Michael Collins, Austin, Tex., Feb. 11, 1993.

8. This and subsequent quotations by Guy Skiles are taken from an undated oral interview conducted by Mavis Bryant at Langtry, Tex., Tapes 20 and 21, Transcript 23, pp. 30–34, Lower Canyons Project Files, Office of the State Archeologist, Texas Historical Commission, Austin, Tex.

9. Interview with Willie Belle Coker, Austin, Tex., Feb. 17, 1993.

10. Telephone interview with Hallie Stillwell, Brewster County, Tex., Feb. 14, 1993.

11. Telephone interview with Dadie Potter, Brewster County, Tex., Feb. 14, 1993.

12. J. Frank Dobie, *Coronado's Children* (New York: Grosset and Dunlap, 1930), 189–90.

13. Ibid., 193.

14. Ibid., 196–97.

15. Interview with Lee Bennett, Marfa, Tex., Sept. 15, 1989; telephone interview, Jan. 29, 1993. As sponsor of the Marfa High School Junior Historian chapter from 1963 to 1980, Bennett received state and national recognition for her creative learning activities.

16. Dobie, *Coronado's Children,* 202.

17. Bennett interview.

18. Ibid.

19. Telephone interview with Herbert F. Hamilton, Huntington, Conn., Jan. 29, 1993.

20. For more information on J. Pendleton Murrah, see Ida Mae Myers, "The Relations of Gov. Murrah, of Texas, With the Confederate Military Authorities,"

master's thesis, University of Texas at Austin, Aug., 1929. J. Pendleton Murrah, who served as Texas governor from Nov., 1863, until the end of the Civil War, grappled continuously with Confederate authorities and a depleted treasury. On June 11, 1865, ill and frustrated, he abdicated both his marriage and the governorship and departed for Mexico. He died of tuberculosis the following month in Monterrey. His burial place is unknown.

21. Hamilton interview, Jan. 29, 1993.

22. Although the treasure site was on private property, its remote location made controlled access difficult.

23. Hamilton interview, Jan. 29, 1993. Dobie had other problems with his buried treasure stories. On Sept. 10, 1925, Lock Campbell, a Southern Pacific railroad conductor and devoted treasure hunter, wrote Dobie as follows: "A friend loaned me your *Legends of Texas,* and I read with interest your story of 'The Lost Nigger Mine.' The story if properly written, would be a very interesting one, but you have certainly got it balled up terribly.... I am sorry you made the reference you did about the Reagan boys. They were rough ... but I never heard of them being suspected of being murderers." Campbell was referring to the following statement that appears on page 65 of *Legends of Texas:* "Their [Reagan's] pasture was full of stolen stock at the time and they did not want the negro to talk; so they forthwith shot him and pitched him into the Rio Grande." Undoubtedly anticipating such a response, Dobie states on the preceding page, "I tell the legend as it is told, not as history would sift it." See "The Nigger Gold Mine of the Big Bend," in *Legends of Texas,* edited by J. Frank Dobie, no. 3 (Austin: Texas Folklore Society, 1924), 54–67.

    Lee Reagan also took exception to the same statement that subsequently appeared in *The Country Gentleman,* and on Jan. 30, 1927, wrote Loring A. Schuler, editor, Curtis Publishing Company: "I have taken the matter up with the largest and most reliable damage suit attorney of my acquaintance in the State of Texas ... it is my opinion and that of my two brothers that we are entitled to damages for such an article.... you will hear from us." Schuler, in turn, wrote Dobie on Feb. 3, 1927: "I'm sending you herewith a copy of a letter just received from Lee Reagan in which he threatens suit for damages because of the LOST NIGGER GOLD MINE article.... What I want is your statement regarding the article as well as your opinion from a knowledge of local circumstance, as to the possibilities of their getting away with a suit for damages in case they bring one." Dobie's response is unknown. Texas Authors Collection—Dobie, Box No. 2.207/ E122, Barker Texas History Center, University of Texas at Austin.

24. According to the U.S. Department of Commerce weather summary for 1956, "The drought which has been in progress in the Plains States from Nebraska southward for several years intensified in 1956. It became one of the worst on record.... *Weekly Weather and Crop Bulletin,* XLIV, 1a, p. 3, showed that the drought has been in progress over western Texas since 1946." Between 1951 and 1957, the Big Bend area recorded annual rainfall deficits of from two to seven inches. The average rainfall for 1956 was only 9.15 inches. *U.S. Department of Commerce Climatological Data, Texas Annual Summary 1956,* vol. 61, no. 13.

25. Interview with Robert Coffee, Austin, Tex., May 21, 1990.

26. Hamilton interview, Feb. 8, 1993.

27. Ibid.

28. Coffee interview, May 21, 1990.

29. Ibid.

30. Roger Conger narrative of the El Muerto Springs treasure hunt. Copy in author's file. All further Conger quotations are from this source.

31. Coffee interview.

32. Ibid.

33. After graduating from the University of Texas at Austin in 1962 with a degree in architectural engineering, Herbert Hamilton posted an enviable record of achievements: structural design of the Toledo Bend Dam, design of the early North Sea drilling platforms, and in 1969, design and construction of 100 more drilling platforms in Angola, while supervising construction of some 250 miles of offshore pipelines. He subsequently formed Planeterra, his own Houston-based engineering consultancy and contracting company. Robert Coffee took two degrees from the University of Texas (journalism, 1956; architectural engineering, 1962), and later formed his Austin-based firm specializing in park, recreational, and historical preservation projects. Don Wukasch graduated from Baylor Medical School in 1962, where he specialized in cardiovascular surgery. His professional associations include Dr. Michael E. DeBakey (seven years) and Dr. Denton A. Cooley (ten years). In 1986 he organized the Houston Medical Clinic. Jim Eller took a degree in engineering at the University of Texas. His whereabouts are unknown. James LeBlond (deceased) subsequently left Waco and entered the banking business in the Lower Rio Grande Valley area. A published author, Roger Conger (deceased) was appointed president of the Texas State Historical Association. A conversation with Roger during which he described his experience in the El Muerto Springs treasure hunt led to my including a chapter on Big Bend treasure hunts in this collection. Roger graciously contributed his narrative for this chapter.

34. *Austin American-Statesman,* May 11, 1964.

35. Hamilton interview, Apr. 16, 1993.

36. Ibid.

37. Ross A. Maxwell, *Big Bend Country: A History of Big Bend National Park* (Big Bend National Park, Tex.: Big Bend Natural History Association, 1985), 6.

38. Interview with Laura Gutierrez-Witt, Austin, Tex., Mar. 4, 1993.

39. Coffee interview, May 21, 1990.

40. Ibid.

Chapter 10. W. D. Smithers: Big Bend Renaissance Man

1. W. D. Smithers, *Chronicles of the Big Bend* (Austin, Tex.: Madrona Press, 1976), xi–xii.

2. Mark H. Bacon and William R. Felton, *The Frontier Years: L. A. Huffman, Photographer of the Plains* (New York: Bramhall House, 1955), 50.

3. Smithers, *Chronicles*, 3.

4. Mary Katherine Cook, "W. D. Smithers, Photographer-Journalist," master's thesis, University of Texas at Austin, 1975, 19; undated letter from W. D. Smithers to Mary Ellen MacNamara (response dated Jan. 8, 1981), Smithers 1981 Correspondence File, Smithers Collection, Harry Ransom Humanities Research Center, University of Texas at Austin, cited hereafter as Smithers Collection, HRC.

5. Ibid., 17.

6. Smithers, *Chronicles*, 9.

7. "58 Years in the Big Bend, 1917–1974," 10–11, W. D. Smithers Manuscript Collection, Box No. 1 of 2, HRC.

8. Smithers, *Chronicles*, 18.

9. Ibid., 29.

10. Interview with W. D. Smithers, El Paso, Tex., Aug. 27, 1975.

11. Ibid.

12. Smithers, *Chronicles*, 65.

13. Cook, "Smithers," p. 50, n. 9.

14. Smithers interview.

15. Interview with Gen. William L. Kennedy, San Antonio, Tex., Jan. 19, 1978.

16. Smithers interview.

17. Ibid. In 1951, Noah Rose and Marvin Hunter published *The Album of Gunfighters* (Bandera, Tex.: Hunter and Rose, 1951), which contained several items from the Rose Collection. Following Rose's death on Jan. 25, 1952, the University of Oklahoma acquired the entire N. H. Rose Collection. For more on McArthur Cullen Ragsdale (apparently no relation to the author), see J. Evetts Haley, *Focus on the Frontier* (Amarillo, Tex.: Shamrock Oil and Gas Corp., 1957).

18. Cook, "Smithers," 30. While working in San Antonio in 1923, Gutzon Borglum, the Mount Rushmore sculptor, engaged Smithers to photograph the sculptor's clay models for him to study the details of facial expressions of the four presidents' images. Smithers recalled he made more than one thousand exposures in the sculptor's Brackenridge Park studio.

19. For more information on Amasa Gleason Clark (1825–1927), see Chris Emmett, *Texas Camel Tales* (1932; Austin, Tex.: Steck-Vaughn, 1969); *Reminiscences of a Centenarian, as Told by Amasa Gleason Clark, Veteran of the Mexican War to Cora Tope Clark* (Bandera, Tex.: n.p., 1930); and Frank Bishop Lammons, "Operation Camel: An Experiment in Animal Transportation in Texas 1857–1860," *Southwest Historical Quarterly* 61, no. 1 (July, 1957).

20. Smithers, *Chronicles*, 67.

21. Ibid., 112.

22. Ibid., 115.

23. W. D. Smithers manuscript, "Pigeons," 115–21, Center for American History, University of Texas at Austin. According to Smithers, that flight established a distance record for a pigeon carrying a message. The program was launched

with six borrowed pigeons, three from the United States Army and three from individuals. (Note: the Center for American History at the University of Texas also holds some of the Smithers manuscript materials.)

24. Ibid., 119–121.

25. Smithers interview. On March 3, 1929, Mexican Gen. Jose Gonzalo Escobar launched a rebellion to gain control of the Mexican government. Fighting flared throughout northern Mexico, threatening the safety of many American citizens living in Texas, New Mexico, and Arizona. The rebellion ended on Apr. 30, 1929, with the surrender of the rebels. For a comprehensive overview of the rebellion from a United States perspective, see Kenneth B. Ragsdale, *Wings Over the Mexican Border* (Austin: University of Texas Press, 1984).

26. For an in-depth study of the Johnson's Ranch airfield, also see Ragsdale, *Wings Over the Mexican Border.*

27. "Reminiscences of W. D. Smithers," an undated interview by Joe Coltharp, typescript in Smithers Collection, HRC.

28. Smithers interview.

29. Smithers, *Chronicles,* 4

30. W. D. Smithers, "Nature's Pharmacy and the Curanderos," *Sul Ross State College Bulletin* 41, no. 3 (1961): 16.

31. Ibid., 38.

32. Ibid., 21.

33. Ibid., 22.

34. Smithers manuscript, "Avisadores and Curanderos," 5-C, Center for American History, University of Texas at Austin.

35. *Austin American-Statesman,* Sept. 19, 1994. Professor Joe Graham, an anthropologist at Texas A&M University at Kingsville, a leader in this field, claimed that a majority of Mexican Americans residing in seven South Texas communities use traditional remedies "instead of—or in addition to—Western medicine." Graham argued that "dietary supplements such as herbs should be judged by the government under a separate category [apart from traditional medicine] recognizing their use for self-medication in many world cultures." Within this context both anthropologists and herbalists argue that Americans should enjoy the same opportunities as citizens of Germany, Japan, France, and Canada. Undated telephone interview with Professor Joe Graham, Kingsville, Tex.

36. Smithers manuscript, "Avisadores and Curanderos," 5-G, Center for American History, University of Texas at Austin.

37. Smithers, *Chronicles,* 88.

38. Ibid., 92.

39. Cook, "Smithers," 39–40. See also "Smithers Reminiscences," Smithers Collection, HRC. Mount Locke is located in the Davis Mountain in West Texas near Fort Davis.

40. Smithers, *Chronicles,* 92–95. Since the service had no prior designation for the assignment, Smithers functioned as an "official investigator." The assignment had an enduring impact on border patrol procedures. Before completing the project, Smithers constructed for the El Paso headquarters a fixed-focus camera

for making identification photographs of aliens, and another for copying fingerprint cards.

41. Cook, "Smithers," 44.

42. *Sul Ross Bulletin,* Sept. 1, 1961, p. 11.

43. Cook, "Smithers," 111.

44. Ibid., 44–46; "Smithers Reminiscences," HRC.

45. Cook, "Smithers," 45–56. Subjects included: No. 1, Roundup: Cattle Drive, Herd, Branding, Chuck Wagon; No. 7, Casa Grande Mountain, Two Cowboys, Yucca in Bloom, Little Donkey in the Desert; No. 40, Yellowstone Falls, Old Faithful, Yellowstone Lake, Mt. and River Scene; and No. 66, San Antonio, Tex.: The Alamo, Sunken Gardens, Lake and Swans, and San Jose Mission. Source: Photo Color Lamp Shade brochure in author's possession.

46. Ibid.

47. "Smithers Reminiscences," HRC.

48. *Alpine Avalanche,* Mar. 17, 1966. The *Avalanche* apparently erred. According to Smithers, his first aerial photographs were not taken until the mid-1920s.

49. Cook, "Smithers," 47–48. On November 24, 1966, Smithers wrote Dr. Joe B. Frantz, then director of the Texas State Historical Association, that "I am still writing Captions and Index of them [the photographs], but the typing costs and photo material are too much to pay from my pension check." W. D. Smithers to Joe B. Frantz, in author's possession.

50. Letter from W. D. Smithers to Texas State Historical Association, Sept. 9, 1968. In author's possession.

51. The addresses are contained in Collectors' Institute Transactions, Fifth Annual Meeting, Nov. 18, 1972.

52. Letter from W. D. Smithers to Kenneth B. Ragsdale, June 22, 1975.

53. Undated letter from W. D. Smithers to Kenneth B. Ragsdale. In author's possession.

54. Ibid., July 18, 1977.

55. Ibid., Feb. 27, 1978. My manuscript with which Smithers was so helpful was published in 1985 by the University of Texas Press as *Wings Over the Mexican Border.*

56. Smithers had experienced previous financial difficulties because of other temporary income. He wrote on January 8, 1979, "I had the same problem in 1967–1968 and 1969 when I printed and indexed the pictures for the Collection, and I lost my pension for two or three years." W. D. Smithers to Kenneth B. Ragsdale, in author's possession. On Nov. 24, 1979, he received $277.92 in royalties from *Chronicles of the Big Bend,* published in 1976. Smithers Day Book entry, Smithers Collection, HRC.

57. Smithers correspondence, June 16, 1979. In Aug. and Sept., 1980, he purchased two desk lamps costing $34.82. Day Book entry, HRC.

58. Ibid., Sept. 7, 1979. Apparently the "big story" Smithers referred to was "An Autobiography of My Seventy Years as a Photo-Journalist, 1910–1980."

59. Entry, Smithers's Day Book, HRC.

60. Ibid.

61. Letter from W. D. Smithers to Mary Ellen MacNamara, May 23, 1981, Smithers Collection, HRC.
62. Entry, Smithers's Day Book, Smithers Collection, HRC.
63. Interview with Mrs. Jimmie Grim, El Paso, Tex., Jan. 6, 1995.
64. Ibid.
65. Ibid. Roy L. Flukinger, senior curator for photography and film, the University of Texas at Austin, Harry Ransom Humanities Research Center, located Rosario Lozoya Gonzalez, who lived in Juarez, Mexico, through Smithers's El Paso attorney, Andrew Guevara. Gonzalez's inheritance was contained in four boxes that included files of his unpublished manuscripts ("A Biography of My Seventy (70) Years as a Photo-Journalist" among them), some photographs, negatives, correspondence, newspaper clippings, books, and magazines. These materials were acquired from Gonzalez by the University of Texas at Austin and incorporated with the Smithers Collection. Copy of inventory in author's files.
66. Interview with Gen. William L. Kennedy, San Antonio, Tex., Jan. 19, 1978.
67. Cook, "Smithers," 38.
68. *Sul Ross Bulletin,* Sept. 1, 1961, p. 5.
69. Copy of book in Smithers Collection, HRC.
70. David Pyle, "The Ethnographic Photography of W. D. Smithers," *Perspectives on Photography* (Austin, Tex.: Humanities Research Center, University of Texas, 1982), 150.
71. Ibid.

Chapter 11.
When Hollywood Came to Marfa

1. Letter from Evelyn Davis to Mark Johnson, KVIA-TV, El Paso, Tex., Dec. 1, 1984. Copy in author's files; *Big Bend Sentinel* (Marfa, Tex.), June 9, 1955, cited hereafter as *Sentinel*. Both Marfa and the state of Texas have a history in filmmaking. In 1950, *High Lonesome* was filmed in the Marfa area. Other major productions that were filmed in the state, and the locations, are Austin, *They Lived by a Slender Thread* (1913); Houston, *North of the 36th* (1924); San Antonio, *The Big Parade* (1925), *Wings* and *The Rough Riders* (1927), *West Point of Air* (1934), and *I Wanted Wings* (1940); Brackettville, *The Alamo* (1959); Claude, *Hud* (1962); and Archer City, *The Last Picture Show* (1971).
2. *Texas Observer,* July 4, 1955.
3. *New York Times,* Sept. 28, 1952.
4. *Dallas Morning News,* Sept. 28, 1952.
5. Partnership Agreement, May 5, 1953, George Stevens Collection, Margaret Herrick Library, Academy of Motion Picture Arts and Sciences and Academy Foundation, Beverly Hills, Calif. Cited hereafter as Stevens Collection. According to *Time* magazine, Ferber's original asking price for the film rights were so high no one was interested. Stevens "decided to do it [produce the film] if the money went into the film rather than in buying the property. So he persuaded

author Ferber to become his producing partner for a percentage of the profits." *Time,* Oct. 22, 1956, p. 112.

Other works by Edna Ferber include *So Big,* for which she won a Pulitzer Prize in 1924, and *Show Boat,* published in 1926, which also became a successful musical.

6. Production Agreement, Dec, 14, 1953, Stevens Collection.

7. George Stevens had worked with Ivan Moffat and Fred Guiol previously. In Stevens's highly successful 1953 production, *Shane,* Moffat served as associate producer and Guiol, who began his film career in 1913, served as associate director. For an in-depth study of George Stevens's filmmaking philosophy, see Bruce Petri, *A Theory of American Film: The Film Techniques of George Stevens* (New York and London: Garland, 1987).

8. Interview with Emma Mallan, Marfa, Tex., Sept. 15, 1989.

9. Telephone interview with J. W. Evans, Marfa, Tex., Mar. 23, 1992.

10. Contract between Giant Productions and Cole A. Means, Apr. 14, 1955. Stevens Collection.

11. Contract between Giant Productions and Ben Avant, no date. Stevens Collections.

12. Inter-Office Communication, Mel Deller to Eric Stacy, Feb. 22, 1955. Stevens Collection.

13. Undated clipping, *San Angelo Standard-Times.* Stevens had previously rejected the King Ranch country because "that is brush country and filming there would look as if you had a hedge behind you," he explained. "You need something to break the horizon or you lose the sense of vastness."

14. Ralph Black, production manager, to Emma Mallan, May 7, 1955. Stevens Collection.

15. Marfa Location Form, Ralph E. Black, Apr. 18, 1955. Stevens Collection. The Crews Hotel housed thirty-six people in fourteen rooms, including construction workers assigned three to a room. The $13.50 daily rate included a $7 room, a $2 breakfast, and a $4.50 dinner. The Toltec Motel housed eighteen people in nine rooms at $6 daily. Personnel housed at the Toltec took meals at the Crews Hotel.

16. Inter-Office Memo, Stars' Residences in Marfa, June 6, 1955. Stevens Collection.

17. Ralph E. Black, Inter-Office Memo, Marfa Location Information, Apr. 18, 1955. Stevens Collection.

18. Ibid.

19. Ibid. "Dailies" or "rushes" are the unedited film sequences recently shot during the filming of a motion picture. These are viewed periodically and critically by the producer, director, technical crew, and actors. These provide for ongoing evaluation of the film during production.

20. *Big Bend Sentinel,* May 5, 1955.

21. "Marfa, Texas—Set Construction Costs," May 22, 1955. Stevens Collection.

22. *Dallas Morning News,* May 20, 1955. The Stevens Collection contains no copy of the company's contract with Elizabeth Taylor.

23. Carroll Baker, *Baby Doll: An Autobiography* (New York: Arbor, 1983), 134–35.

24. Telephone interview with Robert Nichols, Occidental, Calif., Aug. 16, 1993. Nichols received $400 a week, feature billing, with a nine-week guarantee. Contractual agreements with some of the other performers are as follows: Sal Mineo received $1,000 a week with one week guaranteed, feature billing, and round-trip transportation from New York; Carroll Baker, $750 a week with an eight-week guarantee; Jane Withers, $1,000 a week, twelve weeks guaranteed; Mercedes McCambridge, $17,500, star billing, six weeks guaranteed; Rock Hudson and Elizabeth Taylor began work in Los Angeles on May 16, 1955, each with a fifteen-week guarantee; and James Dean began work on May 30, 1955, with a thirteen-week guarantee. James Dean's contract is not included in the Stevens Collection. When George Stevens began casting *Giant*, *Rebel Without a Cause* had not been released; Dean's reputation rested primarily on his work in *East of Eden*.

25. Edna Ferber to Henry Ginsberg, Apr. 23, 1955. Stevens Collection.

26. Ralph E. Black, Inter-Office Memoranda, dated Apr. 18 and May 3, 1955. Stevens Collection.

27. "Giant" Work Schedule. Stevens Collection.

28. The filming that began in Marfa, Texas, on June 6, 1955, was actually the fourteenth camera day. Shooting began in the studio on May 19 and continued on May 31 through June 3 at Charlottesville, Va.

29. "We were Extras in the 'Giant,'" news release prepared by Evelyn Davis. Photocopy in author's files.

30. Baker, *Baby Doll*, 125.

31. Telephone interview with Robert Nichols, Occidental, Calif., Aug. 16, 1993.

32. Telephone interview with Lee Bennett, Marfa, Tex., Mar. 2, 1995.

33. Letter from Lee Bennett to Kenneth B. Ragsdale, Mar. 2, 1987. An outstanding history teacher in Marfa High School, Bennett encouraged her students to collect and write local history. One teenager's paper on the *Giant* location filming described Elizabeth Taylor as follows: "The lady was really stacked."

34. Bennett correspondence, Sept. 15, 1989.

35. Joe Hyams (with Jay Hyams), *James Dean: Little Boy Lost* (New York: Warner, 1992), 221; see also John Howlett, *James Dean: A Biography* (New York: Beaufort, 1975).

36. Bennett to Ragsdale, July 12, 1987. Elizabeth Taylor's personal life may have been a factor in her on-set conduct. At that time she was twenty-three years old, suffering from sciatica, and facing a failed second marriage to actor Michael Wilding, a man twenty years her senior and the father of their two children.

37. Undated clipping in author's files.

38. Sue Flannagan, *San Angelo Standard-Times*. Undated newspaper clipping in author's files.

39. Mallan interview.

40. Telephone interview with Earl Holliman, Studio City, Calif., Feb. 8, 1993.

41. Warner Brothers Publicity Department Records. Stevens Collection.

42. *Big Bend Sentinel*, May 26, 1955.

43. Undated *El Paso Times* clipping. In author's files.

44. Nichols interview.

45. Holliman interview. Other than Earl Holliman, who had lived in Kilgore and Crane, Texas, other Texans in the *Giant* cast were: Monte Hale, San Angelo; Fran Bennett, Fort Worth; Jane Withers, who had lived for eight years in Midland and Odessa; Charlie Watts, former McMurray College professor, Abilene; Ray Whitley, Marfa rancher; Mary Ann Edwards, Austin; and Chill Wills, Seagoville.

46. Letter from Lee Bennett, June 23, 1955. In author's files.

47. Nichols interview.

48. Baker, *Baby Doll,* 125–31.

49. Mallan interview.

50. *Big Bend Sentinel,* June 23, 1955.

51. Baker, *Baby Doll,* 131–32.

52. Holliman interview.

53. *San Angelo Standard-Times,* July 10, 1955.

54. Telegram, George Stevens to Fred Guiol, July 14, 1955. Stevens Collection.

55. Undated telegram from George Stevens to Fred Guiol, Stevens Collection.

56. Mallan to Coryell, Sept. 14, 1955, Stevens Collection.

57. Coryell to Mallan, Sept. 21, 1955, Stevens Collection.

58. *Cause No. 1641, A. R. Eppenauer vs. Warner Bros. Pictures, Inc.* Filed in the District Court of the United States for the Western District of Texas, El Paso Division, on June 27, 1955. Copy in author's files.

59. R. J. Orbringer to Henry Ginsberg, Sept. 9, 1955. Stevens Collection.

60. Interview with Hunter O. Metcalfe, Marfa, Tex., June 6, 1966.

61. Hyams, *James Dean,* 223–24.

62. Howlett, *James Dean,* 149. According to Howlett, Dean mumbled so badly in the drunken "last supper" scene that actor Nick Adams redubbed Dean's lines in the final cut. Robert Nichols said he believed Sheb Wooley drew that assignment.

63. Jess Oppenheimer and Jack Vitek, *The True Story of an American Film Hero* (New York: Villard, 1986), 54.

64. Interview with Rock Hudson, conducted by Susan Winslow in Los Angeles, Aug. 26, 1981. Transcript in the Margaret Herrick Library, Beverly Hills, Calif.

65. *Time,* Oct. 22, 1956, pp. 108–10.

66. *Variety,* Oct. 31, 1956, p. 9.

67. Distribution Records, Margaret Herrick Library, Beverly Hills, Calif. The $14 million represents not gross receipts but the distributor's rental figure, the amount the studio actually received from the exhibitors. The actual gross figure would be $14 million, plus the percentage held by the exhibitors. For a film of this quality during first-run exhibition, a studio would charge rental fees as high as 30 percent of the total box-office gross receipts. Also the above figures represent only United States and Canada distribution. Income from foreign and television distribution and from video rentals is not included.

    Most performers in *Giant* regarded that assignment as a major career move. Rock Hudson received a best actor Academy nomination for his performance in 1956; James Dean, the best supporting actor nomination; and Mercedes McCambridge, the best supporting actress nomination. None won. George

Stevens won his second best director Academy Award for *Giant*. This film was Carroll Baker's first major assignment, which led to her being cast as the lead in *Baby Doll*, for which she received a best actress nomination in 1956, the same year *Giant* was released. Earl Holliman's *Giant* credit led to his being cast in *The Rainmaker*, for which he received the Golden Globe from the Hollywood Foreign Press Association for the best supporting actor. Although favorably mentioned in the reviews, Elizabeth Taylor received no Academy recognition for her *Giant* performance.

68. Dialogue from *Giant* video.

69. Undated letter from Dr. Richard E. Renneker to George Stevens. Stevens Collection. Edna Ferber, *Giant* (New York: Doubleday, 1952), 17.

70. Letter from George Stevens, Jr., to Kenneth B. Ragsdale, Sept. 15, 1992, in author's files.

71. Mallan interview, Feb. 9, 1992.

72. *Big Bend Sentinel,* July 14, 1955.

73. Mallan interview, Jan. 29, 1995.

74. Oppenheimer undated and unidentified newspaper item.

75. Bennett interview, Feb. 9, 1992.

76. Telephone interview with S. E. DeVolin, Ruidoso, N.M., Nov. 28, 1995.

77. Oppenheimer item.

78. Bennett interview.

Index

Note: Pages with illustrations are indicated by italics.